EZEKIEL UNMASKED
A REVELATION
OF
YESHUA'S LOVE
JUSTICE
AND
REDEMPTION

Yeshua's Redemption - Volume III
Chapter 40-48

P. D. DALLING

3G Publishing, Inc.
Loganville, GA 30052
www.3gpublishinginc.com
Phone: 1-888-442-9637

ISBN: 978-1-941247-19-8

Credit to E.W. Bullinger., *Number in Scripture*. Cosimo, Inc. 2005. Brief quotation embodied in review.

Credit to James Strong. Strong's Exhaustive Concordance of the Bible, Massachusetts: Hendrickson Publishers, n.d

Hebrew, Aramaic or Greek words carries an assigned number in brackets which corresponds with its English equivalent to aid the astute reader to a deeper understanding of the broken seal of the book of Ezekiel.

Contents

About the Author

P.D. Dalling was born on the small island of Jamaica West Indies of both African and Jewish lineage. She was commissioned by the LORD to be a voice to the nations of the world through these inspired writings in these final hours of human history. A student of the Word, P.D Dalling was given several visions and dreams starting from the young age of five. The most intriguing of these visions was one given in consecutive order over a period of seven years showing the construction of an enormous temple from the laying of its foundation until the final stages of it being painted in gold. The author later realized that the vision was to prepare her for this assignment as she neared the completion of a six week teaching on *"The Justice of God."*

Prior to completing this series of teachings, the author once more sought Yeshua as she usually does for the next assignment. A few days later on a hot Saturday afternoon, a call came from a devoted Saint of God and watchman living in the State of Florida, who was unaware of the author's prayer request; this devoted follower of Yeshua Jesus shared a message received from the Lord at 2 A.M. that morning. "Tell My child to teach on the book of Ezekiel, it will be tough." The author accepted the challenge but was met with many obstacles and a wrestling in spirit as to the format for something of this magnitude. Then came the answer in a dream to the author; the Lord wanted this work to be put into writing.

P.D. Dalling had to rely on the leading and inner witness of Holy Spirit to begin and complete this project, as He explicitly spoke: "I will teach you." Indeed this was a very difficult task that took on a whole new meaning of what is meant: to have fellowship with Holy Spirit.

Because this work was commissioned by the LORD, P.D. Dalling refrains from offering any personal credentials or academic scholarship. All glory and honor goes to Abba Father, Yeshua Jesus His Son and my great teacher and friend Holy Spirit who will reward their bondservant in heaven.

Preface

The book of Ezekiel will take you on a prophetic journey from the day the LORD GOD called Ezekiel to be His voice to the nation of Israel in exile, unto these present times. Said to be the most intriguing and mysterious book of the Old Testament, there are two clear themes to its interpretation; the literal and the spiritual-prophetic. Psalm 12:6 states: The words of the LORD are pure words: as silver tried in a furnace of earth, purified seven times. This is a fair description of the depth of the interpretation of the book of Ezekiel, because it is given by inspiration and revelation of Holy Spirit. This work offers no preponderance for replacement theology. The book speaks of GOD'S dealings with Israel His people to the unification of the body of Yeshua with their Jewish brothers as One New Man (Ephesians 3). This work flows with GOD'S grace, mercy, and love for a people who rebelled against Him, worshiped other gods, and suffered at the hands of their oppressors. When they repented, like a loving Father, He forgives and reconcile with His beloved.

In the book of Ezekiel the LORD GOD sometimes spoke by the mouth of His prophet using metaphors, allegories, euphemisms, typologies, prophetic role play, analogies, and coded mysteries, which has frustrated readers of this book for centuries. At this time and by GOD'S own providence, He has broken the seal that clouds the mind to reveal divine truths in these last days. This work is presented in three volumes. Volume one covers chapters 1-24 and addresses Israel's past. Volume two covers chapters 25-39 and address Israel's present state and volume three covers chapters 40-48 unveiling Israel's glorious future and the adoption of the Gentiles into the generation of Yeshua Jesus. Yeshua's love, for His beloved people is revealed in volume one; His justice in laid out in volume two and His redemption in volume three. This compilation unmasks the spiritual prophetic content of the book of Ezekiel; it demonstrates the love of Abba Father for all people whom He created in His image and likeness and gives a final call for all to come out of this sin infested world and find rest in Him.

The LORD addresses both good and evil, shepherds and hirelings, the righteous and the unrighteous; leaders of Israel as well as leaders of other nations. Yeshua's suffering and His coming reign as the Prince of peace among His brethren is reveled in the book of Ezekiel. It will be this Prince; the Son of GOD, who will reunite man with Abba Father not as a god, but as ONE NEW MAN in Yeshua HaMashiach, Jesus the Messiah. Ephesians 2:11-15 and 3:1-6 are principal building block for this review on the forty-eight chapters of Ezekiel: *Wherefore remember, that ye being in time past Gentiles in the flesh, who are called Uncircumcision by that which is called the Circumcision in the flesh made by hands; that at that time ye were without Christ, being aliens from the commonwealth of Israel, and strangers from the covenants of promise, having no hope, and without God in the world: but now in Christ Jesus ye who sometimes were far off are made nigh by the blood of Christ. For He is our peace, who hath made both one, and broken down the middle wall of partition between us; having abolished in His flesh the enmity, even the law of commandments contained in ordinances; for to make in Himself of twain ONE NEW MAN, so making peace. . . . For this cause I Paul, the prisoner of Jesus Christ for you Gentiles, if ye have heard of the dispensation of the grace of God which is given me to you-ward: how that by revelation He made known unto me the mystery; (as I wrote afore in few words, whereby, when ye read, ye may understand my knowledge in the mystery of Christ) which in other ages was not made known unto the sons of men, as it is now revealed unto His holy apostles and prophets by the Spirit; That the Gentiles should be fellow heirs, and of the same body, and partakers of His promise in Christ by the gospel.*

As the construction of the temple of man takes shape in volume three of these writings, we will see the manifold grace of Abba Father unfolding. The tabernacle of Moses is a picture of the law or teachings, but the temple of Yeshua Jesus is all about the grace of His Father, which He extends to all. Romans 6:1-14 states: *What shall we say then? Shall we continue in sin, that grace may abound? God forbid. How shall we, that are dead to sin, live any longer therein? Know ye not, that so many of us as were baptized into Jesus Christ were baptized into His death? Therefore we are buried with Him by baptism into death: that like as Christ was raised up from the dead by the glory of the Father, even so we also should walk in newness of life. For if we have been planted together in the likeness of His death, we shall also be in the likeness of His resurrection: knowing this, that our old man is crucified with him, that the body of sin might be destroyed, that henceforth we should not serve sin. Now if we be dead with Christ, we believe that we shall also live with Him: knowing that Christ being raised from the dead dieth no more; death hath no more dominion over Him. For in that He died, He died unto sin once: but in that He liveth, He liveth unto God. Likewise reckon ye also yourselves to be dead indeed unto sin, but alive unto God through Jesus Christ our Lord. Let not sin therefore reign in your mortal body, that ye should obey it in the lusts thereof. Neither yield ye your members as instruments of unrighteousness unto sin: but yield yourself unto God, as those that are alive from the dead, and your members as instruments of righteousness unto God. For sin shall not have dominion over you: for ye are not under the law, but under grace.* The body of Yeshua Jesus, like Israel, is in spiritual exile, but the day will come as you will see step by step unfolding in the book of Ezekiel, when man will once again enjoy fellowship with God face to face.

The unmasking of the book of Ezekiel will bring about a radical change in the way Believers in Yeshua Jesus view Scriptures. It will rattle the conscience of the skeptic and shake the very foundation of Christian dogma. There are lengths, widths, heights and depths in the Word of God that are yet to be revealed. The LORD is waiting to take those who are willing to travel with Him from the surface of His Word and descend to its greatest depths but the choice is ours. Beneath the surface of the Word of God are wonders to behold, this however will be a lifelong task of total abandonment that comes at a great price. The deeper Yeshua takes us in the Word, will make the crushing greater and the judgment stricter, but in the end the natural man will be regenerated and the attributes of the Living God will radiate from his being thereby changing the lives of others. Ecclesiastes 1:9-10 applying the NKJV states: *That which has been is what will be, that which is done is what will be done, and there is nothing new under the sun. Is there anything of which it may be said, "See, this is new"? It has already been in ancient times before us.* As plans are being made for the third temple to be constructed in Jerusalem, God has already begun a parallel work in mankind by preparing us to be His spiritual abode to enter the kingdom of God and the New Jerusalem that comes down from heaven. This temple is therefore referred to as the fourth temple in these writings because it is not natural but spiritual.

Both Jews and Gentile Believers will understand their divine purpose as God reveals something about Himself and His relationship with mankind as He breaks the seal and reveals astounding truths from the Book of Ezekiel. Ezekiel unmasked is therefore God's message to Jews and Gentiles. He addresses our weaknesses and raises the bar to show our strengths. He places the ball labeled "choice" in our court as He motivates us to choose eternal life over death and lasting fellowship instead of damnation. If we accept His calling; He lifts us out of the mire of sin, declares us holy by His grace, and calls us kings and priests. He speaks of Israel as His firstborn and all those who believe in Yeshua Jesus, as been born-again! One day the body of Yeshua will share in the glorious inheritance of Israel as sons and daughters of the King of all kings and Lord of all lords.

God is building a temple

Not made by human hands

The blueprint designed in heaven

A revelation of ONE NEW MAN

Jews and Gentiles called by God to live in unity

Under the eternal banner of love for all the world to see

Both were bought and paid for at a very dear price

Yeshua's poured out blood became their perfect sacrifice.

P.D.Dalling, "A Temple Not Built By Human Hands."

Volume III

Israel's Present:
Yeshua's Redemption

Chapter 40

Verses 1-4

"In the five and twentieth year of captivity, in the beginning of the year, in the tenth day of the month, in the fourteenth year after that the city was smitten, in the selfsame day the hand of the LORD was upon me, and brought me thither. In the vision of God brought He me into the land of Israel, and set me upon a very high mountain, by which was as the frame of a city on the south. And He brought me thither, and, behold, there was a man, whose appearance was like the appearance of brass, with a line of flax in his hand, and a measuring reed; and he stood in the gate. And the man said unto me, Son of man, behold with thine eyes, and hear with thine ears, and set thine heart upon all that I will shew thee; for to the intent that I might shew them unto thee art thou brought hither: declare all that thou seest to the house of Israel."

As the twenty-fifth anniversary of the siege and subsequent captivity of Judah approached and in the fourteenth year to the date of the destruction of Jerusalem; the LORD whisks Ezekiel away in a mighty vision that would unveil great truths relating to the redemption of Israel, the rebuilding of a fourth spiritual temple, and the final blessing that both Jews and Gentiles would receive. Being placed upon a very high mountain, Ezekiel is shown a panoramic view of what appeared to be the outline of a city off in the south that was under construction. Ezekiel was given the opportunity to witness the construction of a vast temple; a magnificent structure that was unique in its design because it was being built to dwell in the New Jerusalem of God. It was far more beautiful than the temple built by King Solomon, yet within its creation was the blueprint of the tabernacle of the wilderness that the LORD God instructed Moses to erect as His visible presence among His people.

In chapters 40 through 48 of the book of Ezekiel, Israel and those who are engrafted into the true vine will receive a final spiritual blessing. This unique city, this massive temple, this splendiferous structure, was not the working of man but a supernatural regeneration of both the bride and body of Yeshua Jesus for His millennial reign here on earth. Ezekiel's vision had three components: first, the prophet was taken to the fourth and final temple which is man himself being transformed into the image of GOD, prepared and made ready for His return. The prophet was next shown the temple that was built by King Solomon lying in ruins in Jerusalem and the truth behind its destruction. And finally, the prophet was allowed to witness the coming redistribution of the land of Israel in which Gentile Believers will also be blessed. Most of the measurements that Ezekiel will receive from here onwards are symbolic in nature, but carries great spiritual significance. It must be mentioned that a third temple will be built in Israel but it will be desecrated, and this will be one of the signs marking the eminent return of Yeshua Jesus, to His fourth and final temple. To retain the intrinsic value and indispensable properties combined with the revelatory understanding of these verses; the measuring system of the KJV is retained to unveil God's message to His people. The seal has been broken and great truths will be revealed as we weigh these unveilings in our hearts. The prophet Ezekiel now prepares to document every detail for this spiritual temple as instructed, and what was about to be explained will be significant for Israel as well as the engrafted Gentiles in these last days.

Gabriel was sent to Daniel to give him understanding regarding the building of a third Temple. The angel spoke of the occurrence of these things beginning in "weeks," however this measure of time is symbolic of years. 2 Peter 3:8 and Psalm 90:4 states: "*But, beloved, be not ignorant of this one thing, that one day is with the Lord as a thousand years, and a thousand years as one day. . . . For a thousand years in thy sight are but as yesterday when it is past, and as a watch in the night.*" There are many signs occurring around us at this very moment that points towards the return of Yeshua. However as horrible things might presently be, sad to say, there is still worse to come. The construction of a third Temple in Jerusalem will be a bitter sweet occasion as it will be desecrated three and a half years later following its completion by the anti-Christ. For those who are alive to see these things; be prepared for great tribulations, but in the midst of mayhem, rejoice and be glad for help is on the way. Yeshua Messiah will come with His mighty angels and declare His Sovereign rule because of His elect. These are the words of Yeshua recorded in Mathew 24:20-22: *"But pray ye that your flight be not in the winter, neither on the Sabbath day: for then shall be great tribulation, such as was not since the beginning of the world to this time, no, nor ever shall be. And except those days should be shortened, there should no flesh be saved: but for the elect's sake those days shall be shortened."*

Daniel 9:20-27 applying the NKJV now lays the prophetic groundwork for the construction of the third temple in Jerusalem and its subsequent defilement three and a half years following its dedication: *"Now while I was speaking, praying, and confessing my sin and the sin of my people Israel, and presenting my supplication before the LORD my God for the holy mountain of my God, yes, while I was speaking in prayer, the man Gabriel, whom I had seen in the vision at the beginning, being caused to fly swiftly, reached me about the time of the evening offering. And he informed me, and talked with me, and said. O Daniel, I have now come forth to give you skill to understand. At the beginning of your supplication the command went out, and I have come to tell you, for you are greatly beloved; therefore consider the matter, and understand the vision: "Seventy weeks are determined for your people and for your holy city, to finish the transgression, to make an end of sin, to make reconciliation for iniquity, to bring in everlasting righteousness, to seal up vision and prophecy, and to anoint the Most Holy. Know therefore and understand, that from the going forth of the command to restore and build Jerusalem until Messiah the Prince, there shall be seven weeks and sixty-two weeks; the street shall be built again and the wall, even in troublesome times. And after the sixty-two weeks Messiah shall be cut off, but not for Himself; and the people of the prince who is to come shall destroy the city and the sanctuary. The end of it shall be with a flood, and till the end of the war of desolations are determined. Then he shall confirm a covenant with many for one week; but in the middle of the week he shall bring an end to sacrifice and offerings. And on the wing of abominations shall be one who makes desolate, even until the consummation, which is determined, is poured out on the desolate."* These things will soon be fulfilled in the city of Jerusalem. Based on the information given in Daniel chapter 9, there will be the signing of a seven year Middle East Peace agreement that will be broken half-way through its ratification. With this in mind, the construction of the temple in the book of Ezekiel could not be that of the third temple, but the fourth and final temple which is man himself. The interpretation of these final chapters of this book of hidden truths will be examined in three ways: spiritual, symbolic and natural. In defiance Judah broke the teachings of the LORD, and a seventy year sentence was decreed, yet the lovingkindness of Abba Father constrained Him and He multiplied His grace with even greater intensity as the house of Israel was being chastised for their rebellion. The prophet now prepares to document all that his chaperone was about to show him because he was instructed to rehearse it to his brethren in captivity.

The mountain range that lies in the south of Israel is called the Judean Mountains and this was the area being viewed by the prophet Ezekiel. On top of this mountain was the ancient ruin of the temple built by King Solomon in Jerusalem and twice destroyed; first by Nebuchadnezzar king of Babylon and in 70 A.D. by the Romans. Jerusalem, Israel's capital, is centrally located on top of the Judean Mountains projecting from its southern ridge about twenty-four hundred feet or approximately seven hundred and thirty meters above sea level. This region of the mountain is called Hebron, Kiriath or Kirjath-Arba that was given to the descendants of Benjamin (Joshua 14:15; 18:28). Judges 1:1-2 once more makes it quite clear that Jerusalem belongs to Israel: *"After Joshua died, the Israelites asked the LORD, "Who should lead the invasion against the Canaanites and launch the attack? The LORD said, "The men of Judah should take the lead. Be sure of this! I am handing the land over to them"* (NET). Three things have been brought to light:

- o Jerusalem was initially given to Benjamin the twelfth son of Israel who incidentally was the only child born in the land of Palestine
- o It was the LORD God who allotted this land to His people
- o Yeshua is a descendant of David from the tribe of Judah, the tribe authorized by Abba Father to take the lead

From his vantage point, Ezekiel could see the silhouette of God's beloved city of Jerusalem on top a plateau in Hebron, located in the southern portion of the Judean Mountains. It is most likely that the prophet was taken to Mount Meron which is located in the Northern District of Israel. Mount Meron is estimated to be approximately 1,208 meters or 3,963 feet above sea level, thereby making it the highest peak within Israel besides the Golan Heights. On a clear day and under the best of conditions, it is possible to view the city of Jerusalem from Mount Meron, which is about 130.6 miles away.

Ezekiel explained that it was the Spirit of God who brought him to the mountain, there he saw a man whose appearance was that of brass. This man who was standing in the gate had a line of flax and a measuring reed in his hand. The Holy Spirit introduces the prophet to the man who was already waiting for his arrival. This was truly a man and his identity is of no secret, because Ezekiel had seen him before in earlier visions of God. This person was none other than Yeshua Jesus Himself! The Hebrew "**Ish**" [H. 376], transliterated "man" was used, which proved that the prophet's tour guide was not an angel, because the Hebrew and Aramaic word for "angel" is **Malakh**. This man was more than a messenger, because the measurements he was about to give Ezekiel were not measurements for a natural temple but a spiritual one. The Word of God makes it clear that man will judge angels (1 Corinthians 6:3). 1 Peter 2:1-6 instructs us: "*Therefore, laying aside all malice, all deceit, hypocrisy, envy, and all evil speaking, as newborn babes, desire the pure milk of the word that you may grow thereby, if indeed you have tasted that the Lord is gracious. Coming to Him as to a living stone, rejected indeed by men, but chosen by God and precious, you also, as living stones, are being built up a spiritual house, a holy priesthood, to offer up spiritual sacrifices acceptable to God through Jesus Christ. Therefore it is also contained in the Scripture, "Behold I lay in Zion a chief cornerstone, elect, precious and he who believes on Him will by no means be put to shame*" (NKJV). The revelation of the next nine chapters will be the reconstruction of the new man in Yeshua Jesus his Savior and Lord, preparing him for the New Jerusalem of God.

As previously indicated, a third temple will be built by man in the city of Jerusalem that will be desecrated, but Yeshua will be building a fourth indestructible temple (Acts 7:48; 17:24).

Hebrews 9:11 quoting the NASB also states: *"But when Christ appeared as a high priest of good things to come, He entered through a greater and more perfect tabernacle, not made with hands, that is to say, not of this creation."* If we live in Yeshua, then our new temple must be just like His, because it will be the new man in Yeshua that will be presented to the Father. 2 Corinthians 5:19-21 and Isaiah 53:4 remind us: *"For God was in Christ, reconciling the world to himself, no longer counting people's sins against them. And he gave us this wonderful message of reconciliation. So we are Christ's ambassadors; God is making his appeal through us. We speak for Christ when we plead, "Come back God!" For God made Christ, who never sinned, to be the offering for our sin, so that we could be made right with God through Christ. . . . Yet it was our weaknesses he carried; it was our sorrows that weighed him down. And we thought his troubles were a punishment from God, a punishment for his own sins"* (NLT). This man can be none other than Yeshua Himself, because He was the only person found worthy by Abba Father to lay down His life for all mankind.

Ezekiel described Yeshua's appearance as being that of brass, but why brass? Brass was always symbolic of the judgment of sin and spoke of our sin that is placed upon Yeshua. Although the KJV translated the word for Yeshua's appearance as resembling "brass," a better rendering is copper. Whenever the word "brazen," "bronze," "brass" or "copper," is used to describe furnishings of the tabernacle built by Moses; the symbolic reference remains the same because copper is tied to the sin offering. The LORD uses parables, typologies, metaphors and other symbolic language frequently throughout Scriptures, but they were never intended to confuse us. Being intimately aware of the propensity of His children, the LORD knows that these applications would be very effective in arousing the thoughts of the seeker of truth, drawing us even closer to Him; the only true source of all knowledge. We must never take one iota of credit for any revelation given to us, but remain humble and ever more available, as we are the LORD'S voice to this generation. Yeshua Jesus is the final temple and in the tabernacles built by both Moses and Solomon copper remained the symbol associated with the sin offering.

Copper was never found in the Inner court or Most Holy Place, it is always associated with the Outer Court. One of the symbolic interpretations of the Outer Court is the place of repentance, our body. The Inner Court is symbolic of thanksgiving and praise: our soul; while the Most Holy Place is symbolic of fellowship and communion with God: spirit to Spirit. Copper is described as an alloy composed of varying types of metal that is resistant to corrosion and can be molded into whatever shape or form one desires. The properties of copper in its symbolic language refers to mankind, we struggle with a multiplicity of sins; we are easily swayed, yet within us lies the potential to resist evil. 2 Corinthians 4:7-11 quoting the NLT puts it this way: "*We now have this light shining in our hearts, but we ourselves are like fragile clay jars containing this great treasure. This makes it clear that our great power is from God, not from ourselves. We are pressed on every side by troubles, but we are not crushed. We are perplexed, but not driven to despair. We are hunted down, but never abandoned by God. We get knocked down, but we are not destroyed. Through suffering, our bodies continue to share in the death of Jesus so that the life of Jesus may also be seen in our bodies. Yes, we live under constant danger of death because we serve Jesus, so that the life of Jesus will be evident in our dying bodies.*"

It is undeniable that man is constantly bombarded by varying negative thoughts and circumstances in life, but we must stand our ground and resist them for they are traps, webs, and ditches, placed there by our adversary to lure us away from the Lord our God. We must stay in close proximity to Him and resist the enemy, for in doing so we have an advocate whose name is Yeshua Jesus our Lord who will strengthen us to endure temptation. Ezekiel describes Yeshua's outward appearance as being copper which speaks of His suffering for our sins. The prophet Isaiah wrote: "*Behold, My servant will prosper, He will be high and lifted up and greatly exalted. Just as many were astonished at you, My people, so His appearance was marred more than any man and His form more than the sons of men. Thus He will sprinkle many nations; Kings will shut their mouths on account of Him; for what had not been told them they will see, and what they had not heard they will understand*" (52:13-15 NASB).

This temple and all that pertains to it will usher in the reign of Yeshua and the newly constructed man will be endowed with His attributes and this is the story of these last nine chapters of the book of Ezekiel. This will be the fourth temple and the number four symbolically points to man as a new creation because he is being reconstructed in Yeshua (2 Corinthians 5:17). Zachariah a prophet of God said: "*...Behold, the man whose name is the* BRANCH! *From His place He shall branch out, and He shall build the temple of the* LORD; *yes He shall build the temple of the* LORD. *He shall bear the glory, and shall sit and rule on His throne; so He shall be a priest on His throne, and the counsel of peace shall be between them both"* 6:12-13. This fourth temple is spiritually significant because everything about it surpasses that of Moses, Solomon and the third temple to be built in Jerusalem. Here are some differences between the natural and spiritual temple:

1. There will be no animal hide coverings.
2. There will be no laver, table of shewbread, lampstand, altar of incense or Ark of the Covenant.
3. There will be no partition or veil.
4. "Sacrificial" ramp is to the east instead of the south.
5. Access to the altar is by stairs only.
6. Rooms or dwelling places are added to the sides of the fourth temple.
7. New allotment of land to the twelve tribes of Israel will surround the temple.
8. Women now have complete access beyond the Outer Court.

Yeshua has the authority to bring great changes to this fourth temple because He is GOD'S sacrificial Lamb that was slain for our sins. It is He that the Overcomers must go through to be presented to the Father. Revelation 3:12 states: "*Him that overcometh will I make a pillar in the temple of My God, and he shall go no more out: and I will write upon him the name of My God, and the name of the city of My God, which is New Jerusalem, which cometh down out of heaven from My God: and I will write upon him My new name.*" Notice, Overcomers will be made pillars in the temple of God; this fact will become clearer as the fourth temple is being built in these closing chapters. There are three simple yet important facts in Ezekiel 40:3 that must be explained because they hold spiritual truths that will affect the symbolic interpretation of these chapters:

1. A line of flax is in His hand
2. A measuring reed is in His hand
3. He stood <u>in</u> the gate

A line of flax is in His hand

In the ancient world flax linen was very popular as its fiber is much stronger than cotton. The Lord is seen here holding a line in his hand made from flax; but why was He holding a line of twined flax? What was the flax symbolic of? First of all the blooming of the flax plant comes in two colors; pale blue and also deep red. The symbolic interpretation of both colors speaks of Yeshua's suffering. He was bruised for our transgressions and some of His inflictions also caused hemorrhage. Yeshua was slapped in the face while blindfolded, a crown of thorns was pressed into His head, and He received many lashes which caused severe bruising and bleeding. To prove that He was dead a spear was thrust in His side and this was His reality for the sins of all; Isaiah 53:4-5; Luke 18:31-33; 22:63-64; Matthew 26:67-68; 27:24-31; Mark 14:65; 15:15-20; John 19:1-5. The twined flax cord therefore is a memorial of His suffering. He became our living sacrifice that we might be presented to the Father through His finished work for our salvation. This is not all there is to the flax plant because it also produces an edible oil; a symbol of Yeshua's office as High Priest. He was crushed, and poured out that we might become beneficiaries of the kingdom of God. The final fact about flax lies in the interpretation of its name, which is "most useful." Our Lord was most useful unto His Father by laying down His life for all. Our eternal hope was paid by one who became sin for all. Our sin was far too great for us to bear, so a loving Father gave us all that He had to snatch us back from the dragnet of hell which we truly deserve and declared us not guilty.

A measuring reed is in His hand

The Lord also had a measuring reed in His hand, (see Revelation 21:15-16). A reed is a rod or ruler used for measuring lengths and its symbolic meaning speaks of the measurement of man in Yeshua our hope of glory and the new man in Yeshua Jesus is the embodiment of this hope (see Colossians 1:26-28; Ephesians 4:4-32). Yeshua is the only foundation that both Israel and Believers are built on. The prophet Isaiah said of Yeshua: *"Therefore thus saith the Lord GOD, Behold, I lay in Zion for a foundation a stone, a tried stone, a precious corner stone, a sure foundation: he that believeth shall not make haste"* (28:16, for further reading see also Psalm 118:22; Matthew 21:42; Acts 4:11; 1 Peter 2:4-9).

He stands in the gate

Yeshua was on top of a mountain where Ezekiel saw Him in this mighty vision of GOD standing in the gate. A better rendering for gate is "opening or door." The man whom the prophet saw was none other than the pre-incarnate Son of GOD; He was not standing "by" or "at" the door; He was standing "in" the door, which means: He had already crossed the threshold. The gate is symbolic of Yeshua being the only way to His Father and that way is called righteousness. In Psalm 118:19-23 it is stated: "*Open to me the gates of righteousness: I will go into them, and I will praise the LORD: This gate of the LORD, into which the righteous shall enter. I will praise thee: for thou hast heard me, and art become my salvation. The stone which the builders refused is become the head stone of the corner. This is the LORD'S doing; it is marvelous in our eyes*" (see also John 14:6). Israel had many pitfalls, but one day they will be made the righteousness of GOD in Yeshua Messiah and this gift is extended to believing Gentiles. We are likened to a building and our foundation is in Yeshua (Ephesians 2:18-22) and these facts were about to be revealed to Ezekiel the prophet. Yeshua began His sanctifying work in His people on Shavuot. Acts 2:1-4 states: "*Now when the day of Pentecost had come, they were all together in one place. Suddenly a sound like a violent wind blowing came from heaven and filled the entire house where they were sitting. And tongues spreading out like a fire appeared to them and came to rest on each one of them. All of them were filled with the Holy Spirit, and they begun to speak in other languages as the Spirit enabled them*" (NET). Reflecting on Ezekiel 39:29 and at a time known only to Abba Father, there will be a second out pouring of Holy Spirit and this will occur on one of the celebrations of Shavuot which is the same as Feast of Weeks or Pentecost. Yeshua through His Eternal Spirit, is preparing His people to be presented unto His Father as one new man in Him. These chosen ones are from many nations, tribes and languages and in this final temple the glory of God will reside perpetually.

The next point of equal importance is the fact that Yeshua is the door! John 10:1, 9, 14-16 states: "*Most assuredly, I say to you, he who does not enter the sheepfold by the door, but climbs up some other way, the same is a thief and a robber. . . I am the door. If anyone enters by Me, he will be saved, and will go in and out and find pasture. . . I am the good shepherd; and I know My sheep, and am known by My own. As the Father knows Me, even so I know the Father; and I lay down My life for the sheep. And other sheep I have which are not of this fold; them also I must bring, and they will hear My voice; and there will be one flock and one shepherd"* (NKJV). Yeshua is the only door by which both Jews and Gentiles may enter into Abba Father and our eternal hope of being reconciled to Him is built on these foundational truths. The fourth temple is therefore a picture of Yeshua's regenerating and reconstructing work in mankind to make him approved unto His Father and not be castaways.

Ezekiel had a message and a mandate to view this coming temple; listen carefully to all that Yeshua was about to reveal to him, ponder them in his heart and rehearse them to his brethren; the true test of Ezekiel's obedience will now be known. Will he remember the instructions he received at his ordination as a prophet? Will he boldly rehearse the words of the LORD without fear whether his brethren would believe him or not? This last vision however will tip the scale, because what was about to be revealed to the prophet, would shake or shape the faith of the Jews in Babylon and indeed, this generation. Ezekiel wasted no time, in his heart he firmly decided to inform his brethren of all the things he was about to be shown, but would they truly understand his message?

Verse 5

"And behold a wall on the outside of the house round about, and in the man's hand a measuring reed of six cubits long by the cubit and a hand breadth: so he measured the breadth of the building, one reed; and the height, one reed."

In this vision Ezekiel was taken to the top of a mountain and he was surprised to note that there was a wall enclosing what appeared to be a house. All that will transpire from here on is symbolic in nature. First of all, there was a wall surrounding the house. If you think of a very expensive home, there is usually a wall or gate of some kind around the perimeter of the property to keep away intruders. In this instance, the wall not only symbolizes protection but it also speaks of relationship because the key Hebrew word used here is **Chowmah** [2346], this Hebrew word establishes the fact that Israel is joined or betrothed unto God as the transliteration for "wall" means "to

27

join" or "a wall of protection." Isaiah 49:14-16 states: "*But Zion said, "The LORD has forsaken me, and my Lord has forgotten me. Can a woman forget her nursing child, and not have compassion on the son of her womb? Surely they may forget, yet I will not forget you. See, I have inscribed you on the palms of My hands; your walls are continually before Me*" (NKJV).

The next Hebrew word used in conjunction with the word "wall" is **Bayith** [1004]; it means a house, but can also be defined as a mansion, a temple, a palace or a dwelling place. Yeshua Jesus declares in John 14:2-3: "*In My Father's house are many mansions: if it were not so, I would have told you. I go to prepare a place for you. And if I go and prepare a place for you, I will come again, and receive you unto Myself; that where I am, there ye may be also.*" This was no ordinary wall or house, but the unfolding of the temple of man. Taking these findings into consideration, this construction is spiritual in nature and of epic proportion because this mansion or house is not being built for just a friend but for a bride! The LORD is telling us that not only is He in a covenant relationship with Israel as a betrothed bride, but that He is their wall of protection against all enemies. The joy of the Gentiles is the fact that they, too, are included as His honored guests.

Yeshua Jesus began the measuring of the building with the reed and its length was given as six cubits long by the cubit and a hand breadth. Man was created on the sixth day (Genesis 1:26-31), and the measurement of the reed was six cubits, which is the measurement of man. Man is assigned the number six which is one greater than five and also one less than seven. Seven is the all-encompassing perfect number of the LORD and therefore points towards His rest from a spiritual standpoint. Man will one day in the reign of Yeshua Jesus, become perfected both morally and spiritually and find a resting place in his Kingman Redeemer and this belief will be revealed in the building of this fourth and final spiritual temple.

Man is represented as being six cubits long by the cubit and a hand breadth; "by" indicates that something is been multiplied. The breadth or width; speaks of a measurement extending from one side to the other and symbolically represents the revelation of the fullness of man in Yeshua as He measures the width of the temple; 1 Corinthians 3:11-17, applying the NASB states: "*For *no man can lay a foundation other than the one which is laid, which is Jesus, Christ. Now if any man builds on the foundation with gold, silver, precious stones, wood, hay, straw, each man's work will become evident; for the day will show it because it is to be revealed with fire, and the fire itself will test the quality of each man's work. If any man's work which he has built on it remains, he will receive a reward. If any man work is burned up, he will suffer loss; but he himself will be saved, yet so as through fire. Do you not know that you are a temple of God and that the Spirit of God dwells in you? If any man destroys the temple of God, God will destroy him, for the temple of God is holy, and that is what you are."* This fourth temple is the total embodiment of man in Yeshua Jesus. The Holy Spirit is feverishly working to prepare a sanctified and regenerated man who is both morally and spiritually holy, and He has already begun this work in us. The temple is about to be measured and all four sides will complete a square, which speaks of perfect unity: the ultimate desire of the Father will be accomplished and Yeshua's prayer asking Abba Father to unite us unto Himself will finally be answered (John 17).

Verses 6-8

"Then came he unto the gate which looketh toward the east, and went up the stairs thereof, and measured the threshold of the gate, which was one reed broad; and the other threshold of the gate, which was one reed broad. And every little chamber was one reed long, and one reed broad; and between the little chambers were five cubits; and the threshold of the gate by the porch of the gate within was one reed. He measured also the porch of the gate within, one reed."

The role of numbers in Scripture is very important but can easily be misunderstood. Many of these numbers unlock valuable biblical truths that the Lord wants to reveal to us. The mystery in the construction of this fourth temple will be demystified. In these verses, the first and most important fact to be noted is Yeshua entering by the eastern gate; this is very significant because it speaks of the uniqueness of this entrance as it relates to Yeshua Jesus, which proves that it was not a messenger angel who took the prophet Ezekiel on this virtual tour but Yeshua HaMashiach Himself. This entrance re-emphasizes the point that Yeshua is the only way to Abba Father. As noted in these verses all the measurements given are ONE REED; from the threshold to the chambers and to the porch is one reed. This numerical value, speaks of the unity of the Godhead and the final unity of man in Yeshua Jesus. The number one stands alone, it is solid in its decisions and not double-minded; to stand as one is to be united as one.

Yeshua ascends the stairs of the eastern gate and at this point, commenced His measurements. The eastern gate is the designated entrance prepared for Yeshua: let's take a peek at Ezekiel 43:6-7: "*So the Spirit took me up, and brought me into the inner court; and, behold, the glory of the LORD filled the house. And I heard Him speaking unto me out of the house; and the man stood by me. And he said unto me, Son of man, the place of My throne, and the place of the soles of My feet, where I will dwell in the midst of the children of Israel forever, and My holy name, shall the house of Israel no more defile, neither they, nor their kings, by their whoredom, nor by the carcasses of their kings in their high places*". Here is the undeniable proof that the pre-incarnate Son of the Living GOD was Ezekiel's tour guide. He alone can enter the eastern gate. He alone as both Son of Man and Son of God can judge, He alone can present man before the throne of GOD, and He alone is found worthy to break the seal (Revelation 5:1-10).

In this vision Ezekiel watches as Yeshua goes up the stairs, indicating that it is only through Him that man can achieve a deeper relationship with God. This however does not mean that man will gain knowledge esoterically, because all mankind are equal in the LORD's eyes. The Hebrew transliteration for stairs used in this context is **Maalah** [4609] and it speaks of one's upward journey in his thought process. This is a humbling experience of spiritual growth and maturation where a prideful and haughty spirit has no place. As Yeshua ascends the stairs, His actions are symbolic of man's regenerative thought pattern becoming more and more like His. Philippians 2:1-11 shows this clearly: "*Therefore, if there is any encouragement in Christ, any comfort provided by love, any fellowship in the Spirit, any affection or mercy, complete my joy and be of the same mind, by having the same love, being united in spirit, and having one purpose. Instead of being motivated by selfish ambition or vanity, each of you should, in humility, be moved to treat one another as more important than yourself. Each of you should be concerned not* only about your own interests, but about the interests of others as well. You should have the same attitude toward one another that Christ Jesus had, who though he existed in the form of God did not regard equality with God as something to be grasped, but emptied himself by taking on the form of a slave by looking like other men, and by sharing in human nature. He humbled himself, by becoming obedient to the point of death even death on a cross! As a result God exalted him and gave him the name above every name, so that at the name of Jesus every knee will bow in heaven and on earth and under the earth and every tongue confess that Jesus Christ is Lord to the glory of God the Father"(NET). This is a righteous climbing, a holy and sanctified climbing where man understands how sinful he really is and how desperate he is in need of reconciliation and the re-establishment of fellowship with his LORD. Yeshua's ascension paves the way for man's redemption; to ascend without Yeshua is to descend into the depths of Sheol without Yeshua!

Recalling that the reed is symbolic of the unity of man in Yeshua, we will observe His divine nature being woven into the spirit of man. These rooms otherwise called chambers are in fact the many compartments of the soul which measured one reed in both its length and width, indicating that all four sides are of equal measurement, otherwise a reflection of cohesiveness. This reveals the notion also that its end-product is the framework of unity. As observed "chambers," is in its plural form and denotes the all-inclusiveness of the unity of all compartments of the soul of mankind into Yeshua. The Apostle Paul wrote: "*For this cause I bow my knees unto the Father of our Lord Jesus Christ, of whom the whole family in heaven and earth is named, that He would grant you, according to the riches of His glory, to be strengthened with might by His Spirit in the inner man; that Christ may dwell in your hearts by faith; that ye, being rooted and grounded in love, may be able to comprehend with all saints what is the breadth, and length and depth, and height; and to know the love of Christ, which passeth knowledge, that ye might be filled with all the fullness of God*" (Ephesians 3:14-19). This is the unveiling of a picture of one new man, both Jews and Gentiles being united in love and the unifier is Yeshua Jesus Himself. King Solomon had this revelation regarding the rooms or chambers: "*By wisdom a house is built, and through understanding it is established; by knowledge its rooms are filled with all kinds of precious and pleasing treasures*"(Proverbs 24:3-

4 NET). Mankind will one day be united as one with the Lord. Evil and chaos are rapidly increasing and now that the door of grace is opened, the sons of God must shine forth having no fear of death, because to be absent from the body is to be present with the Lord 2 Corinthians 5:8; Revelation 12:11.

Every facet of Ezekiel's description of the temple is important as the prophet described the rooms or chambers of this building as being "little." The use of this word however, is not referring to the size of the rooms but rather the symbolic nature of humility. Ezekiel goes on to say that the measurements between these rooms were five cubits and the number five points towards the grace of God. Because five is referring to the cubit measurement, the grace of God is here bound to man at his entering into a deeper fellowship with Yeshua; this form of fellowship is that which joins him into a relationship as family. The word transliterated "cubit" is the Hebrew **Ammah** [520], which describes the measure of the entry of a door, but another meaning of **Ammah** speaks of a mother. The new man in Yeshua will walk in the nurturing grace of El-Shaddai, the all sufficient God who supplies, nourishes, and satisfies our needs; it is this kind of grace that allows mankind to enter and remain in fellowship with God. With fellowship comes revelation and the chambers or rooms are the starting point of the unfolding of Divine knowledge. The Lord GOD will be man's instructor who will download untold truths into the soul of man thereby removing the veil from his understanding. 1 Corinthians 13:12 applying the NLT states: "*Now we see things imperfectly, like puzzling reflections in a mirror, but then we will see everything with perfect clarity. All that I know now is partial and incomplete, but then I will know everything completely, just as God now knows me completely.*" That which we are unable to fully comprehend presently will be crystal clear through a revelatory download.

Man is inquisitive by nature, and for this reason he delves into dark satanic understandings for illumination, instead of waiting upon his Creator who knows far greater things than the master of the underworld. 1 John 3:1-3 reminds us: "*Behold what manner of love the Father has bestowed on us, that we should be called children of God! Therefore the world does not know us, because it did not know Him. Beloved, now we are children of God; and it has not yet been revealed what we shall be, but we know that when He is revealed, we shall be like Him, for we shall see Him as He is. And everyone who has this hope in Him purifies himself, just as He is pure."* We are presently divided in fragments of religious groups and dogmas under the banner of Yeshua but the times of refreshing are at hand. As the world unites to persecute the body of Yeshua Jesus, Believers will unite to exalt the Lord GOD and put aside their differences. We are neither Catholics nor Baptists; Protestants or Pentecostals or any other names we choose to call ourselves. We are the body of Yeshua and every part is uniquely designed to both walk and work in unity, because this is the only way that our effectiveness will become profitable.

The Apostle Paul reminds us of our purpose as we walk in the unity of the Spirit: *"Therefore I, a prisoner for serving the Lord, beg you to lead a life worthy of your calling, for you have been called by God. Always be humble and gentle. Be patient with each other, making allowance for each other's faults because of your love. Make every effort to keep yourselves united in the Spirit, binding yourselves together with peace. For there is one body and one Spirit, just as you have been called to one glorious hope for the future. There is one Lord, one faith, one baptism, one God and one Father of all who is over all, in all, and living through all"* (Ephesians 4:16 NLT).

Verses 9-10

"Then measured he the porch of the gate, eight cubits; and the posts thereof, two cubits; and the porch of the gate was inward. And the little chambers of the gate eastward were three on this side, and three on that side; they three were of one measure: and the post had one measure on this side and on that side."

Two more measurements are given in verse nine for the vestibule of the temple which is also known as the porch of the gate. These are very important measurements, because it is a part of the construction of the new man or temple in Yeshua Jesus. The Apostle Paul wrote in 2 Corinthians 5:17: *"Therefore if any man be in Christ, he is a new creature: old things are passed away; behold, all things are become new."* These mysteries are foreshadows of the new birth and a renewed relationship between God and man. The measurement of the entrance is given and recorded by Ezekiel as eight cubits. Yeshua is the entrance or way to GOD and the number eight speaks of a fresh start or a new beginning. As seven is the completion of a matter, the number eight perfects it. The seventh day brings to an end a week, while the eighth starts its cycle all over again.

The posts located by the entrance are symbolically speaking of Yeshua Himself, and the measurement was two cubits. The number two stands for witness, therefore, a testimony of the New Covenant or *B'rit Chadashah* of reconciliation between the Lord GOD and man. Proverbs 8:34-35 states: *"Blessed is the man who listens to me, watching daily at my gates, waiting at the posts of my doors. For whoever finds me finds life, and obtains favor from the LORD"* (NKJV). These posts are the support for the temple or new man in Yeshua; it gives balance to his framework as the perfection of the Lord is being woven, upheld and sustained by them. Both posts also points towards unity being reinforced since both look exactly alike, opposite from each other at the entrance.

The little chambers mentioned earlier are the various compartments of the soul being reconstructed as a symbol of humility, because pride has no place in the new man or in the New Jerusalem of God. Being symbolically small, these chambers bear no element of arrogance, prejudice or disdain, but a thankful disposition knowing that the knowledge gained was not of their own doing. There were three pairs of these small chambers on either side of the gate facing eastward. The understanding of the significance of these numbers will reveal a wealth of information, and as we continue, the number of chambers will also increase signifying our spiritual growth and maturity. There were three pairs of chambers at this level, which indicates completeness, as man regains fellowship with God.

That which was severed because Adam and Eve sinned is now being renewed. A pillar is load bearing therefore, man is now the picture of a structurally sound being whose ways of thinking has been completely revolutionized. He is now reconciled to God and his understanding is legally enlightened by his Creator. Man is assigned the number six; being created on the sixth day in the image and likeness of God (Genesis 1:26-28). It must be stressed here that man is not GOD, neither will he someday be God, but he is the symbol of his perfect unity with GOD. Because the chambers or rooms were three on either side, indicates that man's humility is now perfected and his knowledge benevolent because he is made free from the strongholds of competition and pride.

Verse 11

"And he measured the breadth of the entry of the gate, ten cubits; and the length of the gate, thirteen cubits."

Yeshua now measures the width of the entrance and Ezekiel records ten cubits. So much is revealed because the number ten being coupled with thirteen points towards the Divine order of the LORD in its perfection and embedded in this perfection is the stamp of the manifold grace of God, in that when we walked in rebellion, He is ever gracious to forgive us when we repent. Five is the symbol of grace, therefore ten is grace doubled 5+5=10. The number ten speaks of the Lord's approval of His perfection and absolute order within man. The number thirteen on the other hand can only be divided by itself or by numbers equal to its value. Because the number thirteen is fractionalized, if divided by one, itself, or an even number it expresses negative emotions such as controversy, rebellion, disputation and disagreement.

Hidden in the number ten is the unification of body, soul and spirit as the new man in Yeshua Jesus will no longer be compartmentalized because of sin, but the regenerative work of his Redeemer will make him presentable unto God as His bride and also His body. The head is of no use without the body and the body is of no use without the head. Abba Father loves us so much that He extended His grace by offering His only Son to die for the sins of both Jews and Gentiles. That which could not have been achieved by the repeated sacrifice of animals was accomplished once and for all times for mankind by a living sacrifice, Yeshua Jesus. Abba Father extended His grace and consummated it all at the same time through His Divine order thereby forgiving our rebellious ways. John 1:12-14 states: *"But as many as received Him, to them He gave the right to become children of God, to those who believe in His name: who were born, not of blood, nor of the will of the flesh, nor of the will of man, but of God. And the word became flesh and dwelt among us, and we beheld His glory, the glory as of the only begotten of the Father, full of grace and truth"*(NKJV). The measurement of the width of the entrance is therefore the foreshadowing of the LORD'S restoration of Divine order in the bride and also the body of Yeshua and this is achieved by His abounding grace towards us.

The length of the gate measured thirteen cubits, which is a mark and memorial of man's rebellion against his Creator. Although thirteen carries a negative connotation, because it is associated with ten cubits; the width of the same entry, the symbolic meaning reveals the depth of God's grace towards mankind. With this in mind the great Ruach HaKodesh (Holy Spirit) revealed something special about the measurement of the entry of the gate because its area is equal to 130 cubits (10x13=130). This measurement is telling a greater story; first of Yeshua the Son of God and secondly of His redemptive plan for Jews and Gentiles. Let's look at two references to the number 130 in Scripture and its symbolic interpretation, remembering that these last nine chapters of the book of Ezekiel unfolds the construction of a special temple of a spiritual kind. One hundred and thirty is memorialized in heaven as a special number and everything that is associated with it points to Yeshua Jesus and His dealing with man in one way or another.

Genesis 5:3

"And Adam lived a hundred and thirty years, and begat a son in his own likeness, after his image; and called his name Seth":

After the death of Abel who was murdered by his brother, Adam was left bereft of two sons, Abel was dead and Cain was banished from his parents (Genesis 4:9-16). At the age of one hundred and thirty Adam's joy was restored and he was blessed with a son named Seth who was his carbon copy and the same was said about Yeshua and His Father; Colossians 1:12-15 states: "Giving thanks to the Father who has qualified you to share in the saints' inheritance in the light. He delivered us from the power of darkness and transferred us to the kingdom of the Son he loves, in whom we have redemption, the forgiveness of sins. He is the image of the invisible God, the firstborn over all creation" (NET, see also 2 Corinthians 4:4). As we compare the Genesis account of the death of Abel, the severing of family ties with Cain and the birth of Seth a picture of redemption can be seen. Adam gained a third son that brought him joy; and so is Yeshua unto Abba Father: Mathew 3:17; 12:18; 17:5;

Isaiah 42:1-4; Mark 1:11; Luke 3:22; 2 Peter 1:17. He is the expressed image of GOD and we who were once dead in sin were given a second chance, being brought back to life through Him. Yeshua redeemed and reconciled us unto Abba Father through the offering of Himself for all mankind (see Colossians 2:13-14).

One hundred and thirty is 10x13, a picture of the grace of God towards mankind that we see throughout the Scriptures giving us a free choice to live forever in His kingdom or a life of misery in Sheol. What then is the spiritual significance of one hundred and thirty? First of all 100 is 1 followed by two zeros [00], which is the regenerative life we have in Yeshua. There is no beginning or ending of the Godhead. Just like a seed planted produces after its kind, so will we be the offspring of the Self-existing GOD. Next is the spiritual value of 30; this number declares the flawless Divinity and absolute perfection of the Lord GOD and when added to 100 we see appearing the Oneness of the Godhead and their absolute Divine perfection, paving the way for our grand homecoming as their offspring. This is the understanding of 130, the measured area of the entrance of the door. Yeshua declares that He is the only door to Abba Father (John 10:1-9); therefore He is our Kinsman-Redeemer and great High Priest. Hebrews 2:16-18; and 4:14-16 states this fact about Yeshua Jesus: "*For indeed He does not give aid to angels, but He does give aid to the seed of Abraham. Therefore, in all things He had to be made like His brethren, that He might be a merciful and faithful High Priest in things pertaining to God, to make propitiation for the sins of the people. For in that He Himself has suffered, being tempted, He is able to aid those who are tempted. . . . Seeing then that we have a great High Priest who has passed through the heavens, Jesus the Son of God, let us hold fast our confession*" (NKJV). Yeshua is the only one found honorable to measure the temple, no other man was worthy for this propitious task. This knowledge validates the fact that it was the pre-incarnate Son of GOD, the Master Builder and foundation of our faith who chaperoned Ezekiel. He was assigned the task of building this fourth temple and all measurements of the new man are found in Him. We must therefore be faithful ambassadors to the end to be found deserving to be measured in Him. The Apostle Paul in his first letter to the Corinthians wrote: "*We are coworkers belonging to God. You are God's field, God's building. According to the grace of God given to me, like a skilled master builder I laid a foundation, but someone else builds on it. And each one must be careful how he builds. For no one can lay any foundation other than what is being laid, which is Jesus Christ"* (1 Corinthians 3:9-11 NET).

<u>Numbers 7:13-85</u>

Once again we see the number 130 as the weight of the offering of each silver dish presented by the leaders of the twelve tribes of Israel after Moses reared up the Tabernacle in the wilderness and dedicated it unto the LORD. Twelve silver dishes each weighing 130 shekels reveals the equality of the Oneness of the Godhead and their absolute Divine perfection. Twelve is the number that is perfect both in its quality as well as its nature and completes the government of God, while silver is symbolic of redemption. The weight of each dish had to be the same, because of the equality of the price for our redemption that was found in one man; Yeshua: the same yesterday, today, and forever (Hebrews 13:8).

Verse 12

"The space also before the little chambers was one cubit on this side, and the space was one cubit on that side: and the little chambers were six cubits on this side, and six cubits on that side."

The measurements for the space before the little chambers is given as one cubit on both sides unlike the chambers in verse seven that measured five cubits; these chambers are six cubits square. A square has all its sides equal and this is a picture of man's progressive growth and maturity in God, he cares not for preeminence, but the unified participation of each other for their common good, which is also a sign that the chambers of the soul is overcoming carnality and becoming spiritually mature.

Verse 13

"He measures then the gate from the roof of one little chamber to the roof of another: the breadth was five and twenty cubits, door against door."

This measurement of twenty-five cubits from door to door is a picture of the super abounding and all-encompassing grace of GOD towards mankind. God looks upon man whom He created from the dust of the earth and submerges him into His grace that was made available by Yeshua's sacrifice. Yeshua laid down His life for this very reason so that He could take it again, therefore presenting us to the Father as not guilty (see John 10:14-18), because He poured out His soul for the soul of all mankind (Isaiah 53:12). The spirit of man is one hundred percent owned by God, but the battle rages for the soul: the faculties of man's thoughts, emotion and power to choose.

Verse 14

"He made also posts of threescore cubits, even unto the post of the court round about the gate."

Yeshua takes a break from measuring and for the first time since He took the prophet on this tour to view the reconstruction of the new man as a temple, Ezekiel now observes Him making something different. Isaiah said: *"Do not call to mind the former things, or ponder things of the past. "Behold, I will do something new, now it will spring forth; will you not be aware of it? I will even make a roadway in the wilderness, and rivers in the desert"* (43:18-19). Yeshua now makes posts of sixty cubits (one score equals 20 cubits). Notice Ezekiel did not document how many posts were made because the focus was not about the number of posts but its measurement which is a picture of the new man in Yeshua Jesus being upright as a pillar in the temple of GOD.

In Revelation chapter 3:7-12 the church in Philadelphia is said to be of little strength yet obeyed Yeshua Jesus and did not deny His name. He told them how much He loved them because of their obedience to endure without wavering. Revelation 3:12 states: *"Him that overcometh will I make a pillar in the temple of My God, and he shall go no more out: and I will write upon him the name of My God, and the name of the city of My God, which is New Jerusalem, which commeth down out of heaven from My God: and I will write upon him My new name."* This is just what Yeshua is doing here; the posts or pillars are those Believers whom Yeshua has endorsed as being worthy to be the support beam for the framework of this temple. The measurement of the posts are sixty cubits and 60 is the spiritual value of man's progress; arising to a level of perfection and productivity in his Savior which is His ultimate goal. These posts that are built by Yeshua are His personal gift to those described in Revelation 3:7-12; they will stand as a memorial all around the courtyard of the gate because they endured and kept the faith to the end.

Verse 15

"And from the face of the gate of the entrance unto the face of the porch of the inner gate were fifty cubits."

Here unveils a jubilee above all jubilees, the debt of mankind has been paid in full by Yeshua and the unveiling of the new man is taking shape. Verse 15 mentions "the face of the gate." The Hebrew word for face is **Panim** or **Paneh** [6440] and speaks of the emotions. When bound with fifty or the jubilee the expressive understanding is a welcoming entrance into Abba Father as man's perpetual joy is restored and this joy is reflected on his face. This is a celebratory entrance as Psalm 100 declares: *"Make a joyful shout to the LORD, all you lands! Serve the LORD with gladness; come before His presence with singing. Know that the LORD, He is God; it is He who has made us, and not we ourselves; we are His people and the sheep of His pasture. Enter into His gates with thanksgiving, and into His courts with praise. Be thankful to Him and bless His name. For the LORD is good; His mercy is everlasting, and His truth endures to all generation"* (NKJV). The new man in Yeshua is now free of all worries and cares and worships the Lord GOD uninhibited.

Verse 16

"And there were narrow windows to the little chambers, and to their posts within the gate round about, and likewise to the arches: and windows were round about inward: and upon each post were palm trees."

It is said here that the little chambers had "narrow windows:" The little chambers is a picture of the humbling of the soul. The word transliterated "narrow," will shed light on this belief because its Hebrew rendering is **Atam** [331]. **Atam** also expresses an action of closing the lips or plugging the ears, which is the most appropriate rendering. With humility there is a degree of silence, this is not stupidity but an act of unselfish restraint. Proverbs 17:27-28 explains this quite well: "*A truly wise person uses few words; a person with understanding is even-tempered. Even fools are thought wise when they keep silent; with their mouth shut, they seem intelligent*" (NLT). The new man in Yeshua will not usurp his brother but takes pleasure in the cohesive service and worship of the Lord his GOD in this new spiritual temple.

So far we see knowledge appearing restrained symbolically by the act of closing the lips or plugging the ears. Windows are mentioned in its plural form in Ezekiel 40:16; its Hebraic root is **Challown** [2474], which may be defined as that which is perforated or pierced. Piercing comes with pain, it points to sanctification and regeneration. Piercing is therefore necessary to transform the new man from the kingdom of darkness into the kingdom of light. With these piercing small holes are created that allows light to shine through much the same as windows. Light is that which sustains life and Yeshua who is the light of the world is also the light of this temple! These are His words about Himself recorded in John 8:12: "*... I am the light of the world: he that followeth Me shall not walk in darkness, but shall have the light of life":* and of His followers He said in Matthew 5:14, 16: "*Ye are the light of the world. A city that is set on a hill cannot be hid. . . . Let your light so shine before men, that they may see your good works and glorify your Father which is in heaven.*"

Sanctification and regeneration are the prerequisites for revelation and with this type of revelation the knowledge of the glory of God is understood through the working of Holy Spirit within. Knowledge is sometimes referred to as enlightenment or one might use the phrase "all of a sudden it was like a light bulb went on." This imagery is used to describe a revelation. However, the knowledge of the new man in Yeshua Jesus takes the form of a download into his soul by the all-knowing God and therefore man cannot credit any revelation or enlightenment as his own. Remember the words of Yeshua to His disciples in Mathew 5:14: "*Ye are the light of the world. A city that is set on a hill cannot be hid.*" For this reason Yeshua took Ezekiel and showed him the city of Jerusalem a figure of the coming elevation of man in Him, as he takes up his own cross and follow his Savior daily. The narrow windows of the little chambers were necessary to allow an intense stream of light to flood the arches. Notice these rays of light were also shining through their posts. These were the support beams for the framework of the temple's foundation that has already been identified as the Overcomers who kept the faith and endured to the end. Rays of light also radiated the circumference of the gate which is a symbol of Yeshua Himself.

Lastly we see the perforations or windows allowing a stream of light (knowledge) within the arches that were hidden from public view. Philippians 2:3-11 states: "*Instead of being motivated by selfish ambition or vanity, each of you should in humility, be moved to treat one another as more important than yourself. Each of you should be concerned not only about your own interests, but about the interests of others as well. You should have the same attitude toward one another that Christ Jesus had, who though he existed in the form of God did not regard equality with God as something to be grasped, but emptied himself by taking on the form of a slave, by looking like other men, and by sharing in human nature. He humbled himself, by becoming obedient to the point of death even death on a cross! As a result God exalted him and gave him the name that is above every name, so that at the name of Jesus every knee will bow in heaven and on earth and under the earth and every tongue confess that Jesus Christ is Lord to the glory of God the Father*" (NET). In the coming reign of Yeshua Jesus, the new man will have no time to display knowledge in a selfish way because he will be aware of its source, and with this awareness comes thankfulness and humility. The narrow windows of the little chambers can be expressed as knowledge with humility, because it is given and sustained by the light that emanates from none other than Yeshua his Redeemer!

Windows otherwise called porches were also in the arches and the reason for this is the fact that the new man in Yeshua will be pure light: he will be pure as his Redeemer is pure. As the regenerated and reconstructed man enters into Yeshua Jesus by this walkway, he will continue to be bathed in light which radiates from the presence of God. He will no longer strive for worldly pleasures or the praises of men, but identifies himself with Yeshua, as Yeshua identifies Himself with Abba Father. Ezekiel also observed that the posts were palm trees, and the Hebrew word used here is **Timmor** [8561], which is taken from its root **Tamar** [8558]. This word can be defined as that which is upright, in right standing, honorable, honest and just, and these are character traits of the Overcomers in Yeshua.

Palm trees remain resilient in very hot and arid climatic conditions and produces a wide range of products, from food to drink and edible oils. Symbolically palm trees are a picture of righteousness, jubilation, felicitation and worship (John 12:12-13; Matthew 21:1-11; Mark 11:1-11; Luke 19:28-40). Because of the adverse conditions under which these palm trees grow, we see a picture of the overcoming Believer being perfected and progressing in maturity; bearing fruit as trees of righteousness. Even under great duress, he continues to rejoice in the LORD and the power of His might. In Ezekiel 40:16 the post did not look like palm trees, neither were they engraved with palm trees; they were actually palm trees, which meant they were planted by someone. Isaiah 61:3 describes this class of Overcomers who have come through great tribulation and are given the symbolic name "palm trees;" the verse states: *"To console those who mourn in Zion, to give them beauty for ashes, the oil of joy for mourning, the garment of praise for the spirit of heaviness; that they may be called trees of righteousness, the planting of the LORD, that He may be glorified"* (NKJV). Man will enjoy a perpetual Sabbath of rest as he celebrates the eternal Feast of the Passover Lamb of God; for such is his privilege as an Overcomer.

The righteous will grow like the palm trees and flourish in the presence of the LORD (Psalm 92:12-13). As the palm trees flourish and remain productive under the heat of adversity, so did these Overcomers. Every part of the palm tree is useful and so are these Saints of God. In the fourth temple, the Believers who are symbolically called "palm trees," will gracefully project like pilasters at the entrance of the temple, but this is only the beginning of his experience as a new creation of God. This phase of reconstruction is taking place in the outer court or body as man presents himself unto the Lord as a living sacrifice, holy and acceptable unto the Lord, which is his due diligence (Romans 12:1). As the regenerating and renewing work of Holy Spirit continues to transform man within, this perfecting work is demonstrated in his character for all to see.

Of much importance is the association of palm tree with Sukkoth, also known as the Feast of Booth or Tabernacles celebrated in the 15th day of Tishrei (around late September or October). This mandatory Jewish festival is a seven day observation connected with the pilgrimage to the temple in Jerusalem. Each day during this festive occasion members of households would recite a blessing holding a palm frond that is wrapped in willow and myrtle, symbolic of the end of the wandering of man from Abba Father.

The posts, which are actually palm trees, makes up the foundational blocks of the Overcomers at the entrance of the new man into Yeshua Jesus. The Lord then begins a makeover, preparing man's outer court (his body), inner court (his soul), and most holy place (his spirit), to be a regenerated and unified whole that will be totally free from sin! This is the beginning point of man's spiritual experience which is to come. As Yeshua Jesus continues His reconstructive work in man whom He loves so much, the depth and degree of man's makeover will only intensify, and by the end of the building of the temple of man, he will look just like Yeshua in his character.

These posts were actually living palm trees, the symbolic foundation of the Overcomers who have been declared righteous and most useful and whose entrance into Yeshua is marked by jubilant worship in holiness. Yeshua Messiah will present this new temple of man to His Father who will be well pleased to welcome him into his new home and the glorious kingdom of His Son. Eden was a great place to be before the fall of man. When man returns to the Lord GOD, he has in fact returned to the Paradise of GOD, being redeemed by the blood of Abba Father's perfect sacrifice, our Yeshua HaMashiach who was slain before the foundation of the world. At man's re-entry point into the holy kingdom, his relationship and fellowship with his Creator will be fully restored, never to be estranged from the Lord again! This re-entry will be one of great celebration as man is received with pleasure and hospitality back into Abba Father never to leave again.

Verses 17-18

"Then brought He, me into the outward court, and lo, there were chambers, and a pavement made for the court round about: thirty chambers were upon the pavement. And the pavement by the side of the gates over against the length of the gates was the lower pavement."

The construction of the wall of the temple of man is being completed, his walls are now resistant to pride, corrupt proof and impenetrable to the forces of evil. No other man is worthy enough to build this new temple but the Son of GOD, therefore, only the Son of GOD is worthy enough to measure it; for it is through Him and not an angel that mankind is redeemed. Yeshua now takes Ezekiel to what is called the outward court which is also known as the outer or utter court; the place where the brazen altar once stood. As the laver is symbolic of our total abandonment and death to self; the brazen altar is symbolic of the yielding of our will to God and death to sin. Ezekiel 40:10 records six chambers located in the eastern gateway. To Ezekiel's amazement and delight, as he continues to observe the reconstruction of the man in Yeshua Jesus he noticed that the number of chambers had increased from six to thirty. These thirty chambers are indicative of man's spiritual growth, as the perfection of God's grace is being justified in him.

If five speaks of the grace of God towards mankind, then six sets of five speaks of a greater perfection as every atom of self is regenerated. Total transformation is beginning to appear just like the art work of a great master sculptor. Titus 3:3-7 states: *"For we also once were foolish ourselves, disobedient, deceived, enslaved to various lusts and pleasures, spending our life in malice and envy, hateful, hating one another. But when the kindness of God our Savior and His love for mankind appeared, He saved us, not on the basis of deeds which we have done in righteousness, but according to His mercy, by the washing of regeneration and renewing by the Holy Spirit, whom He poured out upon us richly through Jesus Christ our Savior, so that being justified by His grace we would be made heirs according to the hope of eternal life"* (NASB). Grace is increasing and here it is six folds. First man had to be unified as one; having all things equal with each other and expressing the pure love of Abba Father, being built up in Yeshua by the grace of the Almighty. Man's transformation within and without is thereby lengthened, widened, heightened and deepened! The Apostle Paul prayed: *"For this reason I ask you not to lose heart because of what I am suffering for you, which is your glory. For this reason I kneel before the Father, from whom every family in heaven and on earth is named. I pray that according to the wealth of his glory he may grant you to be strengthened with power through his Spirit in the inner person, that Christ may dwell in your hearts through faith, so that, because you have been rooted and grounded in love, you may be able to comprehend with all the saints what is the breadth and length and height and depth, and thus to know the love of Christ that surpasses knowledge, so that you may be filled up to all the fullness of God. Now to him who by the power that is working within us is able to do far beyond all that we ask or think, to him be the glory in the church and in Christ Jesus to all generations, forever and ever, Amen"* (Ephesians 3:14-21 NET). Man is here being perfected by grace as the number six is assigned to him from the beginning of his creation (6x5=30); and he will continue to be perfected until he is made complete. Six is man, whereas five is grace; and the product of both is the reflection of the intricate working of God in man which produces yet another number: thirty.

The number thirty reveals that at this stage of man's reconstruction, his perfection and resemblance to the character of Yeshua Jesus is becoming more evident. He does not see himself through the eyes of his peers; neither measures himself against the esoteric rudiments of his earthly teachers who know only in part. He is now humbled by the Omniscient Abba Father and through Yeshua's imbibed wisdom, he will know as he is known. I Corinthians 2:6 and 8:2-3 declare: "*For who has known the mind of the Lord, so as to advise him? But we have the mind of Christ. . . . If someone thinks he knows something, he does not yet know to the degree that he needs to know. But if someone loves God, he is known by God*" (NET). Knowledge is only partial in mankind. He may be well informed but not all knowing; this is the propensity of man. The temple of the new man in Yeshua is established and built upon Him, therefore flowing with His perfect character and His perfect knowledge. Man will be firmly rooted and grounded in his Savior Yeshua Messiah who has paved the way for his grand re-entry into Abba Father never to be separated from Him again. "*God was in Christ Jesus reconciling the world unto Himself: not counting their trespasses against them, and He has committed to us the word of reconciliation. . . . He made Himself who knew no sin to be sin on our behalf, so that we might become the righteousness of God in Him*" (partially taken from 2 Corinthians 5:19, 21 NASB).

Romans 8:35-39 gives us hope for tomorrow as it bears the attributes of the Overcomer: "*Who will separate us from the love of Christ? Will trouble, or distress, or persecution, or famine,* or nakedness, or danger, or sword? As it is written, "For your sakes we encounter death all day long; we were considered as sheep to be slaughtered. No, in all these things we have complete victory through him who loved us. For I am convinced that neither death, nor life, nor angels, nor heavenly rulers, nor things that are present, nor things to come, nor powers, nor height, nor depth, nor anything else in creation will be able to separate us from the love of God in Christ Jesus our Lord" (NET, see also 2 Corinthians 5:14-21; Ephesians 3:1-19 and 1 Timothy 1:14-15).

Ezekiel observed thirty chambers on the lower pavement, but now his gaze is fixed towards the next level; the higher pavement, which is yet another step towards man's completeness in his Savior. Surprisingly the Hebrew word used here for pavement is **Ritspah** [7531], it is a feminine noun transliterated, "hot stones," "red hot," or "glowing stones." Remarkably **Ritspah** is also transliterated in English to describe a female Israeli! This fact symbolically reveals something quite grand, because Yeshua is preparing His bride whom He will present to the Father following her cleansing. This cleansing will be rather painful, but in the end it will produce reconciliation, healing and renewal.

In Esther 1:5-6 it is recorded: "*And when these days were expired, the king made a feast unto all the people that were present in Shushan the palace, both unto great and small, seven days, in the court of the garden of the king's palace; where were white, green, and blue, hangings, fastened with cords of fine linen and purple to silver rings and pillars of marble: the beds were of gold and silver, upon a* <u>pavement</u> *of red, and blue, and white, and black marble.*" In verse six **Ritspah** is also used for "pavement" and it is clearly associated with an invitation for a celebration where both rich and poor alike are invited to attend. In 2 chronicles 7:1-3 **Ritspah** now focuses on a celebration that breaks out in jubilant worship and praise unto the LORD: "*When Solomon had finished praying, fire came down from heaven and consumed the burnt offering and the sacrifices; and the glory of the LORD filled the temple. And the priests could not enter the house of the LORD, because the glory of the LORD had filled the LORD'S house. When all the children of Israel saw how the fire came down, and the glory of the LORD on the temple, they bowed their faces to the ground on the* <u>pavement,</u> *and worshiped and praised the LORD, saying; For He is good, for His mercy endures* *forever."* As seen in these verses a much deeper meaning for the word "pavement" is revealed. It expresses the desire that Yeshua Jesus is extending an open invitation to great and small to attend the celebration of the marriage supper of the Lamb and what a festive occasion that will be.

Verses 19-23

"Then he measured the breadth from the forefront of the lower gate unto the forefront of the inner court without, an hundred cubits eastward and northward. And the gate of the outward court that looked toward the north, he measured the length thereof. And the little chambers thereof were three on this side and three on that side; and the posts thereof and the arches thereof were after the measure of the first gate: the length thereof was fifty cubits, and the breadth five and twenty cubits. And their windows, and their arches, and their palm trees, were after the measure of the gate that looketh toward the east; and they went up unto it by seven steps; and the arches thereof were before them. And the gate of the inner court was over against the gate toward the north, and toward the east; and he measured from gate to gate an hundred cubits."

Yeshua measures the width that was in front of the lower gate to the position that was regarded the most important of all. This was the entrance into the Holy Place, which symbolically refers to the soul; because it is the soul of man that Yeshua reclaimed. Isaiah 53:10-12 states: *"But the LORD was pleased to crush Him, putting Him to grief; if He would render Himself as a guilt offering, He will see His offspring, He will prolong His days, and the good pleasure of the LORD will prosper in His hand. As a result of the anguish of His soul, He will see it and be satisfied; by His knowledge the Righteous One, My Servant, will justify the many, as He will bear their iniquities. Therefore, I will allot Him a portion with the great, and He will divide the booty with the strong; because He poured out Himself to death, yet He, Himself bore the sin of many, and interceded for the transgressors"* (NASB). The soul is extremely important to Abba Father and for this reason it is the area of our tripartite being where all spiritual wars are waged. Yeshua Jesus died to reconcile the soul of man to GOD as the enemy of man, who is Satan, wages war to dominate the soul of man. Yeshua made this point clear: "*The thief does not come except to steal, and to kill, and to destroy. I have come that they may have life, and that they may have it more abundantly*" (John 10:10 NKJV).

Our soul is the seat of our emotions and for this reason whatever is happening within us is unconsciously displayed by our body language, facial expression, and by the tone of our voice in a variety of ways such as; joy, sorrow and anger. What comes out of our mouth is one of the manifestation or pouring out of the soul so to speak. The measuring of the forefront of the gate is the measurement of the soul: the seat of our emotions, intellect and will, which is the driving force of our personality and nature. The Hebrew word **Panim** or **Paneh** [6440] is means "forefront." This very important word refers to the face where the expressions of our emotions are visibly communicated. These responses are the manifestations of the soul, which adverbially and symbolically refers to the seat of our emotions that is in desperate need of regeneration and for this reason, the soul is measured first.

The conversion of the soul is therefore the focus of Yeshua Jesus because it is the prime target of the once anointed Cherub who rebelled. Satan, the name he is commonly known by, and the angels who participated in this foolish insurrection has no soul, and because of this very reason they cannot be redeemed by Yeshua. Demonic entities can attach themselves to any compartment of the soul where there is sin, because these are the areas where we are the weakest and most vulnerable. Demonic activities are evident in a multiplicity of ways, from the influence of one's behavior, to the possession of man; to the more complex organization of ruling powers over cities, provinces or nations. Repentance along with fasting and prayer are useful tools to ensure deliverance, freedom and peace (Ephesians 6:10-18; Mark 5:1-15; 9:17-29; Luke 8:1-2, 26-35; 9:38-42; Matthew 12:43-45; and Luke 11:24-26). The diabolic war which began in the Garden of Eden was for the soul of man and Yeshua has given us the tools and authority to overcome (Luke 10:19). Just as fruits on a tree are not ripened all at once; each chamber or compartment of the soul is at varying levels of spiritual growth and maturity as the reconstruction and measurement of man in Yeshua Jesus continues to unfold.

The measurement from the vestibule of the lower gate to the inner court was a hundred cubits eastward and also northward. North is symbolic of the place occupied by man whereas east pertains to Yeshua. The combined measurement eastward and northward unveils a picture of man in Yeshua Jesus that is to come! The measurement of man in Yeshua is here given as a hundred cubits. If fifty is the symbol of man's freedom from bondage and the public celebration of that freedom is called the jubilee, then a hundred is its reinforcement or double jubilee: The year of total restoration and rest for the soul that has been redeemed by Yeshua and the atonement of His blood reclaiming the lost.

These were the LORD's command to His servant Moses: "*In addition you must count off seven Sabbath years, seven sets of seven years, adding up to forty-nine years in all. Then on the Day of Atonement in the fiftieth year, blow the ram's horn loud and long throughout the land. Set this year apart as holy, a time to proclaim freedom throughout the land for all who live there. It will be a jubilee year for you, when each of you may return to the land that belonged to your ancestors and return to your clan. This fiftieth year will be a jubilee for you. During that year you must not plant your fields or store away any of the crops that grow on their own, and don't gather grapes from your unpruned vines. It will be a jubilee year for you, and you must keep it holy. But you may eat whatever the land produces on its own. In the Year of Jubilee each of you may return to the land that belonged to your ancestors*" (Leviticus 25:8-13 NLT). The observation of the Year of Jubilee is set forth in these verses and Yeshua is preparing man for the perfect jubilee which is his everlasting rest in his Lord. This rest is achieved by the cleansing work of the Holy Spirit transforming man from a carnal baby to a fruit bearing branch of the vine (John 15:1-8). It is the abiding presence of Holy Spirit that prepares the soul of the redeemed (John 15:26-27; 16:13-14). The Holy Spirit is preparing mankind to be reconciled unto Abba Father which is our final spiritual resting place. Isaiah 32:15-18 applying the NKJV speaks of these things: "*Until the Spirit is poured upon us from on high, and the wilderness becomes a fruitful field, and the fruitful field is counted as a forest. Then justice will dwell in the wilderness, and righteousness remain in the fruitful field. The work of righteousness will be peace, and the effect of righteousness quietness and assurance forever. My people will dwell in a peaceful habitation, in secure dwellings, and in quiet resting places."*

Man's resting in the LORD was procured by Yeshua so that he could be welcomed back into the family of God. The first measurement made by the Lord was a hundred cubits eastward; this is a picture of Yeshua's freewill offering to all mankind to come and rest in Him forever. Yeshua proceeds to measure northward, therefore making this rest available to all mankind as a voluntary act. The prophet Isaiah wrote: *"The Spirit of the Lord GOD is upon Me, because the LORD has anointed Me to preach good tidings to the poor; He has sent Me to heal the brokenhearted, to proclaim liberty to the captives, and the opening of the prison to those who are bound; to proclaim the acceptable year of the LORD, and the day of vengeance of our God; to comfort all who mourn, to console those who mourn in Zion, to give them beauty for ashes, the oil of joy for mourning, the garment of praise for the spirit of heaviness; that they may be called trees of righteousness, the planting of the LORD, that He may be glorified." And they shall rebuild the old ruins, they shall raise up the former desolations, and they shall repair the ruin cities, the desolations of many generations. Strangers shall stand and feed your flocks, and the sons of the foreigner shall be your plowmen and your vinedressers. But you shall be named the priests of the LORD, they shall call you the servants of our God. You shall eat the riches of the Gentiles, and in their glory you shall boast"* (61:1-6 NKJV, see also Isaiah 42:7; Luke 4:18-21). Yeshua makes no mistake with His measurements as Hebrews 12:2 applying the NET states: *"Keeping our eyes fixed on Jesus, the pioneer and perfecter of our faith. For the joy set out for him he endured the cross, disregarding its shame, and has taken his seat at the right hand of the throne of God."* Here Yeshua set forth the measurement being the Jubilee for our atonement, giving unto us that which our works alone could not have obtained. Yeshua is our High Priest and honors man as the royal priesthood of God.

The Lord our Messiah continues His measurement of the coming new man: a holy temple unto God. In Ezekiel 40:20-21, it is recorded that Yeshua measures the gate of the outer court northward that included its chambers, posts and arches and these were all identical. The gate was fifty cubits long and twenty-five cubits wide; the same measurement documented in Ezekiel 40:13

and 15 which shows man coming up to the same measurements of his Redeemer. This measurement however gives the length as fifty cubits and the width, twenty-five cubits. Fifty being the jubilee, can also be viewed as 10x5=50, which signifies the perfection of God's Divine order which is multiplied by His grace. In this instance, twenty-five must not be viewed as a half-way point but the self, same multiplication of God's grace 5x5=25, which shows that man has no power to redeem his own life. The Apostle Paul wrote: *"And although you were dead in your transgressions and sins, in which you formerly lived according to this world's present path, according to the ruler of the kingdom of the air, the ruler of the spirit that is now energizing the sons of disobedience, among whom all of us also formerly lived out our lives in the cravings of our flesh, indulging the desires of the flesh and the mind, and were by nature children of wrath even as the rest … But God, being rich in mercy, because of his great love with which he loved us, even though we were dead in transgressions, made us alive together with Christ by grace you are saved! And he raised us up with him and seated us in the heavenly realms in Christ Jesus, to demonstrate in the coming ages the surpassing wealth of his grace in kindness toward us in Christ Jesus. For by grace you are saved through faith, and this is not from yourselves, it is the gift of God; it is not from works, so that no one can boast. For we are his workmanship, having been created in Christ Jesus for good works that God prepared beforehand so we may do them"* (Ephesians 2:1-10 NET). All of man's measurements in Yeshua will be equal because He is the Artisan that is producing this temple and its finished work will be displayed before the Father with great joy.

In the construction of the Tabernacle in the wilderness by Moses, the Lord GOD gave His servant specific instructions and in these instructions there were no steps to ascend. In this fourth and permanent temple, the Lord takes Ezekiel up seven steps, which signifies a new beginning of man's ascension into Yeshua, as the number seven indicates his spiritual perfection and rest. Notice in these verses, Ezekiel did not ascend these steps alone, he was led by Yeshua, because man cannot attain this standard on his own. Isaiah 61:1-3 speaks of the completion of man's perfection in Yeshua: *"The Spirit of the Lord GOD is upon Me, because the LORD has anointed Me to preach good tidings to the poor; He has sent Me to heal the brokenhearted, to proclaim liberty to the captives, and the opening of the prison to those who are* bound; to proclaim the acceptable year of the LORD, and the day of vengeance of our God; to comfort all who mourn, to console those who mourn in Zion, to give them beauty for ashes, the oil of joy for mourning, the garment of praise for the spirit of heaviness; that they may be called trees of righteousness, the planting of the LORD, that He maybe glorified" (NKJV, see also Luke 4:18-21). There is a time coming when the oppression and deception of our arch enemy, the prince of darkness will be exposed, broken and shattered forever. Every struggle with sin and every battle in the flesh will be conquered and finally placed under our feet. One day we will all walk in the empowerment of Yeshua Jesus our King and High Priest who enables us to be victorious as we place our trust in Him wholeheartedly and at that time all our measurements will be alike because we will overcome as He overcame.

Verses 24-27

"After that he brought me toward the south, and behold a gate toward the south: and he measured the posts thereof and the arches thereof according to these measures. And there were windows in it and in the arches thereof round about, like those windows: the length was fifty cubits, and the breadth five and twenty cubits. And there were seven steps to go up to it, and the arches thereof were before them: and it had palm trees, one on this side, and another on that side, upon the posts thereof. And there was a gate in the inner court toward the south: and he measured from gate to gate toward the south an hundred cubits."

Ezekiel follows the Lord from the outer court and makes his way towards the inner court, which is the second level of man in Yeshua. This is a picture of man progressing and being perfected spiritually as he puts off the old man for the new because the light of Yeshua radiates in every chamber of his soul. Man is not measured against his own merit or achievements, but based on his position in Yeshua Messiah who has the power to save or destroy both the soul and body in hell (Matthew 10:28). The posts have already been identified as the support beams for the framework of the temple of man because the foundational blocks of his entrance is made available by Yeshua. The living palm trees and posts being one, points to the unification of the Overcomer and unveils his triumphant victory over sin. The temple of man is being stabilized as his foundation is settled in the Bedrock, who is Yeshua Jesus. Man's stability is only achieved by being in Yeshua, because it is by His sustaining Spirit of grace that man is able to live an overcoming and victorious life. Man therefore has to decide for himself whom he will serve and if he chooses the Lord, Yeshua Jesus petitions the Father to empower him by His Spirit (John 14:15-17). In the new temple it is upon Yeshua that man's foundation will be built. It is stated in 1 John 3:2 applying the NKJV: *"Beloved, now we are children of God; and it has not yet been revealed what we shall be, but we know that when He is revealed, we shall be like Him, for we shall see Him as He is."* Yeshua is the mirror by which man sees himself and every facet of the new man in Yeshua, will be a reflection of His character. Notice throughout the construction of the new temple of man, windows are a very important feature, because his light and enlightenment comes from no other source but Yeshua Jesus who is man's pillar of support in this new temple.

Whether we use the word "porches" or "arches" to describe the pillars of the temple, the Hebrew word transliterated for both is **Eylam**, **Elam** or **Elammah** [361], which alludes to the act of bearing a load and therefore symbolic of Yeshua who was found worthy by Abba Father to carry the weight of our sins Isaiah chapter 53. These magnificent arches symbolically speak of Yeshua the High Priest who is also our burden bearer. Because He carries the weight of our sins, He is the bridge or doorway that leads to eternal life. In the tabernacle of Moses and Solomon, man was the designated high priest and man will also be the high priest in the third temple soon to be built in Israel. In the fourth and final temple however, Yeshua will be the High Priest and each building block of man's new creation will serve a dynamic purpose in the New Jerusalem. In this final temple that Yeshua now takes the prophet Ezekiel to view in this tremendous vision, Yeshua Himself is its builder! This will be the resting place where Abba Father, Yeshua the Son and the ever abiding Holy Spirit will take up their holy throne. King Solomon prayed this powerful prayer recorded in 2 Chronicles 6:40-41 applying the NET: *"Now, my God, may you be attentive and responsive to the prayers offered in this place. Now ascend, O LORD God, to your resting place, you and the ark of your strength! May your priest, O LORD God, experience your deliverance! May your loyal followers rejoice in the prosperity you give."* Yeshua Jesus breathes His peace over us as we struggle to maintain our peace in this life. There will be a coming tranquility in which we will live perpetually, being partakers in Yeshua's suffering and also His Divine nature. This coming glorious temple as we see in Ezekiel's vision is the architectural creation of Abba Father; a blueprint that is sealed with the resurrecting power of the blood of His Son. It is He who bears our burdens, supports our frail beings, and anchors us into His heart and nothing will ever separate us from His love.

The grace and peace of Abba Father is perfected and also multiplied in us, as 2 Peter 1:2-4 states: *"Grace and peace be multiplied unto you through the knowledge of God, and of Jesus our Lord. According to His divine power hath given unto us all things that pertain to life and godliness, through the knowledge of Him that hath called us to glory and virtue: whereby are given unto us exceeding great and precious promises: that by these ye might be partakers of the divine nature, having escaped the corruption that is in the world through lust."* When change is truly desired, deliverance will come. Sin is a shackle that binds us to this old carnal flesh but when we cast all our cares upon Yeshua Jesus our burden bearer, support beam, strong tower and arch support, we will be liberated and find rest for our troubled soul. The multiplied grace of God towards us is 5x5=25, which symbolically leads us towards the perfected seventh step: a place in Yeshua where all our tears will be wiped away. Revelation 7:17 states: *"For the Lamb in the center of the throne will be their shepherd, and will guide them to springs of the water of life; and He will wipe every tear from their eyes"* (NASB).

We who have hope must resist hopelessness and put on the whole armor of God as we are instructed in Ephesians 6:10-18; fighting the good fight of faith to the end. Like the palm trees we must endure all things. In Ezekiel 40:24-27 the new man in Yeshua is led to the south gate which is symbolized by the eagle and represented by the prophet or watchman in the body of Yeshua. Here we will see things from above as we gain a greater height in Yeshua where we observe and achieve a better understanding of all things from this dimension as He enlightens us. When we are earth bound our sight is limited, our vision skewed and our understanding partial, but when we rise in the perfect holiness of Yeshua, revelation is perceptual because we are seated with Him in heavenly places. Sin is useless baggage that keeps the soul earth bound, but when we conquer sin we rise in purpose and value, being adopted in the household of faith.

Verses 28-37

"And he brought me to the inner court by the south gate: and he measured the south gate according to these measures; and the little chambers thereof, and the posts thereof, and the arches thereof, according to these measures: and there were windows in it and in the arches thereof round about: it was fifty cubits long, and five and twenty cubits broad. And the arches roundabout were five and twenty cubits long, and five cubits broad. And the arches thereof were toward the utter court; and palm trees were upon the posts thereof: and the going up to it had eight steps. And he brought me into the inner court toward the east: and he measured the gate according to these measures. And the little chambers thereof, and the posts thereof, and the arches thereof, were according to these measures: and there were windows therein and in the arches thereof round about: it was fifty cubits long, and five and twenty cubits broad. And the arches thereof were toward the outward court; the palm trees were upon the posts thereof, on this side, and on that side: and the going up to it had eight steps. And he brought me to the north gate, and measured it according to these measures; the little chambers thereof, the posts thereof, and the arches thereof, and the windows to it round about: the length was fifty cubits, and the breadth five and twenty cubits. And the posts thereof were toward the utter court; and palm trees were upon the posts thereof, on this side, and on that side: and the going up to it had eight steps."

The south is the domain of the eagle, the visionary, the watchman, the revealer of hidden truths in the spiritual realm. Here he is at a vantage point where he is aware of things that man counts as foolishness. 1 Corinthians 1:20-31 states: *"Where is the wise man? Where is the scholar? Where is the philosopher of this age? Has not God made foolish the wisdom of the world? For since in the wisdom of God the world through its wisdom did not know him, God was pleased through the foolishness of what was preached to save those who believe. Jews demand miraculous signs and Greeks look for wisdom, but we preach Christ crucified: a stumbling block to Jews and foolishness to Gentiles, but to those whom God has called, both Jews and Greeks, Christ the power of God and the wisdom of God. For the foolishness of God is wiser than man's wisdom, and the weakness of God is stronger than man's strength. Brothers, think of what you were when you were called. Not many of you were wise by human standards; not many were influential; not many were of noble birth. But God chose the foolish things of the world to shame the wise; God chose the weak things of the world to shame the strong. He chose the lowly things of this world and the despised things and the things that are not to nullify the things that are, so that no one may boast before him. It is because of him that you are in Christ Jesus, who has become for us wisdom from God that is, our righteousness, holiness and redemption. Therefore, as it is written: "Let him who boasts boast in the Lord"* (NIV). These revelations and interpretations are not for the proud, nor the self-promoting who are but modern day scribes and Pharisees; enemies of the truth (see Mathew 23:13-39). Self must be humbled and nailed to the Cross. Yeshua states in Matthew 23:12, applying the NKJV: *"And whosoever exalts himself will be humbled, and he who humbles himself will be exalted."* As Yeshua is light, so are those who believe in Him. As He humbled Himself, so we are expected to humble ourselves."

Everything about the fourth temple points to Yeshua; His finished work on the Cross as well as His continued sanctifying work in the new man to return to the Paradise of God where he will once again be united with Abba Father. The measurements given for the south gate is fifty cubits by twenty-five, here too, and throughout the fourth temple, the atonement of Yeshua's poured out blood is recorded and celebrated as His grace being multiplied unto those who receive and profess Him. Remembering that the arches are symbolic of Yeshua, the one who carries our burdens, He now gives another set of measurements for these supporting arches; twenty-five cubits long and five cubits wide. This is a powerful statement that everything about this new man, this newly constructed temple, is cemented by the mortar of God's grace!

In Ezekiel 40:31 the palm trees are seen for the first time upon the posts which is symbolically speaking of Yeshua Jesus taking His rightful place in man. Ezekiel's first ascension of the seven steps with Yeshua is a picture of man's coming perfection. As man completes this level, we see Yeshua taking the prophet one more step which completes the first and begins the next as he ascends the eighth step with his Lord. These eight steps are a signal of man's spiritual progress or elevation and points towards the unveiling of his tenacity and fortitude to be identified with Yeshua Jesus in every aspect of His life, being not only perfected but also completed in Him. So far these measurements in Ezekiel chapter 40 are designated for the east, north and south sections of the temple of man. As we continue on this journey we will observe the completion of the new man in Yeshua; holy and righteous.

The budding of this new man can be likened to a flower: as its petals are opened by the warmth of the rays of sunlight washing over its delicate surface, it voluntarily unveils itself, releases its fragrance and displays its beauty. The flower could not have done this of its own free will; it is totally dependent upon the sun. Man is no different; he is like a delicate petal in the hands of his Creator, ready to release the fragrance of the Son. The light of God's perfect Son washes over mankind and the warmth of His glory initiate a response. Man being overwhelmed by the relentless flow of God's love, surrenders his will to the LORD knowing that he bears the sin-free aroma of his Redeemer. The Word of God is sure; it reveals length, width, height and depth. Macroscopically we grasp an understanding of the written Word but it is the desire of Holy Spirit to unveil the depths of its truth also. Life is all about choices: the Lord will never force anything upon us, neither will He require of us that which we are incapable of attaining. Our gifts and talents must be chaperoned by love, displayed by love and maintained by love because it is the power of love that nourishes the gifts thereby changing the world. Pride is the offspring of death but love never fails and gives life!

Verses 38-43

"And the chambers and the entries thereof were by the posts of the gates, where they washed the burnt offering. And in the porch of the gate were two tables on this side, and two tables on that side, to slay thereon the burnt offering and the sin offering and the trespass offering. And at the side without, as one goeth up to the entry of the north gate, were two tables; and on the other side, which was at the porch of the gate, were two tables. Four tables were on this side, and four tables on *that side, by the side of the gate; eight tables, whereupon they slew their sacrifices. And the four tables were of hewn stone for the burnt offering, of a cubit and an half long, and a cubit and an half broad, and one cubit high: whereupon also they laid the instruments wherewith they slew the burnt offering and the sacrifice. And within were hooks, a hand broad, fastened round about: and upon the tables was the flesh of the offering."*

Beginning from this point onward, there is a paradigm shift as Yeshua continues His discussion regarding the size of the temple and its prescribed sacrificial offerings. More will be said about the temple and its offerings from chapters forty-two through forty-six. How will these offerings tie in with the new man in Yeshua Jesus? Should their significance be taken literally? Should animal sacrifice be re-instituted when Yeshua has already paid that price in full by the shedding of His blood? All these questions will be answered shortly as the prescribed offerings points to Yeshua's finished work on the Cross and His final resting place in man.

The measurements given for this temple indicates that they were not intended for the architectural plan designated for the third temple proposed to be constructed in Jerusalem. If these measurements were to be taken literally, the construction of the third temple would surpass the glory of the Seven Wonders of the World. This massive structure would be larger than the city of Jerusalem itself, which is a little over forty-eight square miles. These measurements must therefore be applied to the construction of the most important temple of all... and that is the temple of man. We are a temple and the LORD did make it quite clear to His servant King David in the Old Covenant that the construction of a physical temple would be a place for His name only and clearly explained by Stephen and Paul in the New Covenant. Acts 7:44-48 and 17:24-28 states: *"Our fathers had the tabernacle of witness in the wilderness, as He had appointed, speaking unto Moses, that he would make it according to the fashion that he had seen. Which also our fathers that came after brought in with Jesus into the possession of the Gentiles, whom God drove out before the face of our fathers, unto the days of David; who found favor before God, and desired to find a tabernacle for the God of Jacob. But Solomon built Him a house. Howbeit the Most High dwelleth not in temples made with hands; as saith the prophet. . . . God that made the world and all things therein, seeing that He is Lord of heaven and earth,* dwelleth not in temples made with hands; Neither is worshipped with men's hands, as though He needed anything, seeing He giveth to all life, and breath, and all things; and hath made of one blood all nations of men for to dwell on all the face of the earth, and hath determined the times before appointed, and the bounds of their habitation; that they should seek the Lord, if haply they might feel after Him, and find Him, though He be not far from every one of us: for in Him we live, and move, and have our being; as certain also of your poets have said, For we are also His offspring"* (see also 2 Samuel 7 and 1 Kings 8: 27-27).

For the LORD to dwell in us He must reconstruct our spiritual temple and this is accomplished by the ever-present Holy Spirit who encourages those who acknowledge Yeshua Jesus as their Lord and Savior. Philippians 3:20-21 applying the NKJV informs us: "*For our citizenship is in heaven, from which we also eagerly wait for the Savior, the Lord Jesus Christ, who will transform our lowly body that it may be conformed to His glorious body, according to the working by which He is able even to subdue all things to Himself.* It is the responsibility of Holy Spirit to prepare us by cleansing our conscience from dead works as it is in our genetic blueprint to be holy as the Lord is holy" (Hebrews 9:14;1 Peter 1:15-16; Romans 6:22; Exodus 19:6; Leviticus 20:26); this is a personal choice which we all have to make.

In this section of the review Israel's future and that of the body of Yeshua Jesus (the Church), will focus on the holiness of God and His redemptive plan for mankind. Yeshua's prime interest is the temple of man which we will see in these final chapters. For centuries many scholars have been mesmerized by the Book of Ezekiel, but the LORD God has chosen this season in history; over twenty-five hundred years later to break its prophetic seal. As the LORD God has promised, He is now fulfilling; that in the last days He will pour out His Spirit upon all flesh in prophesies and dreams and visions (see Joel 2:28-29; Acts 2:17-18). The Believer is now approaching a place in Yeshua Jesus where his body must be presented as a living sacrifice, holy and acceptable unto Abba Father.

In the tabernacle constructed in the wilderness, the LORD instructed His servant regarding the purpose of the laver. Exodus 30:17-21 states: "*And the LORD spoke unto Moses, saying, Thou shalt also make a laver of brass, and his foot also of brass, to wash withal: and thou shalt put it between the tabernacle of the congregation and the altar, and thou shalt put water therein. For Aaron and his sons shall wash their hands and their feet thereat: When they go into the tabernacle of the congregation, they shall wash with water, that they die not; or when they come near to the altar to minister, to burn offering made by fire unto the* LORD: *so they shall wash their hands and their feet, that they die not; and it shall be a statute forever to them, even to him and to his seed throughout their generations"* (see also 40:30-32). The purpose of the laver was for the washing of the hands and feet of the priests before they ministered unto the LORD. In the second temple that was built by King Solomon, not only were the number of lavers increased but it was used also for the washing of the burnt offering. A very large basin called a "sea," filled with water was set aside for the priests to perform these ceremonial washings. 2 Chronicles 4:6 states: *"He made also ten lavers and put five on the right hand, and five on the left, to wash in them: such things as they offered for the burnt offering they washed in them; but the sea was for the priests to wash in"* (see also 1 Kings 7:38-40).

There is no mention that the LORD found displeasure with the added function of the laver, instead, the very opposite happened. As Solomon dedicated the temple, the glory of the LORD so filled it, that even the priests were unable to carry out their ceremonial duties. 2 Chronicles 7:1-3 states: *"Now when Solomon had made an end to praying, the fire came down from heaven, and consumed the burnt offering and the sacrifices; and the glory of the* LORD *filled the house. And the priests could not enter into the house of the* LORD, *because the glory of the* LORD *had filled the* LORD'S *house. And when all the children of Israel saw how the fire came down, and the glory of the* LORD *upon the house, they bowed themselves with their faces to the ground upon the pavement, and worshipped, and praised the* LORD, *saying, For He is good; for His mercy endureth forever."* Surprisingly however, in the vision of Ezekiel no laver was mentioned as the place designated for the washing of the burnt offering. Ezekiel 40:38 states: *"And the chambers and the entries thereof were by the posts of the gates, where they washed the burnt offering."* By the posts of the gates and near the chambers at the entrance, was the designated location for the washing of the burnt offering for sacrifice.

The chambers have already been identified as the area of knowledge, and humility (see Proverbs 24:3-4); it represents the exalted position of the righteous Saints of the LORD. He lavishes them with many gifts, because they endured to the end. The Lord then welcomes them into the kingdom of His Father and the partial knowledge of the deeper things of God are revealed to them. It must be explained here that another word used for "posts," is the Hebrew **Ayil** [352] which means strong. It infers to the strength of a chief, and endorses Yeshua Jesus as the highest ranking leader over GOD'S chosen people. Yeshua Jesus is referred to as the "chief cornerstone" in Scripture. Ephesians 2:13-22 speaks of our relationship as a new man in Him: *"But now in Christ Jesus you who formerly were far off have been brought near by the blood of Christ. For He Himself is our peace, who made both groups into one broke down the barrier of the dividing wall, by abolishing in His flesh the enmity, which is the Law of commandments contained in ordinances, so that in Himself He might make the two into one new man, thus establishing peace, and might reconcile them both in one body to God through the cross, by it having put to death the enmity. AND HE CAME AND PREACHED PEACE TO YOU WHO WERE FAR AWAY, AND PEACE TO THOSE WHO WERE NEAR; for through Him we both have access in one Spirit to the Father. So then you are no longer strangers and aliens, but you are fellow citizens with the saints, and are of God's household, having been built on the foundation of the apostles and prophets, Christ Jesus Himself being the corner stone, in whom the whole building, being fitted together, is growing into a holy temple in the Lord, in whom you also are being built together into a dwelling of God in the Spirit"* (NASB). Can you now see the fourth (spiritual) temple taking shape?

Now let's contemplate what the Apostle Peter had to say about the body of Yeshua, which is the congregation of Abba Father. *"Like newborn babies, long for the pure milk of the word, so that by it you may grow in respect to salvation, if you have tasted the kindness of the Lord. And coming to Him as to a living stone which has been rejected by men, but is choice and precious in the sight of God, you also, as living stones, are being built up as a spiritual house for a holy priesthood, to offer up spiritual sacrifices acceptable to God through Jesus Christ. For this is contained in Scripture: "BEHOLD, I LAY IN ZION A CHOICE STONE, A PRECIOUS CORNER stone, AND HE WHO BELIEVES IN*

HIM WILL NOT BE DISAPPOINTED." This precious value, then, is for you who believe; but for those who disbelieve, "THE STONE WHICH THE BUILDERS REJECTED, THIS BECAME THE VERY CORNER stone," and, A STONE OF STUMBLING AND A ROCK OF OFFENSE"; for they stumble because they are disobedient to the word, and to this doom they were also appointed" (1 Peter 2:2-8 NASB). The coming ONE NEW MAN represents both Jews and Gentiles as a perfect building designed and built by a perfect Lord and GOD. To procrastinate or walk in unbelief is a dangerous thing. A time is coming when the Great Judge will separate unbelievers from the righteous. It is better to lose one's life in this sin infested world, than to have the soul eternally separated from Yeshua Jesus who poured out His soul for us. Life is short but eternity is forever! We will either experience perpetual peace or torment and the choice is entirely up to us.

The offerings in this new temple as stated in Ezekiel 40:38-43 are not animal sacrifices. This is a spiritual sacrifice because Yeshua Ha Mashiach has already paid that price in full when He laid down His life for us. The temple that will be built in Israel will be desecrated, and it is guaranteed that Yeshua will never set up His holy throne in any temple that has been desecrated. Sometime after the profanation of the third temple, the veil of time will come to a dramatic close thereby unveiling the fourth temple. This will be the holy habitation of the Living God within us through the re-establishment of the kingdom of God and His Son. This new kingdom will be the dwelling place of all Overcomers because the Spirit of God will declare him holy unto the LORD and Yeshua will present His blood bought bride unto the Father for a blessing: a spiritual temple of ONE NEW MAN with Yeshua Jesus living on the inside(Colossians 1:27; 1 Corinthians 3:16; 2 Corinthians 6:16).

Ezekiel 40:38 gives us a glimpse of what is to come; the sacrifices will be of a spiritual nature memorializing Yeshua's finished work on the cross. Isaiah 4:3-6 states: *"And it shall come to pass that he who is left in Zion and remains in Jerusalem will be called holy everyone who is recorded among the living in Jerusalem. When the Lord has washed away the filth of the daughters of Zion, and purged the blood of Jerusalem from her midst, by the spirit of Judgment and by the spirit of burning, then the LORD will create above every dwelling place of Mount Zion, and above her assemblies, a cloud and smoke by day* and the shining of a flaming fire by night. For over all the glory there will be a covering. And there will be a tabernacle for shade in the daytime from the heat, for a place of refuge, and for a shelter from storm and rain" (NKJV). Here is a prophetic picture of the spiritual house of the new man in Yeshua; 1 Peter 2:4-5 and Titus 3:4-7 applying the NKJV states: "*Coming to Him as to a living stone, rejected indeed by men, but chosen by God and precious, you also, as living stones, are being built up a spiritual house, a holy priesthood, to offer up spiritual sacrifices acceptable to God through Jesus Christ. . . . But when the kindness and the love of God our Savior toward man appeared, not by works of righteousness which we have done, but according to His mercy He saved us through the washing of regeneration and renewing of the Holy Spirit, whom He poured out upon us abundantly through Jesus Christ our Savior, that having been justified by His grace we should become heirs according to the hope of eternal life.*" The temple of man will be perfectly built without hammer or nails and the light of this house will be from the Master Builder Himself. The sacrifices to be offered in this temple will not be the blood of animals, but a broken spirit and a broken and contrite heart (Psalm 51:17).

The washing of the sacrificial offering is therefore a picture of Yeshua's regenerating and life giving offering of Himself so that all who desire to be partakers in His kingdom will have the legal right to do so. The offering up of Yeshua by Abba Father for our sins, will be memorialized as a sweet smelling aroma ever rising upward eternally. Hebrews 10:1-22 clearly states: "*For the law, having a shadow of the good things to come, and not the very image of the things, can never with these same sacrifices, which they offer continually year by year, make those who approach perfect. For then would they not have ceased to be offered? For the worshipers, once purified, would have had no more consciousness of sins. But in those sacrifices there is a reminder of sins every year. For it is not possible that the blood of bulls and goats could take away sins. Therefore, when He came into the world, He said: "Sacrifice and offering You did not desire, but a body You have prepared for Me. In burnt offerings and sacrifices for sin You had no pleasure. Then I said, 'Behold, I have come in the volume of the book it is written of Me To do Your will, O God,'" Previously saying, "Sacrifice and offerings, burnt offerings, and offerings for sin You did not desire, nor had pleasure in them" (which are offered according to the law), then*

He said, "Behold, I have come to do Your will, O God." He takes away the first that He may establish the second. By that will we have been sanctified through the offering of the body of Jesus Christ once for all. And every priest stands ministering daily and offering repeatedly the same sacrifices, which can never take away sins. But this Man, after He had offered one sacrifice for sins forever, sat down at the right hand of God, from that time waiting till His enemies are made His footstool. For by one offering He has perfected forever those who are being sanctified. But the Holy Spirit also witnesses to us; for after He had said before, "This is the covenant that I will make with them after those days, says the LORD: I will put My laws into their hearts, and in their minds I will write them," then He adds, "Their sins and their lawless deeds I will remember no more." Now where there is remission of these, there is no longer an offering for sin. Therefore, brethren, having boldness to enter the Holiest by the blood of Jesus, by a new and living way which He consecrated for us, through the veil, that is, His flesh, and having a High Priest over the house of God. Let us draw near with a true heart in full assurance of faith, having our hearts sprinkled from an evil conscience and our bodies washed with pure water" (NKJV). Can you now see that these offerings and washings of the sacrifice are truly symbolic in nature?

The Lord GOD has already given up His only begotten Son, who freely gave up His life as a ransom for all. Would He revert to animal sacrifices? Those who have confessed the Lordship of Yeshua and walk after the Spirit of Yeshua will be eternally grateful to Him for His atonement for their sins and in so doing commemorate the Lord's poured out blood once and for all times. Hebrews 6:4-6 reminds us: "*For it is impossible in the case of those who have once been enlightened, tasted the heavenly gift, become partakers of the Holy Spirit, tasted the good word of God and the miracles of the coming age, and then have committed apostasy, to renew them again to repentance, since they are crucifying the Son of God for themselves all over again and holding him up to contempt*" (NET).

The temple that the prophet Ezekiel was shown in a vision by Yeshua was not the building of the third temple in Jerusalem but that of the fourth and final temple: the spiritual man himself. The Lord will prepare this temple of man to rule and reign with Him in the New Jerusalem! 2 Corinthians 5:1-6 points to this fourth temple, the new man in Yeshua: "*For we know that if our earthly house of this tabernacle were dissolved, we have a building of God, a house not made with hands, eternal in the heavens. For in this we groan, earnestly desiring to be clothed upon with our house which is from heaven: if so be that being clothed we shall not be found naked. For we that are of this tabernacle do groan, being burdened: not for that we would be clothed, but clothed upon, that mortality might be swallowed up of life. Now He that hath wrought us for the selfsame thing is God, who also hath given unto us the earnest of the Spirit. Therefore we are always confident, knowing that, whilst we are at home in the body, we are absent from the Lord.*" The measurement of the man of dust is limited because he is mortal and dies, but the spiritual man's measurement is enlarged because he is governed by the Spirit and the life giving Spirit sustains him eternally, never to see death a second time.

The measurements given in Ezekiel's vision are of spiritual significance and therefore caries a much deeper interpretation. For this reason, the Holy Spirit stressed the unveiling of the book from its Hebraic root. The time is now ripe and many servants across the world have been commissioned as scribes to unveil specific mystifying truths that have been hidden from our understanding for hundreds of years. We are now living in the times of great uncertainties and the Holy Spirit is preparing the Saints of God for the birthing pains, woes and distresses that will soon blanket the entire face of planet earth. Will we give up our birthright for food or will we choose death and live eternally as sons and daughters?

As this godly servant of the LORD is escorted by Yeshua through His spiritual temple, he observes that in the passageway between the outer and inner door were tables placed on either sides designated exclusively for the slaying of three types of offerings: the first was the burnt offering, next was the sin offering and the last was the trespass offering; their interpretive meaning will be explained because they are of great value. First let's talk about the tables that were intended for the offering of these very important sacrifices. To recap Ezekiel 40:41 states: "*Four tables were on this side, and four tables on that side of the gate; eight tables, whereupon they slew their sacrifices.*" It is important to note here that the Hebrew word for "slew" is **Shachat** [7819] and one of its prime transliterations refers to Yeshua the slain Lamb of GOD!

In the tabernacles of Moses and Solomon there was only one altar used for offerings but in this temple a total of eight tables were mentioned. The number one is descriptive of unity, harmony and single-mindedness, which describes the relationship between Father, Son, Holy Spirit and also the coming relationship between mankind and the Divine Godhead (see John 10:30; 17:21). As one speaks of the beginning of unity, the number eight is the completion of it, because it is the number that adds to its perfection as in 7+1=8. There are seven days in a week the eight is therefore seen as the overflow or the beginning of its next phase. So it is with the increase of the number of tables or altars from one to eight.

Man has regained a form of completeness by Yeshua's death on the Cross and for this reason he continues onward to unblemished perfection. In the reign of Yeshua, man will be completely pure and holy as the temple of his body will be finally free from carnality and lust. Romans 5:12-19 states: "*When Adam sinned, sin entered the world. Adam's sin brought death, so death spread to everyone, for everyone sinned. Yes, people sinned even before the law was given. But it was not counted as sin because there was not yet any law to break. Still, everyone died from the time of Adam to the time of Moses even those who did not disobey an explicit commandment of God, as Adam did. Now Adam is a symbol, a representation of Christ, who was yet to come. But there is a great difference between Adam's sin and God's gracious gift. For the sin of this one man, Adam, brought death to many. But even greater is God's wonderful grace and his gift of forgiveness to many through this other man, Jesus Christ. And the result of God's gracious gift is very different from the result of that one man's sin. For Adam's sin led to condemnation, but God's free gift leads to our being made right with God, even though we are guilty of many sins. For the sin of this one man, Adam, caused death to rule over many. But even greater is God's wonderful grace and his gift of righteousness, for all who receive it will live in triumph over sin and death through this one man Jesus Christ. Yes, Adam's one sin brings condemnation for everyone, but Christ's one act of righteousness brings a right relationship with God and new life for everyone. Because one person disobeyed God, many became sinners. But because one person obeyed God, many will be made righteous"* (NLT).

The body of Yeshua now shares His righteousness because of the superabundant grace of God towards us. Yeshua therefore became the Porch, Passageway or Way to the Father and only the pure in heart will see Him. Our coming sacrifices will not be that of animals, but one of praise and thanksgiving. 1 Peter 2:4-6 NKJV states: *"Coming to Him as to a living stone, rejected indeed by men, but chosen by God and precious, you also, as living stones, are being built up a spiritual house, a holy priesthood, to offer up spiritual sacrifices acceptable to God through Jesus Christ. Therefore it is also contained in the Scripture, "Behold, I lay in Zion a chief cornerstone, elect, precious, and he who believes on Him will by no means be put to shame."* Yeshua our High Priest offered Himself once, therefore the three offerings we are about to examine is one of great spiritual significance. Hebrews 7:26-27 applying the NASB states: *"For it was fitting for us to have such a high priest, holy, innocent, undefiled, separated from sinners and exalted above the heavens; who does not need daily, like those high priests, to offer up sacrifices, first of His own sins and then for the sins of the people, because this He did once for all when He offered up Himself!"* With this in mind let's examine the meaning of these three sacrificial offerings that speak of Yeshua Jesus our Messiah.

○   *Yeshua our burnt offering*

Exodus 20:24 – *"An altar of earth thou shalt make unto Me, and shalt sacrifice thereon thy burnt offerings, and thy peace offerings, thy sheep, and thine oxen: in all places where I record My name I will come unto thee, and I will bless thee."* This is a picture of Yeshua in a typological setting under the Old Covenant. Isaiah 53:7 states: *"He was oppressed and He was afflicted, yet He opened not His mouth; He was led as a lamb to the slaughter, and as a sheep before its shearers is silent, so He opened not His mouth"* (NKJV). The prophet Isaiah spoke of Yeshua as that sacrifice that was later ratified under the New Covenant. Yeshua states this fact about Himself: *"As the Father knows Me, even so I know the Father; and I lay down My life for the sheep. And other sheep I have which are not of this fold; them also must I bring, and they will hear My voice; and there will be one flock and one shepherd. Therefore My Father loves*

Me, because I lay down My life that I may take it again. No man takes it from Me, but I lay it down of Myself. I have power to lay it down, and I have power to take it again. This command I have received from My Father" (John 10:15-18 NKJV). Again it is said of Yeshua: *"Therefore, when He came into the world, He said: 'Sacrifice and offering You did not desire, but a body you have prepared for Me.' In burnt offerings and sacrifices for sin you had no pleasure"* (Hebrews 10:5-6 NKJV). If Abba Father did not find pleasure in these animal offerings as Yeshua has so stated, why would one believe that Yeshua would re-instate animal sacrifices when He Himself has already fulfilled that requirement? For an in-depth study see Hebrews 9:11-15; 10:1-21; 12:22-29; 13:10-12 and 1 Peter 1:18-21. There must be a much deeper meaning regarding these offerings and to gain understanding in these matters we must once again look to the original text for answers.

The Hebrew word for burnt offering is **Olah** [5930], although the **Olah** or burnt offering is the most frequent form of sacrifice in the Old Covenant symbolizing the transference of sins of the people and priest; **Olah** is also an action whereby one yields their spirit, soul, and body to the Lord as an act of worship. In the tabernacles of both Moses and Solomon the burnt offerings were exclusively designated for the north side of the altar. The north is symbolic of the place of man; it is the place of his authority and right to decide. In Ezekiel 40:38-43 however, the offerings were not only placed on tables made from hewn stone, but the only way to get to this altar was by steps; the opposite of the Lord's instructions to Moses in the construction of the first tabernacle. Exodus 20:24-26 states: *"An altar of earth thou shalt make unto Me, and shalt sacrifice thereon thy burnt offerings, and thy peace offerings, thy sheep, and thy oxen: in all places where I record My name I will come unto thee, and I will bless thee. And <u>if thou wilt make Me an altar of stone, thou shalt not build it of hewn stone: for if thou lift up thy tool upon it, thou hast polluted it. Neither shall thou go up by steps unto Mine altar, that thy nakedness be not discovered thereon."</u>*

The Lord explained to Moses the reason for not making an altar of sacrifice from cut stone as it would be rejected and declared polluted. The stone in Ezekiel is described as being hewn or cut which is a picture of Yeshua's suffering at the hands of men. The cutting of the stone is therefore significant of man's own guilt of sin and Yeshua's affliction to cancel it. It is written in Isaiah 53:3-5, 7, 8, 10 and 11 that Yeshua was wounded for our transgression, bruised for our iniquities and He was rejected and smitten for our sins. Next is the climbing of man up the stairs that is now permitted because man has finally been made perfect; there is no sin in him to be exposed because Yeshua's sacrificial work for the fourth temple was already made. Redeemed, man is now elevated and therefore found worthy to go up the steps having received a spiritual transformation and no longer a slave to sin. Yeshua became our burnt offering thereby bearing our sin as an act of worship unto the Father.

- ○ *Yeshua our sin offering*

Exodus 30:10 – "*And Aaron shall make an atonement upon the horns of it once in a year with the blood of the sin offering of atonements: once in the year shall he make atonement upon it throughout your generations: it is most holy unto the LORD.*" The yearly sin offering was the most important offering made by fire unto the LORD and also the most important offering made by Yeshua for the inhabitants of the earth. All mandatory offerings in the Old Covenant were typologies of Yeshua's finished work on the Cross in the New that was ratified by His death. Hebrews 9:8-17 states: "*The Holy Spirit indicating this, that the way into the Holiest of All was not yet made manifest while the first tabernacle was still standing. It was symbolic for the present time in which both gifts and sacrifices are offered which cannot make him who performed the service perfect in regard to the conscience. Concerned only with foods and drinks, various washings, and fleshly ordinances imposed until the time of reformation. But Christ came as High Priest of the good things to come, with the greater and more perfect tabernacle not made with hands, that is, not of this creation. Not with the blood of goats and calves, but with His own blood He entered the Most Holy Place once for all, having obtained eternal redemption. For if the blood of bulls and goats and the ashes of a heifer, sprinkling the unclean, sanctifies for the purifying of the flesh, how much more shall the blood of Christ, who through the eternal Spirit offered Himself without spot to God, cleanse your conscience from dead works to serve the living God? And for this reason He is the mediator of the new covenant, by means of death, for the redemption of the transgressions under the first covenant, that those who are called may receive the promise of the eternal inheritance. For where there is a testament, there must also of necessity be the death of the testator. For a testament is in force after men are dead, since it has no power at all while the testator lives*" (NKJV). Every aspect of the blueprint of the tabernacle given to Moses by the LORD represents types and shadows that were fulfilled by Yeshua Jesus; if this was not so, these offerings would have continued after His death.

Yeshua gave up His earthly life that the elect might gain eternal life, being reconciled to God. 2 Corinthians 5:17-21 speaks of the demonstration of the love of God towards us: "*Therefore if anyone is in Christ, he is a new creature; the old things passed away; behold, new things have come. Now all these things are from God, who reconciled us to Himself through Christ and gave us the ministry of reconciliation, namely, that God was in Christ reconciling the world to Himself, not counting their trespasses against them, and He has committed to us the word of reconciliation. Therefore, we are ambassadors for Christ, as though God were making an appeal through us; we beg you on behalf of Christ, be reconciled to God. He made Him who knew no sin to be sin on our behalf, so that we might become the righteousness of God in Him*" (NASB). In the new man, all offerings will be a memorial within his being which is the final act of the Lord's reconciliatory work. Psalm 51:15-17 NET states: "*O Lord, give me the words! Then my mouth will praise you. Certainly you do not want a sacrifice, or else I would offer it; you do not desire a burnt sacrifice. The sacrifices God desires are a humble spirit – O God, a humble and repentant heart you will not reject.*" These sacrifices will not be on display, because they are not for show. The burnt offering and sin offering will be within man as an endowment of what Abba Father has done for him and through him. His Son's reconciliatory work was ratified when He died, rose again and on the third day ascended into heaven to make intercession for all. Hebrews 7:19-28 states: "*For the law made nothing perfect; on the other hand, there is the bringing in of a better hope, through which we draw near to God. And inasmuch as He was made priest without an oath (for they have become priests without an oath, but He with an oath by Him who said to Him: "The LORD has sworn and will not relent, 'You are a priest forever according to the order of Melchizedek' "), by so much more Jesus has become a surety of a better covenant. Also there were many priests, because they were prevented by death from continuing. But He, because He* continues forever, has an unchangeable priesthood. Therefore He is also able to save to the uttermost those who come to God through Him, since He always lives to make intercession for them. For such a High Priest was fitting for us, who is holy, harmless, undefiled, separate from sinners, and has become higher than the heavens; who does not need daily, as those high priests, to offer up sacrifices, first for His own sins and then for the people's, for this He did once for all when He offered up Himself. For the law appoints as high priests men who have weaknesses, but the word of the oath, which came after the law, appoints the Son who has been perfected forever"* (NKJV). This is the love of GOD on display for both Jews and Gentiles and this final act took care of all our trespasses.

o   *Yeshua our trespass offering*

Leviticus 5:14-15 – *"And the LORD spake unto Moses, saying, If a soul commit a trespass, and sin through ignorance, in the holy things of the LORD; then he shall bring for his trespass unto the LORD a ram without blemish out of the flocks, with thy estimation by shekels of silver, after the shekel of the sanctuary, for a trespass offering."* The LORD is glorified in the burnt offering, as it signals transformation which is expressed by a new heart and a right relationship with God. It offers reconciliation as our repentance is accepted by the LORD being made possible by our perfect sacrifice: Yeshua Jesus. Next we have the sin offering which points to Yeshua as our intercessor and High Priest. As God's judgment is handed down to sinful mankind, Yeshua steps in declaring unto His Father that He paid for our sins in full, thereby appeasing God's judgment upon our offences through Yeshua's clemency. Now we see Yeshua as our trespass offering; He that was without sin took our sin upon Himself offering us His atonement and forgiveness. 1 Peter 2:21-24 and 3:18 states: *"For to this you were called, because Christ also suffered for us, leaving us an example, that you should follow His steps: "Who committed no sin, nor was deceit found in His mouth"; who when He was reviled, did not revile in return; when He suffered, He did not threaten, but committed Himself to Him who judges righteously; who Himself bore our sins in His own body on the tree, that we, having died to sin, might live for righteousness by whose stripes you were healed. . . . For Christ also suffered once for sins, the just for the unjust, that He might bring us to*

God, being put to death in the flesh but made alive in the Spirit" (NKJV, see also Isaiah 53: 4-6; 1 John 2:2).

These three offerings: the burnt offering; the sin offering and the trespass offering are memorials of Yeshua's finished work in our behalf; a pleasing sight unto His Father who deemed His Son faithful, for through Him we were made reconciled unto GOD. As Hebrews 2:16-18 rightly tells us: "*For assuredly He does not give help to angels, but He gives help to the descendants of Abraham. Therefore, He had to be made like His brethren in all things, so that He might become a merciful and faithful high priest in things pertaining to God, to make propitiation for the sins of the people. For since He Himself was tempted in that which He has suffered, He is able to come to the aid of those who are tempted*" (NASB). Because these offerings were done for mankind, there will be the mark or memorial within mankind of Yeshua's intercession for him and the mark or seal for his redemption will be retained in his soul. Man will not revert to animal sacrifice in this fourth and final temple; his sacrifices will be his benevolent act of thanksgiving, praise, worship, and service.

To recap Ezekiel 40:41-42: the tables were of cut stone, portraying Yeshua's suffering. Next there are four pairs of tables symbolizing man's spiritual completion and God's plan for humanity. The measurements of the tables where the instruments for the burnt offering and sacrifice are laid, carries an element of incompletion being one-half. In other words, the Lord will not totally reveal this portion as it is yet to be fulfilled when He reigns on earth. It is documented that the instruments used for the sacrifices were laid upon the altar, which signified that this was the final burnt offering and also Yeshua's finished work! Yeshua's offering of Himself pleased the Father and the instruments of His offering were now laid to rest. The measurements of the altar will remain incomplete until Yeshua returns and the whole house of faith is reconciled unto God. Note that all three measurements of the length, width and height of the cut stone were of the same measurement; a cubit and a half. These measurements are L x W x H = volume. 1½ cubit x 1½ cubit x 1½ cubit =3.375. An important observation noted is that the volume falls short of the perfect number four (4). This is not a sign of imperfection but rather incompletion as these measurements point to the coming perfection and reestablishment of man in God's kingdom.

His relationship with us that had been severed by sin is now rekindled as the estranged bride of Yeshua comes home. All sides of the altar are of equal measurement; which gives us hope that perfection is coming to the household of God, as He continues to reveal His plan for the house of Israel and believing Gentiles who will partake in their inheritance.

Verses 44-46

"And without the inner gate were the chambers of the singers in the inner court, which was at the side of the north gate; and their prospect was toward the south: one at the side of the east gate having the prospect toward the north. And he said unto me, This chamber, whose prospect is toward the south, is for the priest, the keepers of the charge of the house. And the chambers whose prospect is toward the north is for the priests, the keepers of the charge of the altar: these are the sons of Zadok among the sons of Levi, which come near to the LORD to minister unto Him. So he measured the court, an hundred cubits long, and an hundred cubits broad, foursquare; and the altar that was before the house. And he brought me to the porch of the house, and measured each post of the porch, five cubits on this side, and five cubits on that side: and the breadth of the gate was three cubits on this side, and three cubits on that side. The length of the porch was twenty cubits, and the breadth eleven cubits; and he brought me by the steps whereby they went up to it: and there were pillars by the posts, one on this side, and another on that side."

Here we see the fulfillment of Yeshua's words in John 4:23-24: *"But the hour is coming, and now is, when the true worshipers will worship the Father in spirit and truth; for the Father is seeking such to worship Him. God is Spirit, and those who worship Him must worship in spirit and truth"* (NKJV). This is a celebration in song to the only wise God. The singers all unite in chorus, declaring the wonders and glory of Abba Father. Notice that this celebration in worship is occurring inside the inner court; the designated area of the soul, and those who endured to the end had something worth rejoicing over. Revelation 7:13-15 states: *"Then one of the elders answered, saying to me, "Who are these arrayed in white robes, and where did they come from?" And I said to him, "Sir, you know." So he said to me, "These are the ones who come out of the great tribulation, and washed their robes and made them white in the blood of the Lamb. Therefore they are before the throne of God, and serve Him day and night in the temple. And He who sits on the throne will dwell among them"* (NKJV).

Keeping in mind that the book of Ezekiel contains double references, euphemisms and metaphors, analogies and allegories, coded mysteries and typologies, we will be better able to understand our God given purpose as both Jews and Gentiles are called to the prestigious office as priests unto God like His beloved Zadok. The name Zadok means "righteous," he was a Levite whose descendants were chosen to be the bearers of the ark of the covenant; 2 Samuel 15:24-36; 19:11-14; 1 Kings 1; 1 Chronicles12:26-28; and 27:17. Zadok was described as a young warrior who later became a faithful priest during the reign of both King David and later Solomon his son and successor.

In the opening verses of the book of Revelation, John an Apostle and dear friend of Yeshua Jesus made this statement: "*... from Jesus Christ, the faithful witness, the first born from the dead, and the ruler over the kings of the earth. To Him who loved us and washed us from our sins in His own blood, and has made us kings and priests to His God and Father, to Him be glory and dominion forever and ever*" (1:5-6 NKJV). And again the Apostle Peter reminds the righteous: "*You also, as living stones, are being built up spiritual house, a holy priesthood, to offer up spiritual sacrifices acceptable to God through Jesus Christ. Therefore it is also contained in the Scripture, "Behold, I lay in Zion a chief cornerstone, elect, precious, and he who believes on Him will by no means be put to shame." Therefore, to you who believe, He is precious; but to those who are disobedient, "The stone which the builders rejected has become the chief cornerstone, and a stone of stumbling and a rock of offence." They stumble being disobedient to the word, to which they also were appointed. But you are a chosen generation, a royal priesthood, a holy nation, His own special people, that you may proclaim the praises of Him who called you out of darkness into His marvelous light; who once were not a people but are now the people of God, who had not obtained mercy but now have obtained mercy*" (1 Peter 2:5-10 NKJV).

This priestly class of saints will not offer animal sacrifices, but instead they will offer spiritual sacrifices which is a humbled spirit and a penitent heart that is acceptable unto the Lord. This class of saints will also proclaim or sing the praises of the Lord, being forever grateful for His finished work on the Cross. This is what Ezekiel was viewing; the righteous honoring their King. Yeshua specifically chose Zadok because he was King David's faithful priest and one day Yeshua will sit upon David's throne (Romans 15:12; Revelation 5:5; 22:16). 1 Chronicles 6:8 lists Zadok as a part of the priestly descendants of Levi assigned as singers in the temple of the LORD. Verses 31-32 explains: *"And these are they whom David set over the service of song in the house of the LORD, after that the ark had rest. And they ministered before the dwelling place of the tabernacle of the congregation with singing, until Solomon had built the house of the LORD in Jerusalem: and then they waited on their office according to their order."* Yeshua chose the sons of Zadok from among the sons of Levi to minister unto Him at the altar located in the south which is the designated place of the eagle and the home of the prophet or watchmen. This position will be replaced by the priests as the prophets of God will be honored with this new role (Deuteronomy 18:15; Acts 3:22-23; Luke 13:32-33; Mathew 13:57; 1 Corinthians 13:8-10).

Yeshua explained to Ezekiel that the chambers facing northward were designated for the priests who were supervisors of everything that pertained to the altar. Looking back at the Cherubim in the opening chapters of Ezekiel, the face of a man occupied the northern position. Yeshua informs Ezekiel that the sons of Zadok were chosen to minister unto the LORD at the altar. This is a picture of the sons of God in their newly appointed office as priest; they will offer the sacrifice of praise and thanksgiving unto the Lord. Abba Father had not forgotten Zadok the faithful priest of David who did not abandon his king during the most difficult time of his reign (2 Samuel 15:24-36; 1 Kings 1:28-40). Like Zadok, the Lord will appoint His righteous saints and ordain them as priests unto God. The priestly role will become more clearly defined as we continue to excavate the depth of the mysteries of the book of Ezekiel. This vaguely understood book of the Old Covenant, offers a wealth of information about Yeshua Messiah and His reconstruction of the temple of man. As man's remodeling nears its completion a glorious picture of the Overcomers will be revealed.

Verses 47-49

"So he measured the court, an hundred cubits long, and an hundred cubits broad, foursquare; and the altar that was before the house. And he brought me to the porch of the house, and measured each post of the porch, five cubits on this side, and five cubits on that side: and the breadth of the gate was three cubits on this side, and three cubits on that side. The length of the porch was twenty cubits, and the breadth eleven cubits; and he brought me by the steps whereby they went up to it: and there were pillars by the posts, one on this side, and another on that side."

The courtyard of the inner court was measured and found to be a hundred cubits on all four sides. Again embedded in the measurements of the inner court (soul), is the celebration of a double jubilee occurring as man approaches another level in Yeshua. The structure of his new temple continues to take shape and it has become more apparent of the magnificence of this structure. Man's Sabbath's rest is nearing its completion only to start a new beginning. The soul is the place where the altar of the Lord GOD will be, the holy throne of God will reside, and the glory of Abba Father will descend. The newly constructed temple of man will surpass that of all temples built by man to honor the name of the LORD his God.

The fourth temple will be unique as worship and fellowship with God and man is finally restored as it was before the fall of the first man Adam. This long awaited restoration will be the craftsmanship of Yeshua's eternal Holy Spirit who resides in us. Ephesians 2:18-22 reads: *"For through Him we both have our access in one Spirit to the Father. So then you are no longer strangers and aliens, but you are fellow citizens with the saints, and are of God's household, having been built on the foundation of the apostles and prophets, Christ Jesus Himself being the cornerstone, in whom the whole building, being fitted together, is growing into a holy temple in the Lord, in whom you also are being built together into a dwelling of God in the Spirit"* (NASB, see also 1 Peter 2:3-6).

The measurement of each post is five cubits and the focus must be placed on this number. Five speaks of the grace of God. Since this house or temple is a spiritual one, all its measurements must be viewed as such. As the holy place of man is being constructed, his posts are the support beams of God's grace which upholds him in the framework of this temple. Man is now prepared for the most awesome experience he will ever have, which is to be presented to GOD the Father unblemished and blameless! The gate was now being measured and the prophet gave this measurement as three cubits on both sides. This is the number or mark of completion as the Divine Godhead of Father, Son and Holy Spirit, are once more united in man; and man now gains a clear understanding of what it means to be created in the image and likeness of God as he is remodeled and assumes the attributes of his Maker. Man will never attain the stature of GOD, but when he sees Abba Father, he will be just like Him in character. 1 John 3:1-3 states: *"Behold, what manner of love the Father hath bestowed upon us, that we should be called the sons of God: therefore the world knoweth us not, because it knew Him not. Beloved, now are we the sons of God, and it doth not yet appear what we shall be: but we know that, when He shall appear, we shall be like Him; for we shall see Him as He is. And every man that hath this hope in him purifieth himself, even as He is pure."*

The porch was measured and Ezekiel recorded these measurements as twenty cubits long and eleven cubits wide; note that these measurements were taken just prior to man's ascension to the next level in Yeshua. The passageway was twenty cubits long which represents the completed work of God's grace (5x4=20), which is man's walkway. However, because his width is said to be eleven cubits; there is still room for both improvement and perfection: being one more than ten; the unity of God's grace and one less than twelve; the elected and perfected government of God's kingdom. Man's temple however, will finally be perfected in Yeshua at the completion of his makeover. The number eleven is not about man's imperfections; instead, it shows that more work needs to be accomplished before he will be able to enter the New Jerusalem. There is another way to examine the numbers twenty and eleven; if one subtracts eleven from twenty we get nine (20-11=9) the infamous number which signifies the final judgment of the LORD GOD against the rebellious.

Ezekiel is taken up yet another flight of stairs as the temple of man continues to rise from ground level and his structure is now looking more like a mansion. His external framework is now covered as Holy Spirit continues to prepare him internally for his glorious reunion with God (see John chapter 17). The finishing touches of man's new temple are now underway as his support columns are erected. Pillars speak of the coming responsibilities and position of man in Yeshua. Pillars are located by posts on both sides, a sign that the Overcomers are now standing tall, erect, and fully supported by his Chief Cornerstone Yeshua Himself! Revelation 3:10-12 states: "*Because you have kept My command to persevere, I also will keep you from the hour of trial which shall come upon the whole world, to test those who dwell on the earth. Behold, I am coming quickly! Hold fast what you have, that no one may take your crown. He who overcomes, I will make him a pillar in the temple of My God, and he shall go out no more. I will write on him the name of My God and the name of the city of My God, the New Jerusalem, which comes down out of heaven from My God. And I will write on him My new name*" (NKJV). Yeshua is the post, while the Overcomers are the pillars; there awaits a glorious end as the reconstruction of the temple of man comes to its completion and man is conformed more and more into the image of Yeshua. We are reminded in 1 Peter 3:12 that the Lord watches over the righteous, Yeshua Jesus supports the righteous and helps them to live a victorious life. This does not mean that the righteous is without sin; but that they have an advocate before Abba Father in the person of Yeshua HaMashiach to plead for mercy on their behalf.

Chapter 41

Verses 1-2

"Afterward he brought me to the temple, and measured the posts, six cubits broad on the one side, and six cubits broad on the other side, which was the breadth of the tabernacle. And the breadth of the door was ten cubits; and the sides of the door were five cubits on the one side, and five cubits on the other side and he measured the length thereof, forty cubits: and the breadth, twenty cubits."

Just before entering the Most Holy Place (the spirit of man) Yeshua made a final set of measurements in the inner court (the soul). We see the measurements of the posts in the temple increasing from five cubits to six cubits, a symbolic reflection of man's continued growth and maturity within the soul realm. The Lord GOD has endowed man with His grace which is the connective network of his new frame. These posts now serve as markers to identify the point at which man; represented here by his number six, is being prepared to experience the final reconnection and rewiring of the soul and spirit as one. Man is being reconstructed to hear the voice of the Almighty as he did before sin entered the world.

In Ezekiel 41:2 a portion of the verse states: *"… and the sides of the door were five cubits on the one side, and five cubits on the other side."* Because these measurements are five cubits on both sides; the number assigned to God's grace, man's soul and spirit is being measured and fitted with it. This door is man's entrance into the most holy place and the one by which he approaches Abba Father. This portion of verse two states that the sides of the door measured five cubits and not the door itself, which brings us to the Hebrew equivalent for sides, which is **Katheph** [3802]. **Katheph** means to clothe; it speaks of the shoulders from which one's garment is being suspended. These are the final measurements of man's soul as he is being prepared as a royal priest to walk in the spirit. Man must be first clothed in his priestly garment before he enters the Most Holy Place, and for this reason Yeshua now reconstructs the Most Holy Place or spirit of man in preparation to be reconnected to the soul. The refitting of man's soul is almost completed and his new royal priestly garment is seen suspended from his shoulders, indicating that he is accepted by the Godhead and recognized as family. Man is the epitome of God's beautiful creation and His glorious reentry into man is imminent.

It is the LORD's earnest desire to reconcile us unto Himself through the collaboration of His Son and the Holy Spirit. Ephesians 1:3-14 applying the NKJV states: "*Blessed be the God and Father of our Lord Jesus Christ, who has blessed us with every spiritual blessing in the heavenly places in Christ, just as He chose us in Him before the foundation of the world, that we should be holy and without blame before Him in love, having predestined us to adoption as sons by Jesus Christ to Himself, according to the good pleasure of His will, to the praise of the glory of His grace, by which He made us accepted in the Beloved. In Him we have redemption through His blood, the forgiveness of sins, according to the riches of His grace which He made to abound toward us in all wisdom and prudence, having made known to us the mystery of His will, according to His good pleasure which He purposed in Himself, that in the dispensation of the fullness of the times He might gather together in one all things in Christ, both which are in heaven and which are on earth in Him. In Him we also have obtained an inheritance, being predestined according to the purpose of Him who works all things according to the counsel of His will that we who first trusted in Christ should be to the praise of His glory. In Him you also trusted, after you heard the word of truth, the gospel of your salvation; in whom also having believed, you were sealed with the Holy Spirit of promise, who is the guarantee of our inheritance until the redemption of the purchased possession, to the praise of His glory.*"

The measure of man is God's multiplied grace in him because he has no intrinsic capabilities to save himself. It took Yeshua's poured out blood to ratify man's redemption and reconciliation, as nothing more or less would do. Yeshua's sacrifice took care of our sins, therefore, He became our intercessor and covering before His Father, being our spiritual burnt, sin, and trespass offering. Yeshua's gift of love gave mankind a second chance to be dressed in a new kind of apparel which is his reconstructed temple to appear before God blameless. This will be the reward of those who accept His invitation to be their Savior and Lord. By accepting Yeshua Jesus, man no longer lives a reckless, carefree and careless lifestyle, but pursues holiness, justice and truth, therefore becoming partakers in God's kingdom. Colossians 1:12-14 states: *"Giving thanks to the Father who has qualified us to be partakers of the inheritance of the saints in the light. He has delivered us from the power of darkness and conveyed us into the kingdom of the Son of His love, in whom we have redemption through His blood, the forgiveness of sins"* (NKJV). Man is making headway in Yeshua as the ark of His covenant is removed from the natural realm into the spiritual.

The Apostle Paul wrote: *"There is one body and one Spirit, just as also you were called in one hope of your calling; one Lord, one faith, one baptism, one God and Father of all who is over all and through all and in all. But to each one of us grace was given according to the measure of Christ's gift. Therefore it says, "WHEN HE ASCENDED ON HIGH, HE LED CAPTIVE A HOST OF CAPTIVES, AND HE GAVE GIFTS TO MEN." (Now this expression, "He ascended," what does it mean except that He also had descended into the lower parts of the earth? He who descended is Himself also He who ascended far above all the heavens, so that He might fill all things.) And He gave some as apostles, and some as prophets, and some as evangelists, and some as pastors and teachers, for the equipping of the saints for the work of service, to the building up of the body of Christ; until we all attain to the unity of the faith, and of the knowledge of the Son of God, to a mature man, to the measure of the stature which belongs to the fullness of Christ"* (4:4-13 NASB). Mankind is being recreated in this chaotic world with a brand new spiritual nature. He must now stay focused, and keep his eyes on the final prize no matter what is happening around him. He must continue to move forward in the unity of faith to his eternal home, which is his ultimate rest in God.

Verses 3-4

"Then went he inward, and measured the post of the door, two cubits; and the door six cubits; and the breadth of the door, seven cubits. So he measured the length thereof, twenty cubits;

and the breadth, twenty cubits, before the temple: and he said unto me, This is the Most Holy Place."

Before examining more of the enormity of the grace of God, we must take a step backward to recapture the essence of this open vision. Ezekiel 40:2 authenticates that it was the LORD that brought the prophet into the land of Israel in this mighty vision, while 40:3 revealed that it was a man and not an angel that was waiting to escort the servant of God. The Hebrew word for "man" is **Ish** [376], which not only defines a mere man, but a husband and points to Yeshua the Bridegroom. The measurement of the new man is founded upon Yeshua Messiah in whom man's new temple is being patterned John 2:19; Matthew 26:61; 27:40; Mark 14:58; 15:29; and it will be the Son of man that will judge man, 1 Corinthians 6:3; John 8:15-16; Revelation 6:10; 16:5; 19:2, 11; 20:12, 13. Moving onward to Ezekiel 40:4; it is clearly stated that this message was intended for the house of Israel. Remarkably though, this is not only a message for this country located in the Middle East, but it is also intended for a people called out of idolatry and every known sin, to worship God in righteousness and truth (see John 8:31-58).

The measurements of this new temple were performed by Yeshua Himself, because man's measurements are not only founded in Him but it is by Yeshua's standard whereby man will be judged. Romans 8:27-30 is so fitting here: *"Now He who searches the heart knows what the mind of the Spirit is, because He makes intercession for the saints according to the will of God. And we know that all things work together for good to those who love God, to those who are the called according to His purpose. For whom He foreknew, He also predestined to be conformed to the image of His Son, that He might be the firstborn among many brethren. Moreover whom He predestined, these He also called; whom He called, these He also justified; and whom He justified, these He also glorified"*, (NKJV, see also Ephesians 1:3-7). Ezekiel chapter 41 will reveal more truths, as man is being measured in and by Yeshua Jesus, the one who will present us to GOD as a bride.

The prophet now stands before the Most Holy Place and watches Yeshua measuring the final portion of man's soul. With great delight, Yeshua informs Ezekiel that He was about to measure the Most Holy Place or spirit of man, because this rewiring will complete man's re-birth as sons of GOD. Yeshua proceeds to measure the post which is the upright support column of the Most Holy Place and the framework of man's entrance into it. With these measurements we see the unfolding of the habitation of the Spirit of God taking His permanent residence in the spirit of man. Each of these posts were two cubits; a combined sum of four cubits indicating Yeshua's finished work of uniting man once again to Abba Father.

It must be said here that the combined measurements of the post in Ezekiel 41:1 are twelve cubits (6+6=12), indicating that man is coming into a perfection whereby he will rule and reign with Yeshua as observed in the symbolic interpretation of the number twelve. Notice also that the door which leads into the Most Holy Place in Ezekiel 41:3 has a measurement of six cubits while its width is seven cubits. When both numbers are mentioned together something quite spectacular begins to unfold, because these numbers represents that which pertains to man first, followed by that which pertains to God. Here we see the natural and the spiritual in cohesiveness: Father, Son and Holy Spirit are now ready and eagerly waiting to join with man's body, soul, and spirit. The next observation of equal importance pertains to the door which is six cubits high. This is the distance from the base to the top, which is the symbolic representation of the elevation or promotion of the Son of man demonstrated by the width being seven cubits; the spiritual value of the perfection of our Savior, Yeshua Jesus within man.

Yeshua is the post that supports us. He is the rejected cornerstone that is now established as its chief. All our anchors are found in Him and in Him alone. A spiritual temple being built goes through the same process as it would in the natural. First the site and foundation must be prepared and inspected after the curing period is completed. Next the framing is done followed by inspection once again. After this process has been completed and receives its final approval, installation of a protective heat resistant barrier is installed to maintain an indoor climate that is free from external elements. The walls are erected and finishes are made inside and outside. All internal structures must pass the final inspection before added necessities such as flooring, driveway, and trim completes the building. This may not be exactly how every building is constructed, but the point intended is to demonstrate that the building goes through a series of processes and inspections that must be approved or else the building may be condemned, having failed inspection. This is the temple of the Believer and the owner of the building is GOD. The architect is Yeshua and the inspector of the building is Holy Spirit. If the building does not receive the seal of approval by Holy Spirit, it is condemned by all three because He is the seal and guarantor of the Believer.

The door is measured by Yeshua and it was twenty cubits long and twenty cubits wide before the entrance of the Most Holy Place. Because all sides are equal, this indicates that the temple of the new man was about to experience a special endowment from the Father in the person of none other than Yeshua, His faithful High Priest. Abba Father's good favor is about to overtake man because man's patience and endurance finally reached a point whereby his soul is completely humbled and he has come to a level of perfection where he will see and serve God face to face and Spirit to spirit. Communication and fellowship is about to be permanently restored as it were before the fall of mankind, and this was made possible by Yeshua Jesus. Hebrews 6:13-20 reminds us: *"For when God made the promise to Abraham, since He could swear by no one greater, He swore by Himself, saying, " I WILL SURELY BLESS YOU AND I WILL SURELY MULTIPLY YOU." And so, having patiently waited, he obtained the promise. For men swear by one greater than themselves, and with them an oath given as confirmation is an end of every dispute. In the same way God, desiring even more to show the heirs of the promise the unchangeableness of His purpose, interposed with an oath, so that by two unchangeable things in which it is impossible for God to lie, we who have taken refuge would have strong encouragement to take hold of the hope set before us. This hope we have as an anchor of the soul, a hope both sure and steadfast and one which enters within the veil, where Jesus has entered as a forerunner for us, having become a high priest forever according to the order of Melchizedek"* (NASB). Yeshua is the chief cornerstone from whom this building is being erected, and the faithful Saints in their final glorious state will find all things to enjoy.

Verses 5-7

"After he measured the wall of the house, six cubits; and the breadth of every side chamber, four cubits, round about the

house on every side. And the side chambers were three, one over another, and thirty in order; and they entered into the wall which was of the house for the side chambers round about, that they might have hold, but they had not hold, in the wall of the house. And there was an enlarging, and a winding about still upward to the side chambers: for the winding about of the house went still upward round about the house: therefore the breadth of the house was still upward, and so increased from the lowest chamber to the highest by the midst."

We are now stepping on to holy ground because it is in Yeshua that we live, move and exist (Acts 17:28). The wall being measured here is a type of protection for the enclosure. Psalm 91:1 states: *"He that dwelleth in the secret place of the most High shall abide under the shadow of the Almighty."* This wall can also be described as the Most Holy Place; in fact, it is the secret place of God where the Spirit of God communicates with the spirit of man. This is God's Holy Sanctuary that is pure and untarnished by sin. Man now passes through the dividing veil and by Yeshua's approval found to be worthy to enter GOD's presence because he has been perfected. Man's measurement will symbolically be retained as the number six, although his nature has gone through a series of changes through the purifying blood of the Lamb. This magnificent house, this reconstructed temple now portrays measurements of perfection because Yeshua is without sin and He now recreates man's personality to be identical to His own. The measurement of the width of the chambers is the same on all sides, demonstrating a picture of cohesiveness. Father, Son, and Holy Spirit now interact with man's new body (outer court); soul (inner court or Holy Place) and spirit (Most Holy Place). Ephesians 2:10 declares: *"For we are his workmanship, having been created in Christ Jesus for good works that God prepared beforehand so we may do them"* (NET). We are observing a picture of the perfected man in Yeshua Jesus. The width of the chamber is four cubits square, which is the number of the finished perfected work of the knowledge of God in man. The chambers take on a greater depth of revelation because they are indeed describing the chambers of the heart!

A dual message is given regarding the heart. When one pours out his heart to another; he is actually expressing the depth of his innermost emotions and secrets, and the same principle applies here regarding these very important chambers. The measurements of the chambers are four cubits square, indicating that the LORD wants to reveal to man something about Himself that was not fully understood by man. At this stage of the reconstruction of the new man in Yeshua, his soul has reached a degree of perfection by Holy Spirit who endows him with revelation. Mankind can only understand the deeper things of God by the Spirit of God which He freely gives to the elect. As we continue we will observe that the measurement of the chambers also reflects the poured out knowledge of the LORD upon mankind.

The side chambers were three in number, thirty chambers on each level. This was a total of ninety chambers (3x30=90); this number reveals that man has attained the ultimate level of perfection in the LORD. Salvation is man's engagement to Yeshua Jesus and sanctification is the preparation of his soul (no gender bias intended) by the Holy Spirit who takes him through the cleansing process to present him back to Yeshua white and spotless. Yeshua then presents His betrothed to the Father for final approval. It is now Abba Father's decision to give a date for the wedding and the offer of salvation is the criterion for being an invited guest to the marriage supper of the Lamb.

The redeemed is now prepared for a royal wedding celebration like none other. The betrothed and invited guests have accepted their invitation and the LORD's ultimate purpose for redeemed mankind is about to be revealed. Romans 8:16-17 reminds us: "*The Spirit Himself bears witness with our spirit that we are children of God, and if children, then heirs – heirs of God and joint heirs with Christ, if indeed we suffer with Him, that we may also be glorified together*" (NKJV). Not only will this grand and final event be a marriage supper; the most important aspect of it will be the spectacular return of the glory of the LORD for the first time to a spiritual temple never to depart again. Yeshua Jesus paid a costly price as a demonstration of God's love towards us, that while we rebelled against Him, with open arms He poured out His grace. We are blood bought by the Son of the Living GOD; the second Adam who is Yeshua Messiah, the Anointed One. 1 Corinthians 15:22 and 45 states: "*For as in Adam all die, even so in Christ all shall be made alive. . . And so it is written, "The first man Adam became a living being." The last Adam became a life-giving spirit*" (NKJV). Yeshua Jesus is our only hope for a glorious inheritance.

The chambers are placed one on top of the other indicating that man's maturity has been achieved through his yielding to the cleansing power of Holy Spirit. This symbolic interpretation lies in the fact that both three and thirty are mentioned together (3x30=90), symbolically pointing to the fact that perfection has been intensified to a higher degree. Ezekiel 41:6 gives us an important piece of information about where the chambers were anchored: they were imbedded into the wall, but this was no ordinary wall. The Hebrew word transliterated for "wall" is **Qir** or **Qirah** [7023], which means the walls of my heart; while the word transliterated for "chamber" in Ezekiel 41:6-9 and 11, is **Tsela** or **Tsalah** [6763], referring to a person's side. The symbolic interpretation points to the position of the believer in GOD, through Yeshua Jesus. Not only are we anchored into the heart of Abba Father, we are also positioned at His side free from guilt, condemnation and shame. Romans 8:1-6 states: "*There is therefore now no condemnation to those who are in Christ Jesus, who do not walk according to the flesh, but according to the Spirit. For the law of the Spirit of life in Christ Jesus has made me free from the law of sin and death. For what the law could not do in that it was weak through the flesh, God did by sending His own Son in the likeness of sinful flesh, on account of sin: He condemned sin in the flesh, that the righteous requirement of the law might be fulfilled in us who do not walk according to the flesh but according to the Spirit. For those who live according to the flesh set their minds on the things of the flesh, but those who live according to the Spirit, the things of the Spirit. For to be carnally minded is death, but to be spiritually minded is life and peace*" (NKJV). What great and endless love that flows from the heart of Abba Father upon His children made up of both Jews and Gentiles from all over the world that pursued righteousness and holiness and is now being rewarded.

The anchoring of man into the protective fortress of Abba Father's heart creates a secondary effect as we will see when we dissect Ezekiel 41:7 from its Hebraic root. A word study of this verse brings to light a much deeper understanding as we explore their assigned Hebraic numbers. Ezekiel 41:7 states: "*And there was an enlarging, and a winding about still upward to the side chambers: for the winding about of the house went still upwards round about the house: therefore the breadth of the house was still upward and so increased from the lowest chamber to the highest by the midst.*"

Each of the following numbers in this verse is explained below as they reveal a much deeper meaning from Hebrew to English:

- And there was an **enlarging** [7337] – *Rachab*; make room
- And a **winding about** [5437] – *Cabab; round about on every side*
- **Still upward** [4605] – *Maal; upward*
- To the side **chambers** [6763] – *Tsela/Tsalak*; my side
- For the **winding about** [4141] – *Muwcab*; circuit
- Of the **house** [1004] – *Bayith*; dwelling place
- Went **still upward** [4605] – *Maal; upward*
- **Round about** [5439] – *Cabiyb/Cebiybah*; on every side
- The **house** [1004] – *Bayith*; dwelling place
- **Therefore** [3651] – *Ken*; yes
- The **breadth** [7341] – *Rochab; thickness*
- Of the **house** [1004] – *Bayith; dwelling place*
- Was **still upward** [4605] – *Maal; upward*
- And so **increased** [5927] – *Alah*; ascended
- From the **lowest** chamber [8481] – *Tachtown/Tachton; bottommost*
- To the **highest** [5945] – *Elyon*; the Most High; Exalted One; Supreme God
- By the **midst** [8484] – *Tiykown/Tiykon; center*

Here is a snapshot interpretation of Ezekiel 41:7 from its Hebraic root:

"And there was space to make room roundabout on every side; upward to the Father's side as the circuit of His dwelling-place went still upward on every side; yes, the thickness of His dwelling-place went still upward and so ascend from the very first chamber or lowest point of our understanding and revelation of Him; ascending to El Elyon; the Most High; the Exalted One; the Supreme God, who is in the center of it."

To fellowship with Abba Father and be led by His Spirit brings joy to His heart. It is Holy Spirit who takes us deeper, higher and closer into the revelation of Abba Father and His Son Yeshua Jesus. 1 John 1:1-3 applying the NASB states: *"What was from the beginning, what we have heard, what we have seen with our eyes, what we have looked at and touched with our hands, concerning the Word of Life – and the life was manifested, and we have seen and testify and proclaim to you the eternal life,* which was with the Father and was manifested to us – what we have seen and heard we proclaim to you also, so that you too may have fellowship with us; and indeed our fellowship is with the Father, and with His Son Jesus Christ. These things we write, so that our joy may be complete." Man was created to fellowship with the Father and this is accomplished through the Word of God; not to ingest it in a legalistic manner, but to allow its transforming power to change us through and through.

As spiritual blindness is being removed from the Redeemed, the man in Yeshua Jesus gains understanding and revelation of how much God longs to fellowship with us and how it grieves His heart to see the anguish of the lost soul in Sheol. Man will never fully grasp the depth and understanding of GOD's pain for fallen humanity, whom He created to live with Him eternally. It was never the Father's plan that His children should be separated from His love. His love continues to flow as much as His tears because He did not send His Son to be the last sacrifice for the sins of a few, but the sins of all. Abba Father is ever watchful over the ones who are anchored into the wall of His heart, yet even the soul that desires to have nothing to do with Him; He still loves and yearns for. Ezekiel continues to gain a greater understanding of the love of the LORD towards all of humanity and this he would rehearse to the captives in Babylon who were forsaken for a season, but not forgotten.

Verses 8-9

"I saw also the height of the house round about: the foundations of the side chambers were a full reed of six great cubits. The thickness of the wall, which was for the side chamber without, was five cubits: and that which was left was the place of the side chamber that were within."

The prophet's attention is now focused on the enormity and ever increasing height of the temple and observed that the chambers were built upon more than one foundation as they were described as being a full reed of six great cubits. Six great cubits is another way of referring to seven cubits, which is the measure of man's spiritual perfection. Man has now developed from his outer and inner court experiences of Abba Father, to being exposed to His raw uninhibited glory in the Most Holy Place; spirit to Spirit.

When six and seven are mentioned together, they symbolically express the harmonious relationship between Father, Son and Holy Spirit, to man's renewed body, soul and spirit. This is a true demonstration of the merging of that which is spiritual with that which is natural. Ezekiel describes an increase in the width of the house as it spiraled upward from the lowest chamber to its highest. The Hebrew word used in Ezekiel 41:7 for "increased" is **Alah** [5927]. The term **Alah** means to rise, as in moving upward and refers to the exaltation of GOD above all others. This would be the correct interpretation since Ezekiel 41:7 states that the chambers increased from the lowest to its highest point. The foundation or beginning of man's revelation of the love of Abba Father for him starts at ground level. This is man's entry point into the presence of the Almighty when he accepts Yeshua Jesus as Savior and Lord. As man increases in holiness, righteousness and truth, he also increases in understanding and from this point onward he moves upward on the wings of praise to the exalted throne room of GOD where he experiences the fullness of joy.

Verses 10-11

"And between the chambers was the wideness of twenty cubits round about the house on every side. And the doors of the side chambers were toward the place that was left, one door toward the north, and another door toward the south: and the breadth of the place that was left was five cubits round about."

Between the chambers was a space of twenty cubits wide which encircled the Most Holy Place (spirit of man). The significance of this number lies in the fact that God's grace towards mankind is complete (5x4=20) and those who accepted His Son also accepted His grace. Now the doors to the side chambers which lie towards the north and south are symbolic of the coronation of man as priest. In the Most Holy Place the office of the prophet will cease to exist and the priestly office will take its place. The width that remained was encircled by five cubits which is the shield and protection of God's grace on display that was made available to mankind by Yeshua. The encircling grace of the LORD is now complete by a circuit of three hundred and sixty degree. John 1:14-17 states: *"And the Word became flesh, and dwelt among us, and we saw His glory, glory as of the only begotten from the Father, full of grace and truth. John testified about Him* and cried out, saying, "This was He of whom I said, 'He who comes after me has a higher rank than I, for He existed before me,' " For of His fullness we have all received, and grace upon grace. For the Law was given through Moses; grace and truth were realized through Jesus Christ"(NASB).

Verses 12-21

"Now the building that was before the separate place at the end toward the west was seventy cubits broad; and the wall of the building was five cubits thick round about, and the length thereof ninety cubits. So he measured the house, an hundred cubits long; and the separate place, and the building, with the walls thereof, an hundred cubits long; Also the breadth of the face of the house, and of the separate place toward the east, an hundred cubits. And he measured the length of the building over against the separate place which was behind it, and the galleries thereof on the one side and on the other side, an hundred cubits, with the inner temple, and the porches of the court; the door posts, and the narrow windows, and the galleries round about on their three stories, over against the door, ceiled with wood round about, and from the ground up to the windows were covered; to that above the door, even unto the inner house, and without, and by all the wall round about within and without, by measure. And it was made with cherubim and palm trees, so that a palm tree was between a cherub; and every cherub had two faces; so that the face of a man was toward the palm tree on the one side, and the face of a young lion toward the palm tree on the other side: it was made through all the house round about. From the ground unto above the door were cherubim and palm trees made, and on the wall of the temple. The posts of the temple were squared, and the face of the sanctuary; the appearance of the one as the appearance of the other."

The glorious revelation of man's ascension into the presence of Abba Father continues as he prepares to embark on a new spiritual journey. The west was described in Ezekiel chapter one as the position of the ox or oxen, which is a symbol of man as a bondservant or minister of the LORD; the west is therefore their designated domain. In Yeshua, man will rule and reign; being the embodiment of all that is good. The new man in Yeshua

Jesus will also bear the personal attributes of his Savior and these attributes are the endowment of man's reconstructed new temple.

The building on the west is symbolic of the works of men on earth being memorialized in heaven. Revelation 14:13 states: "*And I heard a voice from heaven saying unto me, Write, Blessed are the dead which die in the Lord from henceforth: Yea, saith the Spirit, that they may rest from their labors; and their works do follow them.*" The measurement given for this location is seventy cubits wide which is a symbol of the super magnification of Abba Father's spiritual order having reached its zenith in man. The wall is next measured and was found to be five cubits. Now this wall is in essence speaking of the walls of the heart, and here the heart is measured by the grace of God, therefore the measurement of the wall is said to be five cubits.

As Yeshua continues His measurement of what will be a glorious temple of the new man: the length of the building is recorded as being ninety cubits, which is the highest degree of God's perfection in man. This is His way of restoring us once again as though we never sinned. We hear His voice absolutely clear, being finally free from our own whisperings and also that of the deceiver. 1 Corinthians 12:12-14, 27 states: "*For as the body is one, and hath many members, and all the members of that one body, being many, are one body: so also is Christ. For by one Spirit are we all baptized into one body, whether we be Jews or Gentiles, whether we be bond or free; and have been all made to drink into one Spirit. For the body is not one member, but many.*" The coming fourth temple or One New Man in Yeshua Jesus will be one of liberation, holiness, righteousness and truth. The new man in Yeshua partakes in His death, burial and resurrection, and is crowned as His sons and daughters. The kingdom of God is flawless and every aspect of man will one day be the same. The time of celebration is drawing near as a number of structures in this temple measures one hundred cubits, a double honor:

- o The temple
- o The building with its walls
- o The width of the front of the temple
- o The separate place towards the east
- o The length of the building towards the east

- o The Most Holy Place
- o The porches of the court

One might ask the question, what really is a separate place? For the best answer we go once more to the Hebrew. **Gizrah** [1508] is the transliteration for "separate place," it also means the cutting out of a form of a person, polishing, as well as separating. Here we see the new man being set a part and purified. This is exactly what is taking place on the east side of the temple because the measurements were one hundred cubits; the number that signifies total deliverance or the jubilee of all jubilees. Yeshua Jesus' ransom price was accepted by His Father and man has finally come to rest in God; being a perfect remodel of the once sin infested temple. Isaiah 61 states: *"The Spirit of the Lord GOD is upon Me; because the LORD hath anointed Me to preach good tidings unto the meek; He hath sent Me to bind up the brokenhearted, to proclaim liberty to the captives, and the opening of the prison to them that are bound; to proclaim the acceptable year of the LORD, and the day of vengeance of our God; to comfort all that mourn; to appoint unto them that mourn in Zion, to give unto them beauty for ashes, the oil of joy for mourning, the garment of praise for the spirit of heaviness; that they might be called trees of righteousness, the planting of the LORD, that they might be glorified. And they shall build the old wastes, they shall raise up the former desolations, and they shall repair the waste cities, the desolations of many generations. And strangers shall stand and feed your flocks, and the sons of the alien shall be your plowmen and your vine dressers. But ye shall be named the Priests of the LORD: men shall call you the ministers of your God: ye shall eat the riches of the Gentiles, and in their glory shall ye boast yourselves. For your shame ye shall have double; and for confusion they shall rejoice in their portion: therefore in their land they shall possess the double: everlasting joy shall be unto them. For I the LORD love judgment, I hate robbery for burnt offering; and I will direct their work in truth, and I will make an everlasting covenant with them. And their seed shall be known among the Gentiles, and their offspring among the people: all that see them shall acknowledge them, that they are the seed which the LORD hath blessed. I will greatly rejoice in the LORD, my soul shall be joyful in my God; for He hath clothed me with the garments of salvation, He hath covered me with the robe of righteousness, as a bridegroom decketh himself with ornaments, and as a bride* *adorneth herself with her jewels. For as the earth bringeth forth her bud, and as the garden causeth the things that are sown in it to spring forth; so the Lord GOD will cause righteousness and praise to spring forth before all nations."*

Man is supported by Yeshua, having all his sins forgiven. The new man in Yeshua Jesus is lost for words to express his gratitude to the one who was sinless; who loved him so much that He took upon Himself the iniquity of us all, and bore our sins in His own body that we might be presented unto Abba Father blameless. It is God's desire for all mankind to be made perfected in His love, for He is the embodiment of perfect love; not desiring that anyone should perish (see 2 Peter 3:9). Following the completion of man in the east zone, he now joins the Cherubim in eternal worship and praise to the LORD Most High, which is depicted in the temple by the Cherubim and palm trees.

Here the Cherub has only two faces: that of a man and also that of a young lion. These faces looked towards the palm trees, which is a symbol of those who had been through great tribulation and were rewarded with the Overcomers' crown. The Cherub and the young lion or cub symbolically tells the story of man's new function as a worshiper of the Most High GOD, giving honor to Him in perpetual praise. Everywhere in the temple the face of a man and young lion towards a palm tree could be seen. A young lion or cub is inexperienced and in need of leadership and this leadership comes from none other but the Lion of the tribe of Judah; a Brother above all brothers: Yeshua Jesus the Messiah (Revelation 5:1-10).

Like palm trees man has endured many adverse circumstances and found to be worthy and useful to be called into the kingdom of GOD and His Son. Man is no longer clothed in his filthy righteous rags but robed in the righteousness of Yeshua who now honors him as kings and priests unto GOD. What a glorious reunion between the Lord and mankind. Man's soul is made up of compartments, which are rooms or chambers of his personality traits. These compartments must be purified from anger, impatience, envy, lust, addictions and so on, because anywhere unrighteousness exists in our soul; it is owned and dominated by the prince of darkness. By the celebration that is now taking place in the Most Holy Place, it is obvious that mankind overcame because the light of the knowledge of God prevailed.

Verses 22-26

"The altar of wood was three cubits high, and the length thereof two cubits; and the corners thereof, and the length thereof, and the walls thereof, were of wood: and he said unto me, This is the table that is before the LORD. And the temple and the sanctuary had two doors. And the doors had two leaves apiece, two turning leaves; two leaves for the one door, and two leaves for the other door. And there were made on them, on the doors of the temple, cherubim and palm trees, like as were made upon the walls; and there were thick planks upon the face of the porch without. And there were narrow windows and palm trees on the one side and on the other side, on the sides of the porch, and upon the side chambers of the house, and thick planks."

Because this temple is the new man in Yeshua, an angel could not have constructed it, as man's salvation can only be achieved by GOD's Son, Yeshua. From the onset of the vision, the "man," or pre-Incarnate Son of the Living GOD was identified as Ezekiel's chaperone. The stage is now set for the unveiling of greater things as they pertain to man and Yeshua, as all things have been given to Him by the Father, something no angel could attest. John 3:31-36 states: *"He who comes from above is above all; he who is of the earth is earthly and speaks of the earth. He who comes from heaven is above all. And what He has seen and heard, that He testifies; and no one receives His testimony. He who received His testimony has certified that God is true. For He whom God has sent speaks the words of God, for God does not give the Spirit by measure. The Father loves the Son, and has given all things into His hand. He who believes in the Son has everlasting life; and he who does not believe the Son shall not see life, but the wrath of God abides on him"*(NKJV, see also Matthew 11:27; 28:18; John 13:3).

If there remains any doubt that the vision of the temple being built is a natural one, all these doubts will soon be put to rest. To build a structure of this magnitude, the city of Jerusalem would have to be relocated as such a temple would be much larger than the city itself. Secondly, Yeshua would never reside in a temple that is defiled, because throughout Scripture it is recorded that the temple of God was destroyed because of its defilement. A third temple will be built by man but it will be made ceremonially unclean, therefore rejected by God. Yeshua is preparing a holy habitation for Abba Father, which is the temple of man. Ezekiel was given the opportunity to tour the reconstructed temple of the new man, and also the natural temple in ruins located in the city of Jerusalem. The prophet was the first man to be educated on the symbolic prototype of the natural temple; its service and relationship as the standard for the new and permanent spiritual temple, which is man himself. The altar is therefore the first place where man is seen as drawing closer to God in intimacy [in-to-me-see], which also reveals these following basic truths:

1. The altar

The altar was constructed of wood which is a symbol of humanity. This is a picture of the redeemed sons of God whom Yeshua now presents to the Father. Galatians 4:4-7 points us to this truth: *"But when the fullness of the time was come, God sent forth His Son, made of a woman, made under the law, to redeem them that were under the law, that we might receive the adoption of sons. And because ye are sons, God hath sent forth the Spirit of the Son into your hearts, crying Abba Father. Wherefore thou art no more a servant, but a son; and if a son, then an heir of God through Christ.* This altar is located in the Most Holy Place; previously identified as the spirit of man. In the building of this prototype, the Lord GOD instructed Moses: *And thou shalt make an altar to burn incense upon: of shittim wood shalt thou make it. A cubit shall be the length thereof, and a cubit the breadth thereof; foursquare shall it be: and two cubits shall be the height thereof: the horns thereof shall be of the same. And thou shalt overlay it with pure gold, the top thereof round about, and the horns thereof; and thou shalt make unto it a crown of gold round about"* (Exodus 30:1-4). Here the altar is overlaid with beaten gold which speaks of Yeshua's Divinity, but the altar of Ezekiel 41 is all wood because man is now being presented to the Father based on what Yeshua had already accomplished for man and in man. Yeshua paid for this reunion with His own blood. Ephesians 2:13-18 states: *"But now in Christ Jesus you who once were far off have been brought near by the blood of Christ. For He Himself is our peace, who has made both one, and has broken down the middle wall of separation. Having abolished in His flesh the enmity, that is, the law of commandments contained in ordinances, so as to create in Himself one new man from the two, thus making peace, and that He might reconcile them both to God in one body through the cross, thereby putting to death the enmity and He came and preached peace to you who were afar off and to those who were near. For through Him we both have access by one Spirit to the Father"* (NKJV). The altar of incense now moves from in front of the Holy Place (man's soul), to inside the Most Holy Place (the spirit of man) since the wall of partition has been broken down (see Exodus 40:26-33). Here is a picture of the merging of the soul and spirit of man that was once fractured by sin! The first Adam sinned and severed the connection between the soul and the spirit, but through Yeshua total fellowship and communion with Abba Father is finally and completely re-established. In the kingdom of God and His Son, this altar will no longer be overlaid with gold, because this is a picture of man that has been redeemed and declared free from sin. The altar is therefore no longer a place for the burning of animal sacrifices, but a place of praise and worship for the wrath of God has been appeased by the last sacrifice of the perfect lamb; Yeshua Jesus our Messiah.

2. The measurements were changed

The first blueprint of the earthly tabernacle given to Moses by GOD had a different set of measurements than the one now shown to Ezekiel by Yeshua. The first altar of incense was a picture of the Oneness of the Godhead which is reflected in its measurement (see Exodus 30:1-4 above). The altar of Ezekiel's vision is a picture of man's singleness and peace with God at last. Being three cubits high and two cubits long, this altar is a reflection of the capacity of equality that is given to all Believers through Yeshua. Three cubits is a picture of the completion of man's stature in Yeshua and two cubits represents his decision and agreement to forever please his Savior. Width speaks of the extent of a given object from side to side therefore a reflection of its boundaries or limitations and for this reason, no width is given for this new altar because it is the symbol of the new man in Yeshua Jesus and he has none. How then could this altar be constructed if it were natural? The only way it could have been accomplished is by man creating his own width and to do so would no longer make this altar a spiritual one. This temple that Yeshua is building is not natural, because it is not an edifice but man himself, the true temple of GOD. Acts 7:44-50 and I Corinthians 3:16-17 applying the NASB clearly shows us: *"Our fathers had the tabernacle of testimony in the wilderness, just as He who spoke to Moses directed him to make it according to* the pattern which he had seen. And having received it in their turn, our fathers brought it in with Joshua upon dispossessing the nations whom God drove out before our fathers, until the time of David. David found favor in God's sight, and asked that he might find a dwelling place for the God of Jacob. But it was Solomon who built a house for Him. However, the Most High does not dwell in houses made by human hands; as the prophet says: 'HEAVEN IS MY THRONE, AND EARTH IS THE FOOTSTOOL OF MY FEET; WHAT KIND OF HOUSE WILL YOU BUILD FOR ME?" says the Lord, 'OR WHAT PLACE IS THERE FOR MY REPOSE? WAS IT NOT MY HAND WHICH MADE ALL THESE THINGS?" . . . . Do you not know that you are a temple of God and that the Spirit of God dwells in you? If any man destroys the temple of God, God will destroy him, for the temple of God is holy, and that is what you are." Being made perfect in Yeshua, the new man has no limitations or boundaries that will prohibit his access to the Father.

Ephesians 2:1-10 reminds us: "*Once you were dead because of your disobedience and your many sins. You used to live in sin, just like the rest of the world, obeying the devil – the commander of the powers in the unseen world. He is the spirit at work in the hearts of those who refuse to obey God. All of us used to live that way, following the passionate desires and inclinations of our sinful nature. By our very nature we were subject to God's anger, just like everyone else. But God is so rich in mercy, and he loved us so much, that even though we were dead because of our sins, he gave us life when he raised Christ from the dead. (It is only by God's grace that you have been saved!) For he raised us from the dead along with Christ and seated us with him in the heavenly realms because we are united with Christ Jesus. So God can point to us in all future ages as examples of the incredible wealth of his grace and kindness toward us, as shown in all he has done for us who are united with Christ Jesus. God saved you by his grace when you believed. And you can't take credit for this; it is a gift from God. Salvation is not a reward for the good things we have done, so none of us can boast about it. For we are God's masterpiece. He has created us anew in Christ Jesus, so we can do the good things he planned for us long ago*" (NLT).

3. The altar was moved to the Most Holy Place (spirit of man)

Yeshua's prayer to His Father is finally answered: "*Sanctify them in the truth; Your word is truth. As You sent Me into the world, I also have sent them into the world. For their sakes I sanctify Myself, that they themselves also may be sanctified in truth. I do not ask on behalf of these alone, but for those also who believe in Me through their word; that they all may be one; even as You, Father, are in Me and I in You, that they also may be in Us, so that the world may believe that You sent Me. The glory which you have given Me I have given to them, that they may be one, just as We are one; I in them and You in Me, that they may be perfected in unity, so that the world may know that You sent Me, and loved them, even as you have loved Me. Father, I desire that they also, whom you have given Me, be with Me where I am, so that they may see My glory which You have given Me, for You loved Me before the foundation of the world*", (John 17:17-24 NASB). Yeshua now carries us through the veil that was left open at His death, into the very presence of the Living God to partake in His glory, which He had with the Father before Genesis. The position of the altar in the Most Holy Place is the conclusion of our sanctification process as we are now made perfect. Hebrews 9:2-4 states: "*For there was a tabernacle made; the first, wherein was the candlestick, and the table, and the shewbread which is called the sanctuary. But after the second veil, the tabernacle which is called the Holiest of all; which had the golden censer, and the ark of the covenant, overlaid round about with gold, wherein was the golden pot that had manna, and Aaron's rod that budded, and the table of the covenant.*" The golden censer mentioned here is the same as the altar of incense. In the New Covenant *(B'rit Chadashah)*, the altar was moved from in front of the Holiest of all and placed inside because it was now the designated area for worship (Revelation 11:1). Here we see the crown of gold, its rings and staves removed as the prodigal son comes home to his Father through Yeshua, no more a wonderer and never to be dismissed from His presence or cast out of His home. Isaiah 32:17-18 states: "*And the work of righteousness shall be peace; and the effect of righteousness quietness and assurance forever. And My people shall dwell in a peaceable habitation, and in sure dwellings, and in quiet resting places.*" This is the final resting place of God's people because this is the finished work of Yeshua; making us presentable and acceptable unto His Father as a sweet aroma. 2 Corinthians

101

2:12-14 states: "*Now thanks be to God who always leads us in triumph in Christ, and through us diffuses the fragrance of His knowledge in every place. For we are to God the fragrance of Christ among those who are being saved and among those who are perishing*" (NKJV). The incense that is being offered here is symbolic in nature and is the result of mankind's acceptance of Yeshua as Savior and Lord.

As Ezekiel follows Yeshua and documents every detail of this coming temple he writes in 41:23 that both the temple and the sanctuary had two doors. Two here is not speaking of controversy or opposition, but instead of witness and agreement.

4. The temple and sanctuary had two doors

Because the temple is a magnificent building and speaks of the end of the regenerated man; the sanctuary is seen as a place of holiness, a place of been chosen, accepted, and set apart. When viewed together a picture of the elect or Overcomer is revealed! The new man in Yeshua will be structured in Yeshua and bearing the likeness of Yeshua. It is through Yeshua Jesus that man gains reentry into the throne room or Most Holy Place where the Spirit of the Father resides. These doors were not described as being side by side as with other descriptions of some of the fixtures in Ezekiel's vision, instead, the second door is the confession that one makes. Ezekiel 41:23 states: "*And the temple and the sanctuary had two doors.*" Two points to one's personal decision or confession that must be made. Because the doors were already apart of the new temple, it must be interpreted that this is the surrendered soul that has made the decision to be Yeshua's disciple and agrees with all the terms and conditions of discipleship. After his confession is made, man enters the second door based on his decision and this door is Yeshua Jesus, and the new man in Yeshua now delights in worshiping the Father. Quoting the NET, Psalm 141:2-3 sets forth the purpose of the second door: the mouth: "*May you accept my prayer like incense, my uplifted hands like the evening offering! O LORD, place a guard on my mouth! Protect the opening of my lips!*" Here prayer is viewed as incense and the lifting of the hands is likened as the evening sacrifice, these are some of the differences between the natural and spiritual temple. In the natural temple the conformity is to the visible, but in the spiritual temple the character and nature of activities are all spiritual! Psalm 24:3-10 gives insight into the activities produced in the spiritual realm when the elect worships the LORD. It also reveals that the gates and doors are really symbolic of the true worshipers of Abba Father; again applying the NET: "*Who is allowed to ascend the mountain of the LORD? Who may go up to his holy dwelling place? The one whose deeds are blameless and whose motives are pure, who does not lie, or make promises with no intention of keeping them. Such godly people are rewarded by the LORD, and vindicated by the God who delivers them. Such purity characterizes the people who seek his favor, Jacob's descendants, who pray to him* (Selah) *Look up, you gates! Rise up, you eternal doors! Then the majestic king will enter! Who is the majestic king? The LORD who is strong and mighty! The LORD who is mighty in battle! Look up, you eternal doors! Then the majestic king will enter! Who is this majestic king? The LORD who commands armies! He is the majestic king!* (Selah)". Gates and doors can be an entrance as well as an exit just like the mouth; Yeshua said: "*A good man out of the good treasure of his heart brings forth good; and an evil man out of the evil treasure of his heart brings forth evil. For out of the abundance of the heart his mouth speaks*" (Luke 6:45 NKJV". These gates and doors are symbolic of the worshipers who are unable to restrain their praise and adoration for the Father. Psalm 100 is the epitome of true worship: "*Make a joyful noise unto the LORD, all ye lands. Serve the LORD with gladness: come before His presence with singing. Know ye that the LORD He is God: it is He that hath made us and not we ourselves; we are His people, and the sheep of His pasture. Enter into His gates with thanksgiving and into His courts with praise: be thankful unto Him and bless His name. For the LORD is good; His mercy is everlasting; and His truth endureth to all generations.*" This new temple of man affords him eternal life which is freely given to him by Yeshua.

To conclude this section let us meditate upon the words of Yeshua Jesus that He so eloquently presented in a conversation with a Samaritan woman about His offering of true worship and everlasting life recorded in John 4:7, 21-24: "*There came a woman of Samaria to draw water. Jesus said to her, "Give Me a drink..." Jesus said to her, "Woman, believe Me, an hour is coming when neither in this mountain nor in Jerusalem will you worship the Father. You worship what you do not know; we worship what we know, for salvation is from the Jews. But an hour is coming, and now is, when the true worshipers will worship the Father in spirit and truth; for such people the Father seeks to be His worshipers. God is Spirit, and those who worship Him must worship in spirit and truth"* (NASB). This conversation between Yeshua and the Samaritan woman will be revisited shortly. The question that needs to be answered is, "Do I qualify to be granted eternal life to worship the Father in spirit and in truth?" The drink that Yeshua was offering her was everlasting life! John 7:37-38 also states: *"In the last day, that great day of the feast, Jesus stood and cried, saying, If any man thirst, let him come unto Me, and drink. He that believeth on Me, as the Scripture hath said, out of his belly shall flow rivers of living water."* The following section will reveal a divine truth regarding Yeshua's conversation with the Samaritan woman by the well which establishes the fact that these new temple furnishings are symbolic of spiritual worship by all Believers who have been granted eternal life.

5. Two sets of turning leaves for each door

First of all, there are two sets of leaves on the door which symbolically points towards the agreement in witness of the Spirit of God with the spirit of man. Two sets are telling us that there were a total of four leaves. The spiritual significance of the number four reflects the physical substance that emerges from the spiritual substance. For example we can create an atmosphere of worship, love, peace, healing, hostility, war, and so on. These emotions are first initiated in the spiritual realm before their response become evident as a physical byproduct. The four turning leaves are a part of the worship of Abba Father: the physical act of worship creating an atmosphere that is tangible. This thought is clearly observed when the text is examined from its Hebraic root. The leaves are described as turning and the Hebrew word used here for turning is **Mucabba** or **Muwcabbah** [4142], this is the action of making a revolution or circuit of three hundred and sixty degrees. That is, as the worship of Abba Father pierces the atmosphere, it initiates a response of love from the Father that can be felt like a gentle shower of rain or liquid slowly pouring over the body. The Father's ardent love ignites more worship and the cycle of showers of blessing mingled with praise and worship both changes and charges the atmosphere in a continual cyclical wave pattern. The Hebrew and Greek text provides an exhaustive word study that can be easily missed in translations. When one thinks of leaves, the picture that comes to mind is a plant or tree, but here in the book of Ezekiel, the Hebraic translation opens a much wider door of understanding by taking the reader from the surface of the word to its depth.

Here is the understanding and revelation of Yeshua's conversation with the woman at the well, which proves that eternal life and spiritual worship is one of the main focuses of the new man in his new body and living in the New Jerusalem. The Hebrew word for leaves is **Deleth** [1817], it is taken from the word **Delah** [1802], which describes the action of letting down a bucket for drawing water; it also points to the mouth from which praise and worship is poured. The use of **Delah** or **Deleth** indicates that spiritual worship flows from the lips of the Believer as if they were buckets of water being poured out. Amazingly the same word transliterated "leaves," is also the same word used for "doors." First of all the leaves on the door were turning, which is a picture of man's transformation following his conversion. Before confessing Yeshua Jesus as his Lord, he was a slave to sin and the power of the prince of the air, but at his conversion he became a joint heir with Yeshua unto GOD the Father. 1 John 3:1-3 states: *"Beloved, what manner of love the Father hath bestowed upon us, that we should be called the sons of God: therefore the world knoweth us not, because it knew Him not. Beloved, now are we the sons of God, and it doth not yet appear what we shall be: but we know that, when He shall appear, we shall be like Him; for we shall see Him as He is. And every man that hath this hope in Him purifieth himself, even as He is pure."* Let's examine once again portions of Yeshua's dialogue with the Samaritan woman. John 4:7-14 applying the NASB: *"There came a woman of Samaria to draw water. Jesus said to her, "Give Me a drink." For His disciples had gone away into the city to buy food. Therefore the Samaritan woman said to Him, "How is it that you, being a Jew, ask me for a drink since I am a Samaritan?" (For Jews have no dealings with Samaritans.) Jesus answered and said to her, "If you knew the gift of God, and who it is who says to you, 'Give Me a drink,' you would have asked Him, and He would have given you living water." She said to Him, "Sir, You have nothing to draw with and the well is deep; where then do You get that living water? You are not greater than our father Jacob, are You, who gave us the well, and drank of it himself and his sons and his cattle?' Jesus answered and said to her, "Everyone who drinks of this water will thirst again; but whoever* *drinks of the water that I will give him shall never thirst; but the water that I will give him will become in him a well of water springing up to eternal life."* The Hebrew word for leaves as well as doors speaks of both letting down a bucket for drawing water as well as the product of the fruit of our lips following our conversion. Yeshua explains that the water that He gives will constantly refresh our lives because of its life giving power! The leaves on the door therefore represent the Saints of God who are granted eternal life because they accepted Yeshua as both Savior and Lord. These Believers worship the Father and thank Him for His lovingkindness in a rhetorical liturgy of poured out praise as Abba Father showers them with His perceptible love.

The Holy Scriptures unifies both the Old and New Covenant in a mutual association whereby questions as well as answers are found in a cross reference pattern thus bridging any gaps between both. The entire cannon of Scripture are God breathed and to reject any section is in essence a rejection of it all. Torah portions are found throughout the New Covenant as Messianic prophesies in the Old Covenant. Therefore, to embrace the entire cannon is to embrace GOD Almighty Himself! Next we will examine the final portion of Ezekiel chapter 41, and what revelation awaits us!

6. Cherubim and palm trees are on the temple doors

We have already discussed that the doors are a picture of the praises poured out from the lips of the redeemed. Now we see the holy angels of the LORD who are also called Cherubim, living creatures or beast, joining the Saints in worship, which is not strange for them. As protectors of things pertaining to Abba Father, the Cherubim worships Him continually. Both mankind and Cherubim are caught up in the marvelous decree of the holiness of the LORD as depicted by the palm branches, which signifies celebration (see Matthew 21:9, 15; Mark 11:9-10; John 12:12-13; Revelation 7:9-12). Palm trees speak of the great adversities that the Saints had to overcome (Revelation 12:11), but palm branches describes their joy. This is all taking place in the Most Holy Place, or spirit of man where true worship emanates. We have been so encumbered by the world and all its cares that we forget Yeshua's instructions; which is to cast all our anxieties upon Him. Worship is a volatile weapon in the arsenal of all Believers, as we are instructed by John the Apostle:

"And this is the confidence that we have in Him, that if we ask any thing according to His will, He heareth us" (1 John 5:14). When we worship the Lord GOD, we are offering Him sacrifice of praise with your lips. When we open our mouths to praise the Lord in spite of all our trials and tribulations, we will see the result of its effect for ourselves. A prescribed daily dose of praise and worship, not only boosts our faith, it also changes the atmosphere around us and pleases our heavenly Father who will perform great wonders in our behalf. The favor of God is better than money because financial freedom is part and parcel with His favor. Favor opens closed doors and does things that we lease expect. Lastly, praise and worship mixed with faith is our greatest weapon that shatters the enemies of our soul.

7. Thick planks were on the front porch

There was an important message that the LORD wanted to convey to Ezekiel because He mention that thick planks graced the forefront of the porch. The Hebrew word for porch is **Uwlam** [197]; it speaks of that which is connected or bound to a house or building. **Uwlam** is a derivative of **Alam** [481]; it means to bind, to make one dumb or put to silence; which is symbolic of the finished work of the Cross for the salvation of mankind. **Ab** [5645] is the Hebrew word used here for "thick" or that which is enveloped in darkness. When added to planks; **Ets** [6083]; a picture of Yeshua's suffering for mankind is revealed. **Ets** in context means tree! Next, the word "face" or its Hebrew rendering **Panim** or **Paneh** [6440], speaks of the manifestation of one's emotions which is evident by the expression on our face. In this case it was one of great agony and grief for our Savior Yeshua Jesus. In the New Covenant it is said of Him: *"For even hereunto were ye called because Christ also suffered for us, leaving us an example, that ye should follow His steps: who did no sin, neither was guile found in His mouth: Who, when He was reviled, reviled not again; when He suffered, He threatened not; but committed Himself to Him that judged righteously: who His own self bare our sins in His own body on the tree, that we, being dead to sins, should live unto righteousness: by whose stripes ye were healed. For ye were sheep going astray; but are now returned unto the Shepherd and Bishop of your souls"* (1 Peter 2:21-25). In the Old Covenant Isaiah also prophesied of these things: *"Behold My Servant, whom I uphold; Mine elect, in whom My soul delighteth; I have put My Spirit upon*

107

Him: He shall bring forth judgment to the Gentiles. He shall not cry, nor lift up nor cause His voice to be heard in the street. A bruised reed shall He not break, and the smoking flax shall He not quench: He shall bring forth judgment unto truth. He shall not fail or be discouraged, till He have set judgment in the earth: and the isles shall wait for His law. . . Behold, My Servant shall deal prudently, He shall be exalted and extolled, and be very high. As many were astonished at thee; His visage was so marred more than any man, and His form more than the sons of men: so shall He sprinkle many nations; the kings shall shut their mouths at Him: for that which had not been told them shall they see; and that which they had not heard shall they consider. . . . . He was oppressed, and He was afflicted, yet He opened not His mouth: He is brought as a lamb to the slaughter, and as a sheep before her shearers is dumb, so He opened not His mouth"* (42:1-4; 52:13-15 and 53:7). Yeshua's suffering is the symbolic interpretation of *"thick planks upon the face of the porch,"* a portrayal of His death, which is the visible demonstration of Abba Father's love for all

Lastly in Ezekiel 41:25 is the word "without," it is the Hebrew **Chuwts** or **Chuts** [2351], which speaks of a dividing wall. Ephesians 2:11-16 states: *"Wherefore remember, that ye being in time past Gentile in the flesh, who were called Uncircumcision by that which is called the Circumcision in the flesh made by hands; that at that time ye were without Christ, being aliens from the commonwealth of Israel, and strangers from the covenants of promise, having no hope, and without God in the world: but now in Christ Jesus ye who sometimes were far off are made nigh by the blood of Christ. For He is our peace, who hath made both one, and hath broken down the middle wall of partition between us; having abolished in His flesh the enmity, even the law of commandments contained in ordinances; for to make in Himself of twain one new man, so making peace; and that He might reconcile both unto God in one body by the cross, having slain the enmity thereby.* Yeshua suffered outside the city wall as our sin offering unto the LORD" (for further reading see Exodus 29:10-14; Leviticus 4:8-12, 20, 21; Hebrews 13:12-15). Ezekiel 41:25 is speaking of the rejoicing of mankind and angels, in celebration of what Yeshua had done by reconciling both Jews and Gentiles to His Father by pouring out His blood upon a tree. Hebrews 13:11-15 tells us: *"For the bodies of those beasts, whose blood is brought into the sanctuary by the high priest for* *sin, are burned without the camp. Wherefore Jesus also, that He might sanctify the people with His own blood, suffered without the gate. Let us go forth therefore unto Him without the camp, bearing His reproach. For here we have no continuing city, but we seek one to come. By Him therefore let us offer the sacrifice of praise to God continually, that is, the fruit of our lips giving thanks to His name."* Mankind will rejoice when his new body, also referred to as a temple, a house, a building, or a tabernacle, is completed as its reconciliatory structure will be a picture of the new man in Yeshua Jesus, and what a glorious picture that will be because man will look like His Savior in His suffering, as well as His victories.

8. Narrow windows and palm trees were on both sides of the porch

The basic truths regarding these elements have already been discussed. Now we will see how well they fit together with the master plan of Abba Father and His personal sacrificial offering for all mankind in the person of His only Begotten Son. The remainder of this section will address these changes, which points to Yeshua as the sacrifice for our sins. To reject such an offering from Abba Father is to reject the Father Himself and also the sanctifying work of Holy Spirit, which culminates in the rejection of the Son and His free offering to grant unto us eternal life. The Apostle John, one of Yeshua's closest friends and disciple wrote: *"Behold what manner of love the Father has bestowed on us, that we should be called children of God! Therefore the world does not know us, because it did not know Him. Beloved, now we are children of God; and it has not yet been revealed what we shall be, but we know that when He is revealed, we shall be like Him, for we shall see Him as He is. And everyone who has this hope in Him purifies himself as He is pure. Whoever commits sin also commits lawlessness, and sin is lawlessness. And you know that He was manifested to take away our sins, and in Him there is no sin. Whoever abides in Him does not sin. Whoever sins has neither seen Him nor known Him. Little children, let no one deceive you. He who practices righteousness is righteous, just as He is righteous. He who sins is of the devil, for the devil has sinned from the beginning. For this purpose the Son of God was manifested, that He might destroy the works of the devil. Whoever has been born of God does not sin, for His seed remains in him; and he cannot sin, because he has been born of God"* (1 John 3:1-9 NKJV).

To recap: "narrow" or **Atam** [H. 331], speaks of one's silence or deliberate act not to offer self-defense. In speaking of Yeshua, it is recorded that no deceit was found in His mouth. He bore the mockery of His brethren and that of the Gentiles as well, yet He made no attempt to defend Himself. Isaiah 53:7 tells of Him being oppressed and afflicted yet He kept silent when maligned: but why did He do this? The answer is: He was more concerned about the great weight of our sins than for His personal safety; His silence became our salvation. Yeshua's Cross became Satan's greatest obstacle and a constant reminder of his defeat, for this reason he will do all that he can to remove the Cross anywhere it is found. There is a mighty lesson that we can learn from our Savior: we win more battles by not saying a single word to defend ourselves.

Windows or **Challown** [H. 2474], is a noun describing perforations or piercings. However it can also be referred to as an entryway. These windows are described as being narrow, (**Atam**) which points to one's silence. When combined we once again see a picture of Yeshua holding His peace to fulfill His Divine purpose, which is to be His Father's sacrifice for all of humanity. Because of this act, there is a perpetual celebration from the beneficiaries both Jews and Gentile Believers as depicted by the palm trees on both porches. The porches were previously explained to be that which is bound or tied much like the ritual performed for sacrificial offerings. Ezekiel documents that these narrow windows and palm trees were also upon the side chambers of the house, which tells us that there was complete silence in this area of the Most Holy Place as the Overcomers (represented by the palm trees), earnestly looks upon the Cross (plank or tree) of Yeshua Jesus speechless. There are at least nine Hebrew words translated as chamber(s), and **Tsela** or **Tsalah** [6763] is translated side chambers; when applied in context with these verses it is referring to the side of a person! This word was also applied in Ezekiel 41:5-9 and 11, where it was used in conjunction with being anchored into the heart of GOD. The sacrificial Lamb, Yeshua Jesus, was pierced in the side to ensure His decease (see John 19:32-37; Psalm 22:16; Zechariah 12:10; Revelation 1:7). The silence we see here is that of the redeemed, because of the revelation of the wisdom of GOD concerning the depth of

110

the Cross and the suffering of Yeshua. The Cross is already an offense and one day this will be fully explained and understood especially by those who suffer persecution and martyrdom for their belief in Yeshua (see 1 Corinthians 1:18-24). His piercing will be memorialized as a tapestry in the Most Holy place, which is the spirit of man. All that we have seen so far in Ezekiel 41:22-26 symbolically portrayed, will be a part of the reconstruction of the new man in Yeshua. 1 John 3:2 states: ". . . *and it has not yet been revealed what we shall be, but we know that when He is revealed, we shall be like Him, for we shall see Him as He is"* (NKJV). This new man will be just like Yeshua. For this reason the temple of man will bear the likeness of Yeshua in His birth, His ministry, His death, His resurrection, His ascension, and not to be forgotten, His glorified body. Man's temple is in its final stages of preparation, to be presented unto Abba Father; holy, acceptable, and glorified.

The LORD God is Omnipotent, Omnipresent and Omniscient; attributes that the gods of this world cannot compete against. He knew of the failures that both angels and mankind would face. His reason for allowing Yeshua to be sacrificed was based upon the fact that all intelligent beings whether angels or mankind were created with the capacity to choose. If the Lord did not give us a will to make decisions, we would be robots and slaves to an austere and autocratic taskmaster! Because we were created in the image and likeness of God, His love, mercy and abundant grace is continually being extended to us. Unlike spirit beings, we have a soul and for this special reason, Yeshua was sent into this world. He poured out His righteous soul for our sins that we might be the righteousness of God in Him. Who can we blame if we choose to reject Abba Father's free offering of love? If we believe the Word of God, it gives us power to overcome, faith to face life challenges, patience to endure, brevity to defeat the giants and the blessed assurance that the battle is not ours, it is the LORD's!

Chapter 42

Verses 1-3

"Then he brought me forth into the utter court, the way toward the north: and he brought me into the chamber that was over against the separate place, and which was before the building toward the north. Before the length of an hundred cubits was the north door, and the breadth was fifty cubits. Over against the twenty cubits which were for the inner court, and over against the pavement which was for the utter court, was gallery against gallery in three stories."

Ezekiel accompanied the Lord from the outer court, to the inner court and then to the Most Holy Place, where measurements of great importance were made. The new temple of man must be completed before he can enter the New Jerusalem of God: the home of both Jews and Gentiles. At the onset of this vision it is recorded in Ezekiel 40:4: *"And the man said unto me, son of man, behold with thine eyes, and hear with thine ears, and set thine heart upon all that I shall show thee; for to the intent that I might show them unto thee art thou brought hither: declare all that thou seest to the house of Israel."* The house of Israel was first privy to hear this wonderful message of hope that was to come. This was not the temple that would be rebuilt in his life time but one that would adorn the kingdom of God and His Son.

Ezekiel's tour of this spiritual temple is about to end and the Lord now takes the prophet back to where they first started at the outer court. These visions were of a prophetic nature, highlighting the coming rule of Yeshua Messiah over all His people. The Lord takes Ezekiel towards the separating courtyard where He brought him into a chamber and another building that was located towards the north. There is much to be grasped from Ezekiel 42:1. A *separate place* was first mentioned in Ezekiel

41:12-15, its Hebrew transliteration is **Gizrah** [1508], which speaks of the setting apart of the new man in Yeshua. This was not an easy task because with perfection comes persecution that prepares humanity to shine forth as Overcomers. These are the words of Yeshua Jesus recorded in John 15:18-23, which states: *"If the world hates you, be aware that it hated me first. If you belonged to the world, the world would love you as its own. However, because you do not belong to the world, but I chose you out of the world, for this reason the world hates you. Remember what I told you, 'A slave is not greater than his master.' If they persecuted me, they will also persecute you. If they obeyed my word, they will obey yours too. But they will do all these things to you on account of my name, because they do not know the one who sent me"* (NET). Man is being prepared to reenter the kingdom of God and the presence of Abba Father; this will culminate in the restoration of broken fellowship, and this process begins in the outer court where his cutting out, polishing and separation from the world begins.

So much has been said about the chambers which points towards the compartments of the soul which is the area in need of redemption. Being the seat of the emotions, the soul needs to be rewired so that we can think and act like Yeshua and Holy Spirit. However, this is not done all at once; as man matures spiritually, the Holy Spirit is his constant Chaperone, Helper and Teacher, who never leaves or fails to instruct him. The complete remodeling of the soul depends upon our desire to fellowship with Holy Spirit, and the longer we linger in His presence, is the more fruitful we become. There might be parts of the soul that is mature while other areas are still making baby steps. For example, we might pass the test of patience but struggle with un-forgiveness or we might overcome addictive behaviors yet struggle with low self-esteem. For reasons such as these we see the chambers or rooms being measured in all three courts; outer (body), inner (soul), and Most Holy Place (spirit), because it is the desire of the Lord that we emulate the spiritual man. Galatians 5:15-18 states: *"But if you bite and devour one another, beware lest you be consumed by one another! I say then: Walk in the Spirit, and you shall not fulfill the lust of the flesh. For the flesh lusts against the Spirit, and the Spirit against the flesh; and these are contrary to one another, so that you do not do the things that you wish. But if you are led by the Spirit, you are not under the law"* (NKJV). It is very important that all our measurements are aligned with that of the Spirit.

The north door measured a hundred cubits long and fifty cubits wide. The length and width symbolizes the Jubilee which is our stamp of approval that all our debts are paid in full. The north is the designated position where man was given authority which Adam carelessly abdicated (see Genesis 3). Opposite to the inner court were galleries three stories high (see also Ezekiel 41:15-16). So far we have observed the construction of the spiritual temple of man given in coded messages by the Lord only to be made known in these last days. The understanding of the meaning of "gallery" will be explained as it is closely related to those mentioned in Ezekiel 41. This transliterated Hebrew word is **Attuwq** or **Attiyq** [862], it is defined as the ledge of a building and a derivative of another Hebrew word **Nathaq** [5423]; meaning to pluck, pull, or rooted out. What is the message been conveyed here?

The measurements of both one hundred cubits and fifty cubits are referring to the forgiveness of our debts as symbolized by the celebration of the year of Jubilee. From the inner court opposite the pavement, to a portion belonging to the outer court stood three story galleries opposite each other and their measurement was recorded to be twenty cubits. First of all twenty is the mark of approval and completion of the grace of God towards mankind. Next the galleries were in two rows facing each other, which signify the unity of man as two speaks of agreement. Six is the total number of galleries and this is the number assigned to man. So far man is seen forgiven and having his debt paid in full by Yeshua Jesus. The revelation and completion of this message is made clear by Yeshua Himself in John 10:27-30: *"My sheep hear My voice, and I know them, and they follow Me: and I give unto them eternal life; and they shall never perish, <u>neither shall any man pluck them out of My hand</u>. My Father, which gave them Me, is greater than all; and <u>no man is able to pluck them out of My Father's hand</u>. I and My Father are One."* Man's sin has been forgiven and his debt paid in full because of the unfathomable grace of God and none can pluck, pull, or root us out of His hand. This is the completed picture of the overflowing grace of God towards mankind. Now we are better able to understand that the choices we make in this life will affect our destination or home in the next.

Verses 4-5

"And before the chambers was a walk of ten cubits breadth inward, a way of one cubit; and their doors toward the north. And the upper chambers were shorter: for the galleries were higher than these, than the lower, and then the middlemost of the building."

In front of the chambers and viewing from its side was a walkway that measured ten cubits wide. The number ten speaks of the perfection of God's Divine order, which is also in agreement with His grace. Mankind has nothing to lose when he choose to walk in love and humility, because the proud will have no part in the kingdom of God. James 4:4b-6 states: *"Whosoever therefore will be a friend of the world is the enemy of God. Do ye think that the Scripture saith in vain, The spirit that dwelleth in us lusteth to envy? But He giveth more grace. Wherefore He saith, God resisteth the proud, but giveth grace unto the humble."* Humility is profitable and should be sought after by everyone; Yeshua states: *"But he who is greatest among you shall be your servant. And whoever exalts himself will be humbled, and he who humbles himself will be exalted"* (Matthew 23:11-12 NKJV, see also Luke 14:11; Isaiah 12:11). It is unwise to follow a destructive pathway, because it is through Yeshua alone that we are guaranteed eternal life.

It is stated in Ezekiel 42:5 that the "upper" chambers or rooms were shorter and the galleries were higher. The Hebrew rendering for "shorter" is **Qatsar** [7114]; it speaks of that which has been curtailed or harvested, whether grain or men. Therefore, these shorter chambers that are before the LORD Most High are a special group of Saints, who abides in the presence of the Almighty, being redeemed from the earth. This is the understanding because "upper," is the Hebrew **Elyon** [5945]; and refers to God as being the Supreme High and Elevated One above all others. The chambers were shorter due to the fact that the upper galleries were higher. Galleries points to those who have been harvested. The Hebrew rendering for galleries is defined as that which has been plucked, pulled, or rooted indicating that these Saints suffered for Yeshua Jesus, now they reign with Yeshua Jesus.

The galleries were observed to be higher and this brings us yet to another revelation. "Upper" refers to the Almighty GOD, while higher, which is **Yakol** or **Yakowl** [3201] means to endure or overcome; to be unmovable; or have power; to prevail even through suffering! These are in fact the Overcomers who have been persecuted and martyred for not renouncing their belief in Yeshua. They choose eternal life by rejecting the temporary offer to spare their natural life, thereby receiving a higher reward by being granted the privilege of dwelling close to the throne of GOD because they refused to denounce Yeshua Jesus their Lord and were martyred.

Verse 6

"For they were in three stories, but had not pillars as the pillars of the courts: therefore the building was straitened more than the lowest and the middlemost from the ground."

Pillars were first mentioned in Ezekiel 40:49, they are the supporters who occupy key positions and responsibilities in the kingdom of God. Notice however in Ezekiel 42:6 that the building had no pillars like those in the courtyard, and for this reason a remarkable feature of this unique structure was discovered: it was more upright than the other two buildings that were previously mentioned. The three stories are presenting to us a picture of restoration and completion of the Saints who had been waiting to be totally restored. This is the reward of the Martyrs'. "Straitened" is the Hebrew **Atsal** [680] and some of its meanings are; to be joined, selected or reserved. Revelation 6:9-11; 20:4 applying the NASB gives us a better understanding of these Saints who were martyred: *"When the Lamb broke the fifth seal, I saw underneath the altar the souls of those who had been slain because of the word of God, and because of the testimony which they had maintained; and they cried out with a loud voice, saying, "How long, O Lord, holy and true, will you refrain from judging and avenging our blood on those who dwell on the earth?" And there was given to each of them a white robe; and they were told that they should rest for a little while longer, until the number of their fellow servants and their brethren who were to be killed even as they had been, would be completed also. . . And I saw thrones, and they sat upon them, and judgment was given unto them: and I saw the souls of them that were beheaded for the witness of Jesus, and for the word of God, and which had not worshipped the beast, neither his image, neither had received his mark upon their* foreheads, or in their hands; and they lived and reigned with Christ a thousand years." Ezekiel documented that this upper most section was straitened, which points to the fact that this selected group of Believers were honored by Abba Father for their outstanding humility, faithfulness and endurance.

Verse 7-9

"And the wall that was without over against the chambers, toward the utter court on the forepart of the chambers, the length thereof was fifty cubits. For the length of the chambers that were in the utter court was fifty cubits: and, lo, before the temple were a hundred cubits. And from under these chambers was the entry on the east side, as one goeth into the utter court."

The enclosure wall and the chambers facing the outer court measured fifty cubits, again indicating that a debt had been paid in full. The indebted jubilantly rejoices as depicted by the Hebrew word **Panim** or **Paneh** [6440] which is used to describe the anterior or front of the chambers. This Hebrew word so frequently used in Ezekiel's vision, once again symbolically refers to the expression of the emotions visibly for all to see, and this time it was that of the Overcomers, rejoicing in the presence of the Lord God Almighty who faithfully rewarded them for refusing to deny His name.

This fourth temple is multifaceted consisting of Believers from all walks of life. When Yeshua Jesus commences His reign over His elect, all Saints of God will be empowered with the gift of supernatural discernment of each other's experiences. This might seem farfetched but it is recorded in several places in the Word of God that the earth will be filled with the knowledge of the glory of God; Isaiah 6:3; 11:9; Habakkuk 2:14; Numbers 14:21; Psalm 72:19. This has begun to take place as mankind makes the conscious choice to abide in the presence of the LORD, who gives His children a glimpse of His knowledge by the revelation of His Spirit.

In this present life, many are exalted and honored for their brilliant ideas and discoveries that may gain them notoriety and the privilege of being invited to sit with the influential. Should such a person come face to face with the True and Living God; he (no gender bias intended), will realize how miniscule his brilliance is in comparison to what will be revealed to him by the Lord. What a mighty temple this will be; as that which was only known in part is fully understood. In the architectural plan of a building its blueprint prototype is of precise measurements. Ezekiel was granted the privilege of viewing a detailed and photographic layout of the new man in Yeshua; the fourth and final temple that will grace a new millennium. Let's once more read two of the Apostle Paul's several letters to see how they fit into this picture. 1 Corinthians 3:16-17 and Ephesians 2:19-22 quoting from the NKJV which states: *"Do you not know that you are the temple of God and that the Spirit of God dwells in you? If anyone defiles the temple of God, God will destroy him. For the temple of God is holy, which temple you are. . . . Now, therefore, you are no longer strangers and foreigners, but fellow citizens with the saints and members of the household of God, having been built on the foundation of the apostles and prophets, Jesus Christ Himself being the chief cornerstone, in whom the whole building, being fitted together, grows into a holy temple in the Lord, in whom you also are being built together for a dwelling place of God in the Spirit."* The fourth temple is a spiritual one, and any attempt to apply these measurements to the building of a natural temple will end in speculation, and confusion.

The measurements of every aspect of this fourth temple are symbolic in nature and a reflection of the measure of man in Yeshua Jesus. For this reason the LORD is equipping many scribes to prepare the body of Yeshua for a final and glorious future. Ephesians 4:7-16 quoting once more from the NKJV states: *"But to each one of us grace was given according to the measure of Christ's gift. Therefore He says: "When He ascended on high, He led captivity captive, and gave gifts to men." (Now this, "He ascended" what does it mean but that He also first descended into the lower parts of the earth? He who descended is also the One who ascended far above all the heavens, that He might fill all things.) And He Himself gave some to be apostles, some prophets, some evangelists. And some pastors and teachers, for the equipping of the saints for the work of ministry, for the edifying of the body of Christ, till we all come to the unity of the faith and of the knowledge of the Son of God, to a perfect man, to the measure of the stature of the fullness of Christ; that we should no longer be children, tossed to and fro and carried about with every wind of doctrine, by the trickery of men, in the cunning craftiness of deceitful plotting, but, speaking the truth in love, may grow up in all things into Him who is the head Christ from whom the whole body, joined and knit together by what every joint supplies, according to the effective working by which every part does its share, causes growth of the body for the edifying of itself in love.*"

Embedded in man's authority are his spiritual gifts, given solely for the edification of the body of Yeshua; because these gifts are the ministerial foundation built on the bedrock of Yeshua who freely gave them. Stressing Ephesians 4:13 once again: "*till we all come to unity of the faith and the knowledge of the Son of God, to a perfect man, to the measure of the stature of the fullness of Christ.*" The word "*measure,*" is the Greek **Metron** [3358], from this we get the word meter, thus a rule of measurement. Now when we think of measurement in this case, we must realize that whomever we are measured by, will be the person whom we are judge by. Measurement actually determines the capacity, process or requirement to perfectly fit into that which has already been pre-determined or predestined.

Ezekiel, after observing and documenting the measurements of the temple and its surroundings, expressed surprise when he was given the measurement for the chambers that were facing the temple. Why was he surprised that this measurement was one hundred cubits? What could have been revealed to him there by Yeshua? Remember one hundred is speaking of a double jubilee and the jubilee is the celebration observed by those whose sins have been forgiven; a priceless gift that cannot be repaid. This measurement of one hundred cubits given to Ezekiel for the chambers that were facing the temple, express our coming rest; not of the land but of the soul (Leviticus 25:11; Revelation 21:3).

The second aspect of the jubilee focuses on restoration, where the poor and oppressed receives redemption and restitution (Leviticus 25:10-34; 27:16-24). Isaiah spoke of this in 61:1-3; Yeshua confirmed it in Luke 4:16-21; the Apostle Paul rehearsed its purpose before King Agrippa in Acts 26:16-19; and drove home this point in Colossians 1:12-22 to the residents of Colossae. The jubilee was indeed necessary, because forgiveness was made available to everyone because it is indeed the Sabbath of all Sabbaths. Embedded in one hundred cubits; the measurement of the chambers that were before the temple, is the revelation not only of celebration, but also a picture of our redemption by the grace of Abba Father being multiplied (20 x 5=100). Yeshua fulfilled this obligation by taking the weight of all our sins; He became our jubilee and rest (for further reading see 1 Peter 2:21-25; 2 Peter 1:2-11; Romans 7 and 8).

The earthly celebration of the jubilee only foreshadows a greater one to come. A climax is on the way and the true essence of the jubilee will be on display before and within the temple. The reason for this display is telling us that before the temple of the new man can be built, he or she must first experience the finished work of the Cross through the multiplied grace of God. Man's new temple is made available to him by having his debt paid in full! No wonder the prophet was amazed, he saw something that no other in his time had ever seen nor was it revealed to any other in such a symbolic way as the soul of man is reconnected to the spirit. Great treasures are awaiting those who wholeheartedly turn to Yeshua, because the jubilee commences the rebuilding of the temple of man. This is revealed in Ezekiel 42:9 which states: *"And from under these chambers was the entry to the east side, as one goeth into them from the outer court."*

The chambers or compartments of the soul (inner court) is said to be the entry way into the east. This is speaking of man's entry into Yeshua, which begins at the inner court (soul). The inner court or soul of man is the starting point of his re-entry into fellowship with God. By his contrite confession of Yeshua Jesus, he is met at the brazen altar by Holy Spirit who washes him at the laver, which is a type of the Cross and our salvation. From this point, Holy Spirit begins to prepare mankind for his spiritual journey of holiness and righteousness which is evident by the spiritual fruit he bears. Titus 3:4-7 applying the NKJV states: *"But when the kindness and the love of God our Savior toward man appeared, not by works of righteousness which we have done, but according to His mercy He saves us, through the washing of regeneration and renewing of the Holy Spirit, whom He poured out on us abundantly through Jesus Christ our Savior, that having been justified by His grace we should become heirs according to the hope of eternal life."*

The soul is very important to God and for this reason the king and ruler of Sheol, is relentless in his diabolical attempt to snatch the soul and plunge it into everlasting damnation because he truly hates mankind and lures us away from the truth through deception. For this reason, Yeshua Jesus poured out His soul for ours. Being without sin, He regained the keys of hell and death from Satan (Revelation 1:18), thereby freely offering us eternal life. Yeshua's death and resurrection was sufficient to reclaim His lost sheep and offer them a life of peace in the kingdom of His Father. What a privilege to know that Abba cares so much for our eternal rest that He commissioned Yeshua to ransom our soul from eternal damnation to live with Him in His kingdom.

Verses 10-12

"The chambers were in the thickness of the wall of the court toward the east, over against the separate place, and over against the building. And the way before them was like the appearance of the chambers which were toward the north, as long as they, and as broad as they: and all their goings out were both according to their fashions, and according to their doors. And according to the doors of the chambers that were toward the south was a door in the head of the way, even the way directly before the wall toward the east, as one entereth into them."

The chambers were said to be in the thickness of the wall, referring symbolically to the width or depth of the compartments of the soul being now anchored, making it unshakable and unmovable. In 1 Corinthians 15:57-58 the Apostle Paul encourages the Saints of God to keep themselves anchored in the Lord: *"But thanks be to God, which giveth us victory through our Lord Jesus Christ. Therefore, my beloved brethren, be ye steadfast, unmovable, always abounding in the work of the Lord, forasmuch as ye know that your labor is not in vain in the Lord."* Ezekiel 42:10 also states that this anchoring occurred towards the east which points towards a picture of man in Yeshua being anchored in a place where none can pluck them from His hands (John 10:27-28).

The way that leads to the chambers located in the east, looked similar to those towards the north in appearance as well as their measurements to those mentioned in Ezekiel 42:4. The order of God's grace is measurable in all courts; outer (body), inner (soul) and holiest of all (spirit). Lastly, there was a door which was located in the head of the way. At first glance one would think that "head of the way" was in reference to a specific location or point, but this is not so. The inference to "head of the way" applied in Ezekiel 42:12 is not referring to a location but rather to a person. The Hebrew word used for "head" is **Rosh** [7218], which means chief from which we get **Roshah** [7222]. Here is a story being told of Yeshua as being **Roshah** or chief cornerstone. Yeshua was despised and rejected of men (Isaiah 53:3), yet became the Chief Cornerstone upon which we are being built. Ephesians 2:19-22 quoting the NKJV clearly shows this: *"Now, therefore, you are no longer strangers and foreigners, but fellow citizens with the saints and members of the household of God, having been built on the foundation of the apostles and prophets, Jesus Christ Himself being the chief cornerstone, in whom the whole building, being fitted together, grows into a holy temple in the Lord, in whom you also are being built together for a dwelling place of God in the Spirit"* (for further reading see Matthew 21:12; Mark 12:20; Luke 20:17; Acts 4:11; 1 Peter 2:6-7). The head of the way is therefore describing Yeshua Jesus our Chief Cornerstone. We are His people, His temple, and the foundation upon whom we are built. To live life carelessly after declaring Yeshua Jesus as Savior and Lord grieves Him. We must never allow cracks to appear in our spiritual foundation or any part of our temple; if they do appear, we must run to the Father and repent as the souls of many are influenced by our conduct. As fellow citizens of the kingdom of God, we must never forget that our whole temple is being erected in Yeshua our Chief Cornerstone.

Verses 13-14

"Then said he unto me, The north chambers and the south chambers, which are before the separate place, they be holy chambers, where the priest that approach unto the LORD shall eat the most holy things: there shall they lay the most holy things, and the meat offering, and the sin offering, and the trespass offering; for the place is holy. When the priests enter therein, then shall they not go out of the holy place into the outer court, but there they shall lay their garments wherein they minister; for they are holy; and shall put on other garments, and shall approach to those things which are of the people."

We fail to realize how important it is and how strict and humbling it is to be called into the priesthood of Yeshua; 1 Peter 2:4, 9 quoting the NKJV states:" *Coming to Him as to a living stone, rejected indeed by men, but chosen by God and precious, you also, as living stones, are being built up a spiritual house, a holy priesthood to offer up spiritual sacrifices acceptable to God through Jesus Christ. . . . But you are a chosen generation, a royal priesthood. A holy nation, His own special people, that you may proclaim the praises of Him who called you out of darkness into His marvelous light; who once were not a people but are now the people of God who had not obtained mercy but now have obtained mercy."* The north and south chambers were set apart as holy. North is symbolic of man as an authoritative figure in Yeshua, while south is the designated domain of man as a prophet or watchman. The office of the prophet will be retired during the reign of Yeshua and they will be known as priests unto the LORD.

With the coming of the Holy Spirit during the Jewish harvest festival called Shavuot or Feast of Weeks or Pentecost (Acts 2); the construction of a spiritual temple began and man commenced a new journey with Abba Father, Yeshua Messiah and the Holy Spirit (see Acts 1:6-8; 2:1-18). The Holy Spirit now takes man through this spiritual journey of reconstruction, which is our hope of glory. The Apostle Paul in his letter to the Believers in Colossae wrote: *"Now I rejoice in my sufferings for your sake, and in my flesh I do my share on behalf of His body, which is the church, in filling up what is lacking in Christ's afflictions. Of the church I was made a minister according to the stewardship from God bestowed on me for your benefit, so that I might fully carry out the preaching of the word of God, that is, the mystery which has been hidden from the past ages and generations, but has now been manifested to His saints, to whom God willed to make known what is the riches of the glory of this mystery among the Gentiles, which is Christ in you, the hope of glory"* (Colossians 1:24-27 NASB).

The Lord now makes a profound statement concerning both the north and south chambers, because this is the court of the tabernacle or temple of congregation which the Lord calls "the separate place." The separate place will be the designated area for the priest to eat the offerings (see Leviticus 5:14-19; 6:8-30). The meat, which is actually a meal offering, is one of the voluntary offerings presented before the LORD as a sweet aroma consisting of fine flour, which is the symbol of a living sacrifice. It must be understood that this offering had no element of a sacrificial animal, but consisted of fine flour as demonstrated in

124

the Levitical teachings of the Old Covenant. Its purpose points towards total surrender of our will, therefore rightly consisting of meal rather than meat. The Hebrew word used for "meat" is **Oklah** [402], which means the eating of food. On the other hand, the sin and trespass offering requires the sacrifice of an animal.

The sin offering (Leviticus 4) as its name applies is offered for sin, while the trespass offering is offered for a specific sin done in ignorance. Yeshua became our meat or meal offering; a living sacrifice that both appease and pleased Abba Father. Yeshua said of Himself: *"Verily, verily, I say unto you, he that believeth on Me hath everlasting life. I am that bread of life. Your fathers did eat manna in the wilderness, and are dead. This is the bread which cometh down from heaven, that a man may eat thereof, and not die. I am the living bread which came down from heaven: if any man eat of this bread, he shall live forever: and the bread that I will give is My flesh, which I will give for the life of the world"* (John 6:47-51). Both the sin and trespass offering are never considered sweet aromas to the LORD because they are petitioned for one's forgiveness.

It is said in Ezekiel 42:13 that the priestly class will eat the most "holy things." The Hebrew word used for "holy" is **Qodesh** [6944] and points towards that which is dedicated or separated unto the LORD. We become what we eat and in this case, when we live a sanctified life, we reflect that which we have ingested: holiness in, holiness out, purity in, purity out. We are all invited to the marriage supper but not all will enter as the choice is personal. Those, whom the Lord chooses for this priestly class, are Believers who have ingested, confessed and demonstrated the Word of God in their lifestyle. They are sanctified by the thorough working of the Holy Spirit and set apart to offer spiritual sacrifices unto the Lord being declared holy as Yeshua is holy.

We cannot miss any information regardless how minute. A portion of Ezekiel 42:13 states: *"The north chambers and the south chambers, which are before the separate place, they be holy chambers, where the priests that approach unto the LORD shall eat the most holy things."* First of all, the *"separate place"* is speaking of the Saints who have been exclusively set apart unto the Lord to perform a specific service. These are the Believers who have reached a great standard in God; they have lived lives that were a memorial in heaven and now are rewarded as priests in the continual service of the LORD. Ezekiel 42:13 tells us that the priests will both consume and also lay the most holy things before Abba Father. 1 Peter 2:4 states the fact that these offerings are spiritual and will be an everlasting commemoration of Yeshua's finished work on the Cross. The outer court is a symbol of the flesh and sin, therefore a profaned place where Yeshua bore our reproach and because of this reason it was prohibited by the LORD for the priestly vestures set apart for performing the holy ceremonial duties to be worn in the outer court. The Lord GOD is holy and He requires all Believers to be holy (Leviticus 11:44-45; 19:2; 20:7, 26; 1 Peter 1:13-16).

The things of the flesh that dominates our lives are the same things that destroy or separate us from having Holy Communion with the LORD. A soul that is liberated from all the filth of this world is a soul that will find favor with God. Hebrews 13:10-16 states: "*We have an altar, whereof they have no right to eat which serve the tabernacle. For the bodies of those beasts, whose blood is brought into the sanctuary by the high priest for sin, are burned without the camp. Wherefore Jesus also, that He might sanctify the people with His own blood, suffered without the gate. Let us go forth therefore unto him without the camp, bearing His reproach. For here have we no continuing city, but we seek one to come. By Him therefore let us offer the sacrifice of praise to God continually, that is, the fruit of our lips giving thanks to His name. But to do good and to communicate forget not: for with such sacrifices God is well pleased.*" The Lord considers doing well and communicating such things as sacrifices that is pleasing to Him. In the kingdom of God the sacrifices to be offered by the redeemed will be one of thanksgiving, worship, and praise.

Verses 15-20

"*Now when he had made an end of measuring the inner house, he brought me forth toward the gate whose prospect is toward the east, and measured it round about. He measured the east side with the measuring reeds, five hundred reeds, with the measuring reed round about. He measured the north side, five hundred reeds, with the measuring reed round about. He measured the south side, five hundred reeds, with the measuring reed. He turned about to the west side, and measured five hundred reeds with the measuring reed. He measured it by the four sides: it had a wall round about, five hundred reeds long, and five hundred reeds broad, to make a separation between the sanctuary and the profane place."*

Here we see the abundance of the life giving, fruit bearing, soul saving grace of God on display: five followed by two zeros (5-0-0). Notice that these are equal measurements in a progressive order:

1. East – man in Yeshua who is his only hope
2. North – man in his delegated authoritative role
3. South – man as a watchman or prophet who is now a priest
4. West – man as a bondservant having one master

The message given in these cardinal points shows Yeshua taking precedence in man as he yields to his Creator; man looks upon himself as being nothing without his Lord. The statement and change in order of the four attributes of man from north, east, west and south: to east, north, south, and west: is a picture of the maturity of man; he is no longer carnal but spiritual and all of his actions now reflects those of Yeshua and for this reason he is set apart because he is now anchored in the heart of Abba Father!

The measurements that are given here, is a reflection of the fullness of grace and that grace was made perfect through the unity of the body of Yeshua. If we revisit the tabernacles of Moses and Solomon we will discover that both were rectangular, which is symbolic of areas in our lives where we missed the mark and this was depicted in these tabernacles by having two long and two short sides. Romans 3:21-26 states: *"But now the righteousness of God without the law is manifested, being witnessed by the law and the prophets; Even the righteousness of God which is by faith of Jesus Christ unto all and upon all them that believe: for there is no difference: for all have sinned, and come short of the glory of God being justified freely by His grace through the redemption that is in Christ Jesus: whom God hath set forth to be a propitiation through faith in His blood, to declare His righteousness for the remission of sins that are past, through the forbearance of God; to declare, I say, at this time His righteousness: that He might be just, and the justifier of him which believeth in Jesus."* In the reign of Yeshua, however, the temple of God will be square because man will be perfected in Yeshua Jesus. The measurement of 500 reeds is therefore symbolic of the crowning perfect number of the grace of God because man's measurements are now found in Yeshua, being purchased by His poured out blood.

These measurements were not intended to engender mathematical or architectural quandary, instead, bound in the numerical value of 500 reeds, the LORD God of the universe is giving us a coded message. Psalm 46:1-8 tells us: *"God is our refuge and strength, a very present help in trouble. Therefore will not we fear, though the earth be removed, and though the mountains be carried into the midst of the sea; though the waters thereof roar and be troubled, though the mountains shake with the swelling thereof. There is a river, the streams whereof shall make glad the city of God, the holy place of the tabernacles of the Most High. God is in the midst of her; she shall not be moved: God shall help her, and that right early. The heathen raged, the kingdoms were moved: He uttered His voice, the earth melted. The LORD of hosts is with us; the God of Jacob is our refuge. Come, behold the works of the LORD, what desolations He hath made in the earth."* The LORD is telling us here not to be afraid. In other words the measurement of 500 reeds is stating a reassuring fact: "A MIGHTY FORTRESS IS OUR GOD!" This is a symbolic message of the protective covering of Abba Father enclosing His people within Himself, because we are His final resting place. As Solomon dedicated the Temple, he pleaded with the LORD to find a resting place in a physical Temple but the Fathers final resting place is indeed within humanity. King Solomon prayed: *"Now Therefore arise, O LORD GOD, to Your resting place, You and the ark of Your might; let Your priests, O LORD God, be clothed with salvation and let Your godly ones rejoice in what is good"* (2 Chronicles 6:4 NASB). The glory of the LORD will return, but His final rest will be within man.

All four sides of the Holy Place or inner house which is a picture of the soul, were of identical measurements and its retaining wall was also five hundred reeds in length and width, which is an indication that man has been consummated with his Maker. The measurement of man in Yeshua was the identical measurement of the protective wall of Abba Father who surrounds and keeps him safe from all danger. The refiner's fire of the Lord GOD is about to transform man once again and for all times, into the image and likeness of Yeshua Jesus our Messiah. Whether the return of Yeshua is at hand or His coming is delayed by the grace of GOD for our sake, be it known that the rejection of Yeshua Jesus does not annul His return.

Chapter 43

Verses 1-7

"Afterward he brought me to the gate, even the gate that looketh toward the east: and, behold, the glory of the God of Israel came from the way of the east: and His voice was like a noise of many waters: and the earth shined with His glory. And it was according to the appearance of the vision which I saw, even according to the vision that I saw when I came to destroy the city: and the visions were like the visions that I saw by the river Chebar; and I fell upon my face. And the glory of the LORD came into the house by the way of the gate whose prospect is toward the east. So the Spirit took me up, and brought me into the inner court; and, behold, the glory of the LORD filled the house. And I heard Him speaking unto me out of the house; and the man stood by me. And He said unto me, Son of man, the place of My throne, and the place of the soles of My feet, where I will dwell in the midst of the children of Israel forever, and My holy name, shall the house of Israel no more defile, neither they, nor their kings, by their whoredom, nor by the carcasses of their kings in their high places."

The prophet was granted the unique opportunity of touring the future re-gathering of Israel as One New Man in Yeshua. Whether he is a Jew or Gentile, he will be adopted as sons of the Most High and the Lord will declare with great delight that indeed they are the Israel of God. The Apostle Paul wrote: "*Who are Israelites; to whom pertaineth the adoption, and the glory, and the covenants, and the giving of the law, and the service of God, and the promises; whose are the fathers, and of whom as concerning the flesh Christ came, who is over all, God blessed forever. Amen. Not as though the Word of God hath taken none effect. For they are not all Israel, which are of Israel: neither because they are the seed of Abraham, are they all children:*

131

but, In Isaac shall thy seed be called. That is, They which are children of the flesh, these are not the children of God: but the children of the promise are counted for the seed" (Romans 9:4-8).

After Yeshua Jesus completed the reconstruction of the temple of man, Holy Spirit transports the prophet in the spirit back to the inner court, which is the soul of the elect now made completely pure and awaiting the return of the glory of the LORD God within them. The Hebrew word used in Ezekiel 43:2 for "earth" is **Erets** [776] and it is speaking of this populated planet, where the inhabitants will be eye witnesses of the return of the glory of the God of Israel on earth as well as within the elect. Ezekiel 43:4 makes it quite clear that the return of the glory of the God of Israel was seen entering the house or temple. The Hebrew word used here for "house" is **Bayith** [1004], which means a dwelling place; the final rest of the Lord God within the elect. The new man will behold the glory of God as He unveils Himself to us, because the reconstructed, recreated new man is now perfected and clothed in a spiritual body that will never decay as it bears the identity of Yeshua Jesus.

In the presence of Yeshua, the LORD God of Israel makes a declaration to Ezekiel: "*The place of My throne, and the place of the soles of My feet, where I will dwell in the midst of the children of Israel forever, and My holy name shall the house of Israel no more defile, neither they, nor their kings by their whoredoms, nor by the carcasses of their kings in their high places*" (43:7). The LORD, the High and Exalted One, now takes up His rightful place as Sovereign Ruler within us. The LORD God so gracious to the Israel of God, now demonstrates His unmerited favor towards the elect for all to see in the spirit of man; the place for the soles of His feet, His newly redesigned throne. The dedication of the temple built by King Solomon, although magnificent in splendor is no match for this spiritual temple, because it was the desire of the Lord GOD not only to dwell among us, but also to dwell within us. The prayer that Solomon offered to the LORD on behalf of himself and the people is now finally answered in its fullness (2 Chronicles 7:1-16).

It is from the Mercy Seat located in the Most Holy Place or spirit of the new man that the LORD will now communicate with the elect (Exodus 25:22). The place of GOD's throne and the soles of His feet are within the new man as the Hebrew word **Kaph** [3709]

132

is designated for "*soles*" of His feet, which goes far beyond its natural expression, because "soles" is interpreted, as that which has been revealed. Ezekiel was observing the re-entry of the LORD God of Israel into the new man and with this re-entry, He makes known His secrets, because man has now finally come to the abiding place: Under the shadow of the Almighty (Psalm 91:1). Jews and Gentiles will see firsthand the wondrous return of Abba Father to a people who have been prepared by the Spirit of God to be a resting place for His eternal abiding presence. At this time all unbelief will be erased from the minds of the heathens as well as God's elect and they will declare that the God of Israel alone is the One true highly exalted and Living God.

Verses 8-12

"*In their setting of their threshold by My thresholds, and their post by My posts, and the wall between Me and them, they have even defiled My holy name by their abominations that they have committed: wherefore I have consumed them in Mine anger. Now let them put away their whoredom, and the carcasses of their kings, far from Me, and I will dwell in the midst of them forever. Thou son of man, shew the house to the house of Israel, that they may be ashamed of their iniquities: and let them measure the pattern. And if they be ashamed of all that they have done, shew them the form of the house, and the fashion thereof, and the goings out thereof, and the comings in thereof, and all the forms thereof, and all the ordinances thereof, and all the forms thereof, and all the laws thereof: and write it in their sight, that they may keep the whole form thereof, and all the ordinances thereof, and do them. This is the law of the house; upon the top of the mountain the whole limit thereof round about shall be most holy. Behold, this is the law of the house.*"

It is now clear that the Lord gave Ezekiel understanding in all that He had shown him, and now he must herald this glorious vision of the future of mankind: the true Israel of God. The Apostle Paul states in Galatians 6:14-17: "*But God forbid that I should glory, save in the cross of our Lord Jesus Christ, by whom the world is crucified unto me, and I unto the world. For in Christ neither circumcision availeth anything, nor uncircumcision, but a new creature. And as many as walk according to this rule, peace be on them, and mercy, and upon the Israel of God. From henceforth let no man trouble me: for I bear in my body the marks of the Lord Jesus.*" The future of the new man in Yeshua is a glorious one. Would the captives who settled by the River Chebar believe Ezekiel's report? What impact would this vision have on the future of God's elect? Would the people rejoice and turn wholeheartedly to the LORD or would they dismiss and ignore the vision as being contrary to nature, reason, or common sense; the product of an overactive imagination. The fight is on to destroy the soul of man as the forces of darkness prods and pulls the weak and carnally minded away from the truth to walk in unbelief.

Ezekiel must depend upon God's message of comfort as he prepares to deliver the most important message given to him by the Lord GOD of Israel: "*...Son of man, I send thee to the children of Israel, to a rebellious nation that hath rebelled against Me: they and their fathers have transgressed against Me, even unto this day. For they are impudent children and stiffhearted. I do send thee unto them; and thou shalt say unto them; Thus saith the Lord GOD. And they, whether they will hear, or whether they will forbear, (for they are a rebellious house,) yet shall know that there hath been a prophet among them. And thou, son of man, be not afraid of them, neither be afraid of their words, though briers and thorns be with thee, and thou dost dwell among scorpions: be not afraid of their words, nor be dismayed at their looks, though they be a rebellious house. And thou shalt speak My words unto them, whether they will hear, or whether they will forbear: for they are most rebellious*" (Ezekiel 2:3-7). Remembering these words, the prophet obediently and humbly does as he is told.

What a glorious future awaits Ezekiel's brethren if they turn to the God of Israel and serve Him only. If they be ashamed of all their wickedness; if they cry out in despair and confess their sins; if they believe his words; this would be the sign that they were truly repentant. The next step would then be to recite every detail of the vision before the people, declaring the coming new temple and the magnification of all that it entails, because this final temple will be the holy habitation of the LORD God of Israel, a spiritual temple to demonstrate His glory in the earth. Yeshua is the fulfillment of both the Old and New Covenant; giving hope and a favorable future to both Jews and Gentiles. The LORD now gives the prophet a coded promise in Ezekiel 43:12 concerning His dwelling-place which is the spiritual temple of man. The verse is broken down and key words underlined to reveal the transliterated message from its Hebraic origin.

- *This is the* <u>*law*</u> **Torah** *[8451] of the* <u>*house*</u> **Bayith** *[1004] –* This is the teaching (law, Torah) of the dwelling-place of the LORD (house, Bayith)

- <u>*Upon*</u> **Al** *[5920-21] the* <u>*top*</u> **Rosh** *[7218] of the* <u>*mountain*</u> **Har** *[2022] –* (upon, Al), the Most High and **Rosh** My leader and Chief Corner Stone Yeshua, whom I have promoted (mountain, Har)

- *The* <u>*whole*</u> **Kol** *[3605],* **Jeremiah 33:8** *– And I will cleanse them from all their iniquity, whereby they have sinned, and whereby they have transgressed against Me* (Kol *is Jeremiah 33:8*)

- *limit thereof round about shall be* <u>*most holy*</u> **Qodhesh** [6944] – I will set them apart in holiness (most holy, Qodhesh)

- *Behold, this is the* <u>*law*</u> **Torah** *[8451] of the* <u>*house*</u> **Bayith** *[1004] –* Look and see, this is the teaching (law, Torah) *of the dwelling-place* of the LORD (house, Bayith).

Here is the revealed coded message of Ezekiel 43:12 made plain:

This is the teaching of the dwelling-place of the LORD, the Most High, and My leader and Chief Corner Stone Yeshua, whom I have promoted. "*And I will cleanse them from all their iniquity, whereby they have sinned, and whereby they have transgressed against Me*". I will set them apart in holiness. Now look and see this is the teaching of the dwelling-place of the LORD.

It must be stressed that "whole," which is **Kol** [3605] was the transliteration of Jeremiah 33:8; a uniquely placed promise.

The vision of the construction of the fourth temple and the future of the new man in Yeshua now comes to an end. The LORD God of Israel now speaks to the prophet concerning the rebuilding of the temple in Jerusalem. Saints of God that which was hidden is now being revealed for the sole purpose of preparing mankind

135

to be perfected in love, because all that is holy and righteous flows from it. The confession of Yeshua is the beginning and ending of this new temple or creation in Abba Father. Man's total surrender is his point of entry into the household of faith and the Israel of God. It cannot be stressed enough that these revelations are not esoteric; neither are they the enablement of the philosophical wisdom of man but by the awesome unveiling of the power of the Almighty God through Holy Spirit, because His lovingkindness towards His people endures forever. Now is the time for us to make sure that we are truly building upon the approved foundation of Yeshua our Lord and Savior, our Prince of Peace.

Verses 13-27

"And these are the measures of the altar after the cubits: The cubit is a cubit and a hand breadth; even the bottom shall be a cubit, and the breadth a cubit, and the border thereof by the edge thereof round about shall be a span: and this shall be the higher place of the altar. And from the bottom upon the ground even to the lower settle shall be two cubits, and the breadth one cubit; and from the lesser settle even to the greater settle shall be four cubits, and the breadth one cubit. So the altar shall be four cubits; and from the altar and upward shall be four horns. And the altar shall be twelve cubits long, twelve broad, square in the four squares thereof. And the settle shall be fourteen cubits long and fourteen broad in the four squares thereof; and the border about it shall be half a cubit; and the bottom thereof shall be a cubit about; and his stairs shall look toward the east. And He said unto me, Son of man, thus saith the Lord GOD; These are the ordinances of the altar in the day when they shall make it, to offer burnt offerings thereon, and to sprinkle blood thereon. And thou shalt give to the priests the Levites that be of the seed of Zadok, which approach unto Me, to minister unto Me, saith the Lord GOD, a young bullock for a sin offering. And thou shall take of the blood thereof, and put it on the four horns of it, and the four corners of the settle, and upon the border round about: thus shalt thou cleanse and purge it. Thou shalt take the bullock also of the sin offering, and he shall burn it in the appointed place of the house, without the sanctuary. And on the second day thou shalt offer a kid of the goats without blemish for a sin offering; and they shall cleanse the altar, as they did cleanse it with the bullock. When thou hast made an end of cleansing it,

thou shalt offer a young bullock without blemish. And thou shalt offer them before the LORD, and the priest shall cast salt upon them, and they shall offer them up for a burnt offering unto the LORD. Seven days shalt thou prepare every day a goat for a sin offering: they shall also prepare a young bullock, and a ram out of the flock without blemish. Seven days shall they purge the altar and purify it; and they shall consecrate themselves. And when these days are expired, it shall be, that upon the eight day, and so forward, the priest shall make burnt offerings upon the altar, and your peace offerings; and I will accept you, saith the Lord GOD."

The Lord now turns to matters at hand, which is the rebuilding of the temple in Jerusalem. The Babylonian exile was approaching its prophesied seventy year end and the returning settlers would recommence the teachings set forth by the Lord, concerning their worship of Almighty God. Isaiah prophesied that the Lord GOD of Israel would raise up for Himself a king named Cyrus who would show favor to the people 44:28; 45:1 (for further reading see 2 Chronicles 36:22-23; Ezra 1:1-4; Jeremiah 29:10). Not only did Cyrus give the decree for the return of the exiles, he also handed over to the returning Jews the vessels and furnishings that were taken from the temple during the Babylonian oppression, to re-establish temple worship in the city of Jerusalem. Ezra 5:12-15 states: "But after that our fathers had provoked the God of heaven unto wrath, He gave them into the hand of Nebuchadnezzar the king of Babylon, the Chaldean, who destroyed this house, and carried the people away into Babylon. But in the first year of Cyrus the king of Babylon the same king Cyrus made a decree to build this house of God. And the vessels also of gold and silver of the house of God, which Nebuchadnezzar took out of the temple that was in Jerusalem, and brought them into the temple of Babylon, those did Cyrus the king take out of the temple of Babylon, and they were delivered unto one, whose name was Sheshbazzar, (a prince of Judah) whom he had made governor; and said unto him, Take these vessels, go, carry them into the temple that is in Jerusalem and let the house of God be builded in his place." Nebuchadnezzar's army had taken all that was considered valuable from the house of the LORD in Jerusalem to Babylon.

Ezekiel is given new measurements for the altar of sacrifice and these measurements were different from those given to

Moses for the construction of the first temple in the wilderness (Exodus 27:1), and also the second temple built by Solomon (2 Chronicles 4:1). These new measurements that were given to Ezekiel are for three altars combined that had a single base and fixtures. If we should fast forward to the return of Judah from their Babylonian captivity, we can clearly see that the new altar was designed from the measurements given to Ezekiel. Ezra 3:1-3 states: *"And when the seventh month was come, and the children of Israel were in the cities, the people gathered themselves together as one man in Jerusalem. Then stood up Jeshua the son of Jozadak, and his brethren the priests, and Zerubbabel the son of Shealtiel, and his brethren, and builded the altar of the God of Israel, to offer burnt offerings thereon, as it is written in the law of Moses the man of God. And they set the altar upon his bases; for fear was upon them because of the people of those countries: and they offered burnt offerings thereon unto the LORD, even burnt offerings morning and evening."*

Ezekiel was instructed by the Lord that the Levite priests who were descendants of Zadok should serve Him in the temple (40:46; 43:19; 44:15; 48:11). The craftsmen for the construction of this new altar that will be set on more than one foundation are listed In Ezra 3:2. Ezekiel 43:13-27 is explicitly referring to the requirements for the rehabilitation of the temple that was in ruins for seventy years in the city of Jerusalem. The LORD stirred Cyrus to liberate Judah and give them all the assistance they needed in the rebuilding of the temple (Ezra 3). He also placed on Ezra's and Nehemiah's heart a burden to supervise this laborious task.

Ezekiel 43:13-27 and also 44:15-31 is referring to the rebuilding of the temple in Jerusalem which had been in ruins since the Babylonian siege. Those who were taken as captives to Babylon and their children, who were born in exile desiring to return home, would resume the sacrificial offerings unto the LORD. With the advent of Yeshua Jesus; Abba Father's final perfect offering to mankind, all animal sacrifices were abolished. His death fulfilled this priestly obligation and His resurrection from the dead became the seal of approval and appropriate benefit for all Believers to approach the Father, being washed in His loving mercy and clothed in His grace. A gracious Father now gives instructions for the temple; its teachings, furnishings and its offerings to the next generation of Jews who were raised in a foreign land. Many relied on oral tradition as their fathers were stripped of everything they owned and carted off to Babylon, including the scrolls. Seventy years in exile was approaching its completion and the Jews that were born in captivity never experienced temple worship or the sacrificial offerings unto the LORD. They never openly observed the feasts and festivals but at the appointed time were granted a second chance to do so. Will these returning Jews fully embrace the God of their father's? Will they worship Him in spirit and in truth? Will they faithfully observe His ordinances and teachings? Regrettably the answer is no, and for this reason a fourth and permanent spiritual temple was in the mind of Abba Father to rescue His people from their sin and iniquities.

Chapter 44

Verses 1-3

"Then He brought me back the way of the gate of the outward sanctuary which looketh toward the east; and it was shut. Then said the LORD unto me; This gate shall be shut, it shall not be opened, and no man shall enter in by it; because the LORD, the God of Israel, hath entered in by it, therefore it shall be shut. It is for the Prince; the Prince, He shall sit in it to eat bread before the LORD; He shall enter by the way of the porch of that gate, and shall go out by the way of the same."

In chapters 40-43, Ezekiel was shown a vision of great importance and interest to scholars throughout the centuries. Many, if not all, believe that this temple will be built in the not so distant future. From an architectural standpoint, such a structure would be the size of the city of Jerusalem. However, the temple shown to Ezekiel in the first portion of this vision was not a physical building, but one of a spiritual kind, which is the temple of the NEW MAN in Yeshua! This vision approaches an end and the LORD now turns His focus on the task at hand, which is the rebuilding of the structurally unsound city walls in Jerusalem and its ruined temple. Seventy years in Babylon was prophesied by Jeremiah the servant of the LORD (Jeremiah 25; 29:10; 2 Chronicles 36:21-22; Ezra 1:1). For his obedience to warn the sin polluted leaders and citizens living in Jerusalem, Jeremiah was treated as a free man by the decree of Nebuchadnezzar king of Babylon.

In a vision the LORD brought Ezekiel by the way of the gate facing the east and makes a profound statement. The eastern gate will be left shut as it is reserved for His Son whom He calls Prince. The Hebrew word used here is **Nasi** [5387], a Prince above all princes exalted above His brethren by His Father, a title reserved for none other but Yeshua. Acts 5:30-31 states: *"The God of our fathers raised up Jesus whom you murdered by hanging on a tree. Him God has exalted to His right hand to be Prince and Savior, to give repentance and forgiveness of sins"* (NKJV, see also Acts 2:53; Philippians 2:9). Yeshua is the gate; no one can gain access to the Father by any other means. A gate that is closed limits or restricts one's entrance or exit, but a gate that is "shut" describes an entrance or exit that is blocked or sealed off thereby making it inaccessible to intruders. This special gate was so designed by the Father for His Son and one day it will be re-opened by the one who ordered its sealing.

The LORD continues His discourse with Ezekiel by informing him that the Prince shall sit in the gate to eat bread before His Father. To understand this statement, we must once again explore its Hebrew association. The word "sit" is **Yashav** [3427], it means to judge as would the wise men in ancient times sit at the gate of the city to judge the people. Deuteronomy 16:18 states: *"Judges and officers shall thou make thee in all thy gates, which the LORD thy God giveth thee, throughout thy tribes: and they shall judge the people with just judgment."* Yeshua has many offices and here He is depicted as Judge. The second part of the verse also offers some very important information: *"to eat bread before the LORD,"* this statement expresses yet another of Yeshua's role. This was no ordinary bread because the word used is **Lechem** [3899], which profoundly means: Bread of the Presence [*lechem hapanim*], Exodus 25:30; Matthew 12:4.

Panim or **Paneh** [6440] is the Hebrew word transliterated "before," as in before the presence of the LORD. Yeshua Jesus is our intercessor as the word **Panim** or **Paneh** can also express the outpouring of His emotions. Yeshua Jesus is therefore our continual offering and High Priest before the LORD, being ceremonially allowed to eat the Bread of the Presence in the Holy Place. He is our *lechem hapanim;* our memorial of being offered upon the altar before Abba Father (Leviticus 24:7-9). In other words: Yeshua is the continual shewbread in the presence of the LORD, He is our bridge of hope and reconciliation. Yeshua made this statement recorded in John 6:27-35 applying the NASB: *"Do not work for the food which perishes, but for the food which endures to eternal life, which the Son of Man will give to you, for on Him the Father, God, has set His seal."* Therefore they said to Him, "What shall we do, so that we may work the works of God?" Jesus answered and said to them, "This is the work of God, that you believe in Him whom He has sent." So they said to Him, "What then do You do for a sign, so that we may see, and believe You? What work do You perform? Our fathers ate the manna in the wilderness; as it is written, 'HE GAVE THEM BREAD OUT OF HEAVEN TO EAT.'" Jesus then said to them, "Truly, truly, I say to you, it is not Moses who has given you the bread out of heaven, but it is My Father who gives you the true bread out of heaven. For the bread of God is that which comes down out of heaven, and gives life to the world." Then they said to Him, "Lord, always give us this bread." Jesus said to them, "I am the bread of life; he who comes to Me will not hunger, and he who believes in Me will never thirst." To reject such an offering, is to reject our final and glorious home.

Ezekiel 44:3 concludes: "He shall enter by the way of the porch of the gate, and shall go out by the way of the same." There is no other way to the Father but through Yeshua His Son (John 14:5-6; Hebrews 9:1-10), for this reason we see the symbol of the eastern gate having no other access. The same goes for the three courts of the temple. We should constantly be moving forward in Yeshua who is faithful; there is no variableness in His character or purpose. His Father has given us a promise and a hope to deliver just as He has spoken. What excuse will we offer when the Son of GOD appears? He has sent people back from the dead, given many visions and dreams of the expressed reality of both heaven and outer darkness. He has sent us apostles and prophets, evangelists, elders, and teachers. What will be our rationale for rejecting Abba Father's priceless offering to the world?

Verses 4-5

"Then brought He me the way of the north gate before the house: and I looked, and behold, the glory of the LORD filled the house of the LORD: and I fell upon my face. And the LORD said unto me, Son of man, mark well, and behold with thine eyes, and hear with thine ears all that I say unto thee concerning all the ordinances of the house of the LORD, and all the laws thereof; and mark well the entering in of the house, with every going forth of the sanctuary."

Ezekiel's tremendous vision continues and the prophet once again gets a glimpse of the spiritual temple known as the new man in Yeshua. He was commanded never to forget what he was shown because the time would come, set on the calendar of God, when these things would be manifested. The eastern gate belongs to Yeshua our High Priest who lives in the presence of Abba Father ever making intercession for mankind of all ethnic groups, languages and religious persuasions. He is the bread of life that came down from the Father and by Him alone will many return and be blessed. Yeshua poured His innocent blood thereby making it unacceptable and abominable for any man or woman to pour out his or her sinful blood as a sacrifice for any cause in the name of GOD. Overwhelmed, the prophet fell prostrate at the appearance of the awesome power and glory of the Father and as before, his frail human body had no capacity to remain upright.

The visions that the LORD gave Ezekiel were also a measure of hope, because there would come a time when mankind would no longer strive with sin. His new temple or house will be the holy habitation of the Lord GOD and man will enjoy living in the presence of the Lord. Here the prophet looks to the north and sees the new man built upon the foundation of Yeshua and reigning in Him. First, it was the East that the prophet was taken where he observed the Prince as the Bread of Life in the presence of His Father as our offering. Yeshua satisfied His Father's judgment against sin, and when the prophet looked towards the north he saw the regenerated man, sanctified and made perfect and acceptable. The soul of man is now transformed; being made pure that the very presence of the Almighty finds a sin free resting place for His home.

Verses 6-14

"And thou shalt say to the rebellious, even to the house of Israel, Thus saith the Lord GOD; O ye house of Israel, let it suffice you of all your abominations, in that ye have brought into My sanctuary strangers, uncircumcised in heart, and uncircumcised in flesh, to be in My sanctuary, to pollute it, even My house, when ye offer My bread, the fat and the blood, and they have broken My covenant because of all your abominations. And ye have not kept the charge of Mine holy things: but ye have set keepers of My charge in My sanctuary for yourselves. Thus saith the Lord GOD;

No stranger, uncircumcised in heart, nor uncircumcised in flesh, shall enter into My sanctuary, of any stranger that is among the children of Israel. And the Levites that are gone away far from Me, when Israel went astray, which went astray away from Me after their idols; they shall even bear their iniquity. Yet they shall be ministers in My sanctuary, having charge of the gates of the house, and ministering to the house: they shall slay the burnt offering and the sacrifice for the people, and they shall stand before them to minister unto them. Because they ministered unto them before their idols, and caused the house of Israel to fall into iniquity; therefore have I lifted up Mine hand against them, saith the Lord GOD, and they shall bear their iniquity. And they shall not come near unto Me, to do the office of a priest unto Me, nor to come near to any of My holy things, in the Most Holy Place: but they shall bear their shame, and their abominations which they have committed. But I will make them keepers of the charge of the house, for all the service thereof, and for all that shall be done therein."

In the book of Ezekiel the LORD used the word "rebellious," a total of sixteen times, which is more than anywhere else in the Authorized Version of the Holy Scriptures. This word gives the idea of one being stubborn, stiff-necked, un-repentant, without remorse, ruthless and perverse. This is not a good thing as rebellion is as the spirit of witchcraft (1 Samuel 15:23). Rebellion was first mention in Deuteronomy 9:7-29 when the children of Israel provoked the LORD, and once again He addresses their waywardness. Israel faced seventy years of exile for their stubbornness; what would they learn from this experience? They were accused of taking foreign youths and placing them in the temple of the LORD which contaminated it. The temple was a holy place but these heathens had complete access there, doing as they pleased to the encouragement of the priests the Levites.

The holy offerings set apart for the priests and the Bread of His Presence which is a symbol of Yeshua being an offering for all was polluted. The fat or choicest part of the burnt offering became food for these pagans; while blood that was prohibited for the house of Israel to consume became their drink (Deuteronomy 12:16, 24; 15:23; Exodus 30:9); breaking the teachings and statutes of the LORD. As custodians and ministers of the temple, the Levites delegated their responsibilities to others not approved by the LORD. The LORD stressed yet again that no such individuals living among them should enter His sanctuary when they returned from captivity. Those priests found culpable of idolatry and who were responsible for the lawless behavior of the children of Israel, would continue to do the required services of the temple, however they were disbarred from the presence of the Lord GOD in the Most Holy Place. The teachings and ordinances prescribed for the high priest were never revoked by the LORD and to enter the Most Holy Place in a debased state would have proven to be fatal (Exodus 30:1-10; Leviticus 16-27; Hebrews 9:7). The Levites would pay for all the evil they had done, but the LORD their God would not totally remove them from their priestly duties which He had ordained and this is called grace!

Verses 15-31

"But the priests the Levites, the sons of Zadok, that kept the charge of My sanctuary when the children of Israel went astray from Me, they shall come near to Me to minister unto Me, and they shall stand before Me to offer unto Me the fat and the blood saith the Lord GOD: They shall enter into My sanctuary, and they shall come near to My table, to minister unto Me, and they shall keep My charge. And it shall come to pass, that when they enter in at the gates of the inner court, they shall be clothed with linen garments; and no wool shall come upon them, whiles they minister in the gates of the inner court, and within. They shall have linen bonnets upon their heads, and shall have linen breeches upon their loins; they shall not gird themselves with anything that causeth sweat. And when they go forth into the utter court, even into the utter court to the people, they shall put off their garments wherein they ministered, and lay them in the holy chambers, and they shall put on other garments; and they shall not sanctify the people with their garments. Neither shall the shave their heads, nor suffer their locks to grow long; they shall only poll their heads. Neither shall any priest drink wine, when they enter into the inner court. Neither shall they take for their wives a widow, nor her that is put away: but they shall take maidens of the seed of the house of Israel or a widow that had a priest before. And they shall teach My people the difference between the holy and profane, and cause them to discern between the unclean and the clean. And in controversy they shall stand in judgment; and they shall judge it according to My judgments: and they shall keep My laws and My statutes *in all Mine assemblies; and they shall hallow My Sabbaths. And they shall come at no dead person to defile themselves: but for father, or for mother, or for son, or for daughter, for brother, or for sister that hath had no husband, they may defile themselves. And after he is cleansed, they shall reckon unto him seven days. And in the day that he goeth into the sanctuary, unto the inner court, to minister in the sanctuary, he shall offer his sin offering, saith the Lord GOD. And it shall be unto them for an inheritance: I am their inheritance: and ye shall give them no possession in Israel: I am their possession. They shall eat the meat offering, and the sin offering, and the trespass offering; and every dedicated thing in Israel shall be theirs. And the first of all the firstfruits of all thing, and every oblation of all, of every sort of your oblations, shall be the priest's: ye shall also give unto the priest the first of your dough, that he may cause the blessing to rest in thine house. The priests shall not eat of anything that is dead of itself, or torn, whether it be fowl or beast."*

The LORD restated the duties of the priests leaving them without excuses. Remembering the faithfulness of Zadok, the LORD reinstates his descendants to be the chief Levites. Their clothing could not produce sweat because body fluid is considered a contaminant. In rabbinical Judaism, shatnez (pronounced shot-nezz) is a combined fabric of wool and linen and the Mitzvah (precepts and teachings commanded by GOD in Torah) still prohibits the wearing of fabric made of such mixtures (see Deuteronomy 22:11). Linen is a breathable fabric that does not cause perspiration and therefore the LORD's choice for the garment of the priest. Until this day, Rabbinical Jews still check clothing labels before purchasing. The Mitzvah comprises six hundred and thirteen (613) commandments that were given to Moses on Sinai and documented in the Torah; this number speaks of man's rebellion against his Creator: in Scripture: 6 is the number assigned to man and 13 is the mark of his rebellion. The mixing of wool and linen is symbolic of a contaminated garment and also points to the contamination in doctrinal teachings and religious practices which the LORD abhors. For this same reason, the belt that was worn for beauty by the priests could not be sweat producing, because, this too, would cause malodor, making the priest unacceptable to perform his duties.

There are many symbolic references to Yeshua which includes what was acceptable and unacceptable for the Levitical priests, as they were Abba Father's earthly representative of His Son. The office of high priest was assigned to a Levite as God's appointed intercessor for the children of Israel (Deuteronomy 10:6-9). The all wise GOD specifically chose the descendants of Levi as his name profoundly means: he who is joined, attached, or united; a portrayal of joy felt by a husband who has been united with his beloved bride (Genesis 29:34).

The Levitical priesthood therefore speaks of the unification between the Almighty God and mankind until Yeshua's inauguration as the sacrifices performed by the priests were foreshadows of better things to come. Almost six hundred years had passed since the LORD spoke to Ezekiel concerning the priests, to the fulfillment of GOD's promised Son; our living sacrifice who was tempted as we are, yet without sin. He was touched by our infirmities and permanently and forever abolished the need for animal sacrifices because He became the only High Priest that was totally pure. These animals were innocent just like Yeshua Jesus, who completed the need for an earthly priesthood of men to intercede in the behalf of another. Hebrews 4:14-16 states: "*Seeing then that we have a great High Priest, that is passed into the heavens, Jesus the Son of God, let us hold fast our profession. For we have not a High Priest which cannot be touched with the feelings of our infirmities; but was in all points tempted like as we are, yet without sin. Let us therefore come boldly unto the throne of grace that we may obtain mercy, and find grace to help in time of need.*" The blood of these animals were only a temporary solution for sin, and for this reason, it was prohibited for the priestly garment to be worn casually as it was a symbol of Yeshua our High Priest being untouched by sin. The LORD continues to instruct Ezekiel on the requirements for the priest, and next on His agenda was the priest's hair.

Shaving of one's head or allowing the hair to grow long was also prohibited (Leviticus 19:27). In Ezekiel's era, the style of one's hair was an identifying mark of nationality or affiliation. Of equal importance is the fact that the instrument used for shaving the head could cause accidental injury to the scalp, and the blood of man is tainted by sin. The requirements for the priest were very strict and absolute adherence was expected. Consuming strong wines or any other drink that was likely to cause poor judgment was also on the list that was prohibited. It is very easy for one to lose self-control when inebriated and more importantly wine was symbolic of Yeshua's poured out blood for the sins of humanity (Leviticus 10:9; 1 Corinthians 10:16-17; 11:25-27).

Included also on the list of priestly requirements was the teaching on marriage. Unmarried priest could only wed a virgin or the widow of a priest as he was separated to perform the holy services of the LORD (Leviticus 21:7, 13, 14). The priestly line is joined unto the LORD, therefore, the inclusion of the priest's widow since she was joined unto her husband who sanctified her. Priests also served as teachers (Leviticus 10:10, 11; Joshua 1:8; James 1:22, 3:1; Romans 2:13; I Timothy 1:7-13). Teaching Torah is a repetitious practice with a double edged sword, as it is the teacher's instructions and meditations as well as that of the people. What excuse can a priest offer the LORD when he breaks the very commands of the LORD he was committed to pattern in his duties as well as his lifestyle? Much was given to the priests therefore much was required of them (Luke 12:48).

The priests were also judges, keepers and sanctifiers of the Sabbaths, ordered to abstain from burial rites with a few exceptions that were followed by strict ceremonial cleansing. The priests belonged to the LORD as much as the LORD belonged to the priest, and certain offerings made unto Him was theirs as well (Leviticus 10:12-19). The body of Yeshua is now called His possession: a chosen generation, a royal priesthood, His holy nation and special people thereby establishing the fourteenth generation of Yeshua Jesus whose birth into this world was not to marry and have a few children, but to seek and save the lost souls of this world and in doing so, enlarged His family through our adoption into the family of God (Matthew 1:1-17; Exodus 19:6; 1 Peter 2:9; Ephesians 1:5; Galatians 4:5; Romans 8:15 and 23).

The Levitical priesthood could not eat anything that died of itself, or its blood was not properly drained, because this would make them ceremonially unclean (Exodus 22:31; Leviticus 22:8). The life is in the blood and the blood is identified with life (Leviticus 17:10-16). Hebrews 9:1-15 quoting the NET speaks of the consummation of these things in Yeshua: "*Now the first covenant, in fact, had regulations for worship and its earthly sanctuary. For a tent was prepared, the outer one, which contained the* lampstand, the table, and the presentation of the loaves; this is called the holy place. And after the second curtain there was a tent called the holy of holies. It contained the golden altar of incense and the Ark of the Covenant covered entirely with gold. In this ark were the golden urn containing the manna, Aaron's rod that budded, and the stone tablets of the covenant. And above the ark were the cherubim of glory overshadowing the mercy seat. Now it is not the time to speak of these things in detail. So with these things prepared like this, the priests enter continually into the outer tent as they perform their duties, but only the high priest enters once a year into the inner tent, and not without blood that he offers for himself and for the sins of the people committed in ignorance. The Holy Spirit is making clear that the way into the holy place had not yet appeared as long as the old tabernacle was standing. This was a symbol for the time then present, when gifts and sacrifices were offered that could not perfect the conscience of the worshiper. They served only for matters of food and drink and various washings; they are external regulations imposed until the new order came. But now Christ has come as the high priest of the good things to come. He passed through the greater and more perfect tent not made with hands, that is, not of this creation, and he entered once for all into the most holy place not by the blood of goats and calves but by his own blood, and so he himself secured eternal redemption. For if the blood of goats and bulls and the ashes of a young cow sprinkled on those who are defiled consecrated them and provided ritual purity, how much more will the blood of Christ, who through the eternal Spirit offered himself without blemish to God, purify our consciences from dead works to worship the living God. And so he is the mediator of a new covenant, so that those who are called may receive eternal inheritance he has promised, since he died to set them free from the violations committed under the first covenant." Yeshua became our firstfruits (Exodus 22:29; 23:19; 34:27). Yeshua Jesus was His Father's most prestigious gift to all (1Corinthians 15:20-23), being the best of the best, the giver of eternal life, our living sacrifice, and the crème de la crème of His Father. He has earned the honor as High Priest and overseer of our soul (1 Peter 2:24-25). Yeshua was a blessing to the Father and to the world because He gave His very best which was His life!

Not only did the LORD speak to Ezekiel concerning the returning Jews to Jerusalem, He was preparing Daniel in the king's palace by giving him revelations of what he had read in the scrolls concerning the time span of their exile. With this understanding Daniel sought the face of the LORD in prayer, supplication, intercession and fasting openly for the people as well as for himself (Daniel chapter 9). During this season the Lord was also stirring Nehemiah's spirit as well as that of Ezra the priest and scribe to organize the rebuilding of their beloved Jerusalem and its temple.

Ezra left Babylon carrying all he could back to the city of Jerusalem, which included the furnishings needed for the rehabilitation of the temple and carefully documented the intricate details regarding the repatriation of the Jewish people (Ezra chapter 7). Nothing happens by chance, the LORD will often times give each of His servant a role to play that may not seem like much at first, but when all the pieces fall into its place, a greater and more glorious picture unfold. Believers in Yeshua Jesus must understand that their gifts and callings are to be a blessing to others. God qualifies each person whom He calls to perform a specific task, yet his or her obedience to do so is only a fragment that fits perfectly into a more grandeur mosaic.

For their move back home Cyrus the new leader of Babylon, would be the agent of change for the exiles (see Isaiah 44:28; 45:1-3). His hand of authority would be in favor of the Jews and stirring in his heart was the Spirit of the Living God to use his new office and influence to fulfill Jeremiah's prophesies. We must never get too comfortable in any system that reflects spiritual Babylon but always be prepared to leave at a moment's notice. Not all Jews left Babylon, many decided to stay for that was their home for seventy years and also their comfort zone. When the LORD God calls His people out of any type of system, obedience is better than to remain and suffer the plagues that will eventually come upon it. We cannot procrastinate and end up being shut out of the blessings of God, for to do so will be to our own detriment. When the Lord stirs His people to move, we must do so without hesitation or questioning.

Chapter 45

Verses 1-6

"Moreover, when ye shall divide by lot the land for inheritance, ye shall offer an oblation unto the LORD, a holy portion of the land: the length shall be the length of five and twenty thousand reeds, and the breadth shall be ten thousand. This shall be holy in all the borders thereof round about. Of this there shall be for the sanctuary five hundred in length, with five hundred in breadth, square round about; and fifty cubits round about for the suburbs thereof. And of this measure shalt thou measure the length of five and twenty thousand, and the breadth of ten thousand: and in it shall be the sanctuary and the most holy place. The holy portion of the land shall be for the priests the ministers of the sanctuary, which shall come near to minister unto the LORD: and it shall be a place for their houses, and a holy place for the sanctuary. And the five and twenty thousand of length, and the ten thousand of breadth, shall also the Levites, the ministers of the house, have for themselves, for a possession for twenty chambers. And ye shall appoint the possession of the city five thousand broad, and five and twenty thousand long, over against the oblation of the holy portion: it shall be for the whole house of Israel."

As the appointed seventy year of Babylonian captivity was approaching its end, the LORD commanded Ezekiel to relay a message to his brethren. It was a message of hope and a bright future if they observed and practiced the teachings of the LORD. Ezekiel was first given a tour of the fourth and final glorious temple which is the regenerated blood bought man, to be the dwelling place of the LORD once again. Until these things are fulfilled, the LORD switches gear to speak to the prophet concerning the third temple, which is yet to be built in Jerusalem. This fact was revealed by the opening portion of the LORD'S conversation with Ezekiel: *"Moreover, when ye shall divide by lot the land;"* the Hebrew word used for *"shall divide by lot"* is **Naphal** [5307], among its meanings are: to overthrow accidentally or by violence and lastly, to fall into the hands of another. This statement is conveying a prophetic message informing us that there will be chaos in the Middle East and the land of Israel will be the focus of this unrest that will lead to portions of it being relinquished to their opponents. However, after a while, Israel will rout their enemies and gain the victorious upper hand; recapturing more land than that which had been previously taken from them. It will be subsequent to these occurrences that the land of Israel will be divided into these allotted portions.

The Lord instructs Ezekiel first of all that a portion of the land of Israel (not Jerusalem), twenty five thousand reeds long and ten thousand reeds wide should be dedicated to Him as His holy portion, including all the borders surrounding it. Roughly the size of New Jersey, the land of Israel is currently about 8019 square miles or 20,770 km^2 which makes these allotments achievable, but let's focus on the spiritual value of the size of the land as the LORD gave specific measurements with a message in mind also. First of all, two important facts are revealed about 25,000. Twenty-five thousand is mentioned eleven times in Scripture and amazingly, all occurring in the book of Ezekiel (45:1, 3, 5, 6; 48:8-10, 13, 15, 20, and 21). Eleven is a significant number as it refers to that which has been compromised; being one more and one less than two perfect numbers, ten and twelve. This is telling us that the third temple; the LORD'S holy portion, will be compromised. The Apostle Paul in a second letter to the Thessalonians spoke of this coming defilement: *"Don't let anyone deceive you in any way, for that day will not come until the rebellion occurs and the man of lawlessness is revealed, the man doomed to destruction. He will oppose and exalt himself over everything that is called God or is worshiped, so that he sets himself up in God's temple, proclaiming himself to be God"* (2:3-4 NIV).

The pattern, measurement, and land allocated for the building of the third temple in Jerusalem is now given. The Lord specifically chose 25,000 reeds, a measurement which has never been used before in the Scriptures to get our attention and also to convey

154

the second important message which is: The Lord GOD is about to do a new thing among His people. Isaiah 43:19 states: *"Behold I will do a new thing: now it shall spring forth; shall ye not know it? I will even make a way in the wilderness, and rivers in the desert"* (see also Revelation 10:5). Although these were literal measurements, there is however a revelatory component to them. The small strip of land that is currently known as Israel is only a portion of its true size and borders, but this will be changed as the Cannon of Scriptures have indicated. Within these measurements of the land allotment are spiritual revelations that will give insight into the LORD's future plans for His people. The focus therefore will be both of its natural measurement as well as its revelatory component.

The first portion of land will be allocated and dedicated to the LORD, which indicates that this new thing that was about to be performed among His people commenced with Himself; His portion being twenty-five thousand reeds long and ten thousand reeds wide. With the breaking down of this measurement; twenty-five is followed by three zeros (25-000) and ten thousand is also followed by three zeros (10-000); this is a message in itself. Here we see the grace of God being magnified in perfection and agreement, as 5 is the number by which grace is either divided or multiplied. From the Hebrew word **Zera** [2233]; we get the word "zero," the seed or offspring. Here we have three zeros (000), which signifies completeness, finality or conclusion; therefore, nothing can be further added or subtracted; this is the LORD's message of redemption to His elect (John 3:16-17). Abba Father gave us Yeshua Jesus, His Son and by His grace we are saved. In Ephesians 2:4-10 and applying the NKJV it is stated: *"But God, who is rich in mercy, because of His great love with which He loved us, even when we were dead in trespasses, made us alive together with Christ (by grace you have been saved), and raised us up together, and made us sit together in the heavenly places in Christ Jesus, that in the ages to come He might show the exceeding riches of His grace in His kindness toward us in Christ Jesus. For by grace you have been saved through faith, and that not of yourselves; it is the gift of God, not of works, lest anyone should boast. For we are His workmanship, created in Jesus for good works, which God prepared beforehand that we should walk in them."* The number 25,000 and 10,000 are both pictures of the abounding grace of GOD, being magnified in His dwelling place and among His people. Grace is given unto the world by the LORD GOD and Yeshua Jesus His Redeemer and Son; His seed – 000.

Yeshua accomplished His Father's wish to reunite His elect by being crucified and shedding His blood on a tree to purchase our salvation. From the measurements of Moses to Solomon and then to Ezekiel's vision of a temple, we can clearly see progression in its size, which reveal the increasing manifestation of not only the grace of GOD, but also His presence among His people. John 1:12-17 reminds us: *"But as many as received Him, to them He gave the right to become children of God, to those who believe in His name: who were born, not of blood, nor of the will of the flesh, nor of the will of man, but of God. And the Word became flesh and dwelt among us, and we beheld His glory, the glory as of the only begotten of the Father, full of grace and truth. John bore witness of Him and cried out, saying, "This was He whom I said, 'He who comes after me is preferred before me, for He was before me,' " And of His fullness we have all received, and grace for grace. For the law was given through Moses, but grace and truth came through Jesus Christ"* (NKJV).

Included in the holy portion of land allotted to the LORD, will be the sanctuary, measuring five hundred (500) cubits long and five hundred (500) cubits broad with the suburbs perimeter measuring in at fifty (50) cubits. The measurement of the sanctuary is separate and apart from the temple as a whole, because it speaks of that which is innermost, indicating that this was the measurement of the Most Holy Place, also known as Holiest of all, Holy of Holies, and most inner court. Notice its measurement has four equal sides; indicating that the grace of God is in unity with His purpose. The encircling suburb of fifty (50) cubits is an extension of Abba Father's covering grace and His grace is stamped in every aspect of the building of the third temple.

The sanctuary and its ministers will be set apart in holiness and any place designated for the worship and ministration unto the LORD must be treated as such. Because the inheritance of the Levites comes from Abba Father, they are given custodianship for the allotted land that is set aside as holy unto the LORD. Once more the mark of God's grace is evident as the Levites are given twenty chambers (rooms) to occupy. This unmerited favor offered immunity for repentant sins as the chambers symbolically speaks of that which has been made known.

The possession of the city of Jerusalem will be five thousand reeds wide and twenty five thousand reeds long which will be located close to the portion of land set apart earlier as a holy offering unto Abba Father; this is revealed in Ezekiel 45:6 as belonging to the house of Israel. The battle over Jerusalem is a spiritual one because it truly belongs to the LORD, and for this reason daily prayers must go up to the Father to procure peace. Psalm 126 states: *"I was glad when they said unto me, Let us go into the house of the LORD. Our feet shall stand within thy gates, O Jerusalem. Jerusalem is builded as a city that is compact together: whither the tribes go up, the tribes of the LORD, unto the testimony of Israel, to give thanks unto the name of the LORD. For there are set thrones of judgment, the thrones of the house of David. Pray for the peace of Jerusalem: they shall prosper that love thee. Peace be within thy walls, and prosperity within thy palaces. For my brethren and companions' sakes, I will now say, Peace be within thee. Because of the house of the LORD our God I will seek thy good."*

There is no other nation on the face of the earth that has received blessings pronounced over it by the LORD Himself as the nation of Israel, His prophetic witness to the final showdown here on earth between good and evil. Although many Jews have rejected Yeshua HaMashiach their brethren and Messiah, Israel will forever be the LORD's trophy even in the midst of continued turmoil and unrest. The LORD God is now calling forth a people unto Himself named the Israel of God: the Overcomers, who have suffered greatly, but have not denied their faith or His name. Pray for the redemption of Judah. Pray for the consummation of the house of Israel that Holy Spirit will sweep over His beloved people bringing forth an awesome revival before Yeshua HaMashiach returns. Abba Father loves His Jewish people and for this reason He has stirred the Gentiles to make them jealous (Romans 11:25). Here is a promise for the house of Israel by David and the prophet Jeremiah, recorded in Psalm 14:7 and Jeremiah 31:31-34 applying the NET: *"I wish the deliverance of Israel would come from Zion! When the LORD restores the well-being of his people, may Jacob rejoice, may Israel be happy! . . . . "Indeed, a time is coming," says the LORD, "when I will make a new covenant with the people of Israel and Judah. It will not be like the old covenant that I made with their ancestors when I delivered them from Egypt. For they violated that covenant, even though I was like a faithful husband to them," says the*

LORD. *"But I will make a new covenant with the whole nation of Israel after I plant them back in the land," says the LORD. "I will put my law within them and write it on their hearts and minds. I will be their God and they will be my people."*

Verses 7-8

"And a portion shall be for the prince on the one side and on the other side of the oblation of the holy portion, and of the possession of the city, before the oblation of the holy portion, and before the possession of the city, from the west side westward: and the length shall be over against one of the portions, from the west border unto the east border. In the land shall be his possession in Israel: and My princes shall no more oppress My people; and the rest of the land shall they give to the house of Israel according to their tribes."

Is the LORD referring to the Prince He had spoken of in Ezekiel 44:3 or is He speaking of another? The answer is found in the book of Genesis. Israel is made up of the twelve sons of Jacob, of which only one tribe was promised a kingdom, and that was the tribe of David's descendants: Judah. Genesis 49:10 states: *"The scepter shall not depart from Judah, nor a lawgiver from between his feet, until Shiloh come; and unto him shall the gathering of the people be"* (see also Numbers 24:17; Luke 1:32-33). If we fast forward to Ezekiel 48:8 and 22 we will see that the prince being referred to in 45:7-8 is actually the tribe of Judah. Ezekiel 48:8, 22 states: *"And by the border of Judah, from the east side unto the west side, shall be the offering which ye shall offer of five and twenty thousand reeds in breadth, and in length as one of the other parts, from the east side unto the west side: and the sanctuary shall be in the midst of it. . . Moreover from the possession of the Levites, and from the possession of the city, being in the midst of that which is the prince's, between the border of Judah and the border of Benjamin, shall be for the prince."* The promises of the LORD are irrevocable, that which He has said He will do and that which He has spoken, is a guarantee that it will be done (see Numbers 23:19). Judah's sins were worse than that of the other tribes (see also Jeremiah 3:11; 2 Kings 21:11 and commentary on Ezekiel 16:15-52 and 23:1-21), yet Abba Father has kept His promise even when Judah broke theirs. Yeshua Jesus is a descendant from the tribe of Judah (Revelation 5:3-5). He alone is given the authority to enter through the eastern gate (Ezekiel 44:1-3) being Abba Father's representative on our behalf before His presence. He is therefore our Bread of the Presence; the *lechem hapanim* of the LORD our God. The mention of the prince in these verses is speaking of the tribe of Judah in general; Yeshua's brethren and not Yeshua who is the head of this tribe.

Verses 9-22

"Thus saith the Lord GOD; Let it suffice you. O princes of Israel: remove violence and spoil, and execute judgment and justice, take away your exactions from My people, saith the Lord GOD. Ye shall have just balances and a just ephah, and a just bath. The ephah and the bath shall be of one measure, that the bath may contain the tenth part of a homer, and the ephah the tenth part of a homer: the measure thereof shall be after the homer. And the shekel shall be twenty gerahs: twenty shekels, five and twenty shekels, fifteen shekels, shall be your maneh. This is the oblation that ye shall offer; the sixth part of an ephah of an homer of wheat, and ye shall give the sixth part of an ephah of an homer of barley: concerning the ordinance of oil, the bath of oil, ye shall offer the tenth part of a bath out of the cor, which is an homer of ten baths; for ten baths are an homer: and one lamb out of the flock, out of two hundred, out of the fat pastures of Israel; for a meat offering, and for a burnt offering, and for peace offerings to make reconciliation for them, saith the Lord GOD. All the people of the land shall give this oblation for the prince in Israel. And it shall be the prince's part to give burnt offerings, and meat offerings, and drink offerings, in the feasts, and in the new moons, and in the Sabbaths, in all solemnities of the house of Israel: he shall prepare the sin offering, and the meat offering, and the burnt offering, and the peace offerings, to make reconciliation for the house of Israel. Thus saith the Lord GOD; In the first month, in the first day of the month, thou shalt take a young bullock without blemish, and cleanse the sanctuary: and the priest shall take of the blood of the sin offering, and put it upon the posts of the house, and upon the four corners of the settle of the altar, and upon the posts of the gate of the inner court. And so thou shalt do the seventh day of the month for every one that erreth, and for him that is simple: so shall ye reconcile the house. In the first month, in the fourteenth day of the month, ye shall have the Passover,

a feast of seven days; unleavened bread shall be eaten. And upon that day shall the prince prepare for himself and for all the people of the land a bullock for a sin offering."

The LORD reiterates the need for justice to be exercised in a manner in which His people conducted themselves in business. All forms of cheating and short changing committed by His elect were known by the LORD. This was one of His final calls for repentance, behooving His people to exercise justice and be a people known for their integrity. He then gives Ezekiel the required measure for the offering; that is the sixth part (1/6th) of an ephah of a homer of wheat and barley. Within this measure is also a message to all.

Sixth part
One-sixth or the sixth part is referring to one of six equal parts. Notice it comes after the fifth (grace) and before the seventh (perfection). The sixth is therefore associated with man's imperfections. Therefore this offering which is made unto the LORD is done to forgive our inadequacies and imperfections.

The ephah
This is a dry measure for grains: 1 ephah = 1/10th of a homer. One tenth is seen as a unit of God's Divine order in a typological setting. This is the order that points to the kingdom of God; that which is done in heaven is replicated here on earth. The ephah although a dry measure for grains; is pointing to the coming perfection of Abba Father's Divine Order here on earth.

The homer (kor)
This is a dry measure of capacity which is equal to 10 baths or 10 ephahs. The homer or kor [Hebrew 2563]; points to that which is bubbling upwards. The homer is all about the number 10 as this number is its unit measure. Within the measure of a homer is the message of the completeness of two messages; the grace of GOD being multiplied as His Divine order being perfected on earth and therefore in earth (mankind).

Wheat
Wheat was discussed in chapter 4:9-17; it is the most common of all cereal grains. The wheat grain is a picture of humility; the full head of grain literally bows itself while that of the tares (weed) which looks almost identical to it, proudly remains erect;

thereby separating itself from the wheat, which is the identifying harvesting marker. The wheat speaks of the sifting rigor of trials that the Believer undergoes by Satan; but that which is meant for evil will produce good when we keep our eyes on Yeshua (Luke 22:31-32). With humility comes grace and with grace comes fellowship and reconciliation. For this reason the wheat offering is symbolic of reconciling us unto Abba Father when we miss the mark.

Barley
Like the wheat, the barley grain was also discussed in chapter 4:9-17. This grain is associated with the jealousy offering (Numbers 5:14-31), as the jealous husband seeks justification because of his wayward wife, much the same as the straying of Israel into the idolatrous practices of the heathens. The word "jealousy" was first mentioned in Exodus 20:4-6 and addressed the consequences of idolatry. The LORD makes known that He is a jealous GOD. The barley offering is associated with the forgiveness of Israel's idolatry with the god's of the heathens.

Bath of oil
This is cold pressed olive oil that points to our act of worship as stated by the Lord in Leviticus 2:15-16: "*And thou shalt put oil upon it, and lay frankincense thereon: it is a meat offering. And the priest shall burn the memorial of it, part of the beaten corn thereof, and part of the oil thereof, with all the frankincense thereof: it is an offering made by fire unto the LORD.*" In Ezekiel 45:14 the LORD makes known that the homer (kor) is equal to 10 baths (or 10 baths = 1 homer). One is the symbol of unity and ten points to the LORD'S Divine Order being bound by His grace. All the offerings done by the Levites points to that which has already been completed in heaven and one day our eyes will behold them in the earth.

All twelve tribes of Israel are here referred to as "prince" but it will be the tribe of Judah that will be elected first to give unto the Levites their burnt offerings; meat (meal) offerings; and drink offerings at the feasts, new moons and Sabbaths of Israel as a reconciliatory act (this will be explained further in chapter 46). Yeshua is from the tribe of Judah; therefore it will be the duty of this tribe to give their offering first. These three offerings, as we will see, are a picture of Yeshua, the lamb without blemish; Abba Father's offering to humanity.

161

The burnt offering

This offering could not be eaten by the priest; it was totally consumed by fire because it was offered for sin. It is documented in 2 Corinthians 5:17-21: *"Therefore if anyone is in Christ, he is a new creature; the old things passed away; behold, new things have come. Now all these things are from God, who reconciled us to Himself through Christ and gave us the ministry of reconciliation, namely, that God was in Christ reconciling the world to Himself, not counting their trespasses against them, and He has committed to us the word of reconciliation. Therefore, we are ambassadors for Christ, be reconciled to God. He made Him who knew no sin to be sin on our behalf, so that we may become the righteousness of God in Him"* (NASB). Yeshua took all our sin upon Himself, thereby reconciling us unto His Father.

The meat (meal) offering

This offering is not a living sacrifice therefore, does not require the shedding of blood. This was a grain offering unto the LORD (Leviticus 2:1-16; 6:14-18; 7:9-10; 10:12-13). The grain offering points to Yeshua as our restitution of peace. If anyone is in Yeshua; he is newly created (2 Corinthians 5:17-18).

The drink offering

Yeshua is seen here as our Sanctifier and Redeemer, being our poured out offering, (Titus 3:5). Yeshua Messiah poured out His soul for ours. Isaiah 53:11-12 states: *"He shall see the travail of His soul, and shall be satisfied: by His knowledge shall My righteous servant justify many; for He shall bear their iniquities. Therefore will I divide Him a portion with the great, and He shall divide the spoil with the strong; because He hath poured out His soul unto death: and He was numbered with the transgressors; and He bare the sin of many, and made intercession for the transgressors."*

The LORD has prescribed set times for these offerings: In the feasts, new moons and the Sabbaths.

The feasts

The feasts are celebrated during the spring and fall and speak so much more than time cycles. Embedded in these seasons are hidden truths concerning Yeshua's second coming. The first four feasts occur during the spring: Pesach (Passover), the Feast of

Unleavened bread, Feast of firstfruits (wave offering) and Feast of Weeks/Shavuot (Pentecost).

Pesach/Passover – Commemorates the end of Israel's slavery in Egypt (Exodus 12). This feast was fulfilled in Yeshua at His death because it freed man from the slavery of sin (1 Peter 1:18-23; Hebrews 9:14-15).

The Feast of Unleavened Bread – In Exodus 12, blood had to be placed at special locations on the door of those who would be saved from the final plague of death and the points were the blood was applied was an outline of a cross. Yeshua became our representation of unleavened bread because no sin was found in Him. John 6:32, 33, 48-51 states: *"Then Jesus said to them, "Most assuredly, I say to you, Moses did not give you the bread from heaven, but My Father gives you the true bread from heaven. For the bread of God is He who comes down from heaven and gives life to the world. . . I am the bread of life. Your fathers ate the manna in the wilderness, and are dead. This is the bread which comes down from heaven, that one may eat of it and not die. I am the living bread which came down from heaven. If anyone eats of this bread, he will live forever; and the bread that I shall give in My flesh, which I shall give for the life of the world"* (NKJV).

The Feast of Firstfruits/ wave offering – Deuteronomy 26:1-11 gives details concerning this feast as it speaks of our thankfulness for all that the Lord has done for us. The feast celebrates Yeshua's resurrection from the dead and our redemption from sin and death. 1 Corinthians 15:20-23 states: *"But now Christ is risen from the dead, and has become the firstfruits of those who have fallen asleep. For since by man came death, by Man also came the resurrection of the dead. For as in Adam all die, even so in Christ all shall be made alive. But each one in his order: Christ the firstfruits, afterward those who are Christ's at His coming"* (NKJV). Both the Feasts of Firstfruits and Unleavened bread are celebrated on the same day

Feast of Weeks/Shavuot/Pentecost – This feast was celebrated when Israel finally made it to the promise land; its observance points to a new covenant or *B'rit Chadashah* being installed (Exodus 34:22; Leviticus 23:15-21), fifty days following the Feast of Firstfruits. Leviticus 23:15-16 states: *"And you shall count for yourselves from the day after the Sabbath, from the day that you brought the sheaf of the wave offering seven Sabbaths shall be completed. Count fifty days to the day after the seventh Sabbath; then you shall offer a new grain offering to the LORD"* (NKJV). This new grain offering unto the LORD speaks of the New Covenant by the indwelling of Holy Spirit and a fresh move of God in the entire earth which continues to this day; Acts 1:1-8. The other feasts as previously mentioned had to fall in place for the Feast of Weeks to be fulfilled and now we have the precious endowment of Holy Spirit until Yeshua Messiah returns to take us home.

Yeshua was crucified on Pesach (Passover) becoming our sacrificial lamb and redeemer and on the Feast of Unleavened Bread; He became our perfect sacrifice for sin. On the Feast of Firstfruits; He offered us eternal life and on Shavuot He indwelled those who believed in Him with Holy Spirit. The fall festivals are yet to be fulfilled, but the rules for their observance have been given by the LORD; these are: Sukkoth (Tabernacles or Feast of Ingathering), Yom Kippur (Day of Atonement) and Yom Teruah (Day of the Shofar, Rosh Hashanah or Feast of Trumpets). Of the three feasts to be fulfilled there is something very special about Yom Teruah because provisions are made for the forgiveness of sin and all un-willful act of unrighteousness, by the mandatory requirement of the affliction of one's soul.

Verses 23-25

"And seven days of the feast he shall prepare a burnt offering to the LORD, seven bullocks and seven rams without blemish daily the seven days; and a kid of the goats daily for a sin offering. And he shall prepare a meat offering of an ephah for a bullock, and an ephah for a ram, and a hin of oil for an ephah. In the seventh month, in the fifteenth day of the month, shall he do the like in the feast of the seven days, according to the sin offering, according to the burnt offering, and according to the meat offering, and according to the oil."

The LORD reinforces the requirements for the burnt offerings, which points to our complete and voluntary surrender in Ezekiel 45:23-25. This offering reflects remorse that was followed by liberating worship for being forgiven. After sorrow is expressed for one's wretchedness, a grain meal is offered. This mixture is made of fine flour and olive oil, which points to the sanctifying process through the working of Holy Spirit in the lives of the forgiven now purged and delivered from foolish pride. Hebrews 2:9-18 states: *"But we do see Him who was made for a little while lower than the angels, namely, Jesus, because of the suffering of death crowned with glory and honor, so that by the grace of God He might taste death for everyone. For it was fitting for Him, for whom are all things, and through whom are all things, in bringing many sons to glory, to perfect the author of their salvation through sufferings. For both He who sanctifies and those who are sanctified are all from one Father; for which reason He is not ashamed to call them brethren, saying, "I WILL PROCLAIM YOUR NAME TO MY BRETHREN, IN THE MIDST OF THE CONGREGATION I WILL SING YOUR PRAISE." And again, "BEHOLD, I AND THE CHILDREN WHOM GOD HAS GIVEN ME." Therefore, since the children share in flesh and blood, He Himself likewise also partook of the same, that through death He might render powerless him who had the power of death, that is, the devil, and might free those who through fear of death were subject to slavery all their lives. For assuredly He does not give help to angels, but He gives help to the descendants of Abraham. Therefore, He had to be made like His brethren in all things, so that He might become a merciful and faithful high priest in things pertaining to God, to make propitiation for the sins of the people. For since He Himself was tempted in that which He has suffered, He is able to come to the aid of those who are tempted"* (NASB). All the offerings in the Old Covenant were types and shadows of good things to come, made available to all through Yeshua who placed into effect the New Covenant. We are His brethren if we follow His examples that He sets for us. No one will be rejected who does the will of the Son for in Him, Abba Father is well pleased.

Chapter 46

Verses 1-8

"Thus saith the Lord GOD; The gate of the inner court that looketh toward the east shall be shut the six working days; on the Sabbath is shall be opened, and in the day of the new moon it shall be opened. And the prince shall enter by the way of the porch of that gate without, and shall stand by the post of the gate, and the priest shall prepare his burnt offering and his peace offering, and he shall worship at the threshold of the gate: then he shall go forth; but the gate shall not be shut until the evening. Likewise the people of the land shall worship at the door of this gate before the LORD in the Sabbaths and in the new moons. And the burnt offering that the prince shall offer unto the LORD in the Sabbath day shall be six lambs without blemish. And the meat offering shall be an ephah for a ram, and the meat offering for the lambs as he shall be able to give, and a hin of oil to an ephah. And in the day of the new moon it shall be a young bullock without blemish, and six lambs and a ram: they shall be without blemish. And he shall prepare a meat offering, an ephah for a bullock, and an ephah for a ram, and for the lambs according as his hand shall attain unto, and a hin of oil to an ephah. And when the prince shall enter, he shall go in by the way of the porch of that gate, and he shall go forth by the way thereof."

As we begin to examine Ezekiel chapter 46, there are portions that will unveil the coming reign of Yeshua Jesus. The LORD has revealed great truths in part to the body of Yeshua Jesus until that which is done in part shall be no more. In 1 Corinthians 13:9-10 it is stated: *"For we know in part, and we prophesy in part. But when that which is perfect is come, then that which*

167

is in part shall be done away." The Saints that are used by God are kept humble knowing that what has been imparted to them by the Holy Spirit is not attributed to their theological or intellectual prowess; he or she operates by the divine gift of a scribe of Yeshua and His Father, through indwelling Holy Spirit. Once more we will embark on truths that will make us draw even closer to Yeshua Jesus who has chosen to break the seal at this time in human history. It is already midnight on the earth and mankind is given yet another chance to turn and acknowledge Yeshua Jesus as Savior and Lord. Now is the time to prepare our bodies as a living sacrifice and a holy habitation for the LORD God because His dwelling place, His holy temple and His personal house is within us!

Ezekiel chapter 46 is much like any other chapter in this great book of mysteries as more revelatory truths are unsealed. This chapter opens with the LORD stating *"The gate of the inner court that looketh toward the east shall be shut the six working days..."* In this statement there is a prophetic revelation. First of all these are not six literal days, instead, it is conveying a period of time in one thousand years blocks of mercy, grace and salvation in which the Lord of the harvest, Yeshua the Messiah, is preparing His people for His millennial reign. It points to a window of opportunity to get things done before darkness, lawlessness, and moral decline fully engulfs the earth as it did in the days of Noah (Genesis 6-7). Yeshua spoke these words recorded in John 9:4 which states: *"I must work the works of Him that sent Me while it is day; the night is coming when no one can work"* (NKJV). This will be a significant occurrence, because the gate will be shut not in the sixth working day which will be the completion of the sixth millennium, but rather during the sixth millennium. This will be the period just before the beginning of the seventh on the Jewish calendar. One must never succumb to worry during these dark hours, but look unto the Lord, who will shorten these days because of the elect; Matthew 24:22; Mark 13:20.

A new century does not commence on the first day of the beginning of that year, but rather after one full year has been completed. This fact must be taken into consideration, because the window of opportunity is not a precise date, but a time frame before the end of the six thousandth year and the official beginning of the seventh. This period will be marked by great tribulations, famines, pestilences and woes, as never before seen upon the face of the earth. Yeshua Jesus states in Matthew 24:36-39 of the coming of these things: *"But of that day and hour knoweth no man, no, not the angels of heaven, but My Father only. But as the days of Noah were, so shall also the coming of the Son of man be. For as in the days that were before the flood they were eating and drinking, marrying and giving in marriage, until the day that Noah entered into the ark, and knew not until the flood came, and took them all away; so shall also the coming of the Son of man be* (see also Genesis 7:10-24; Mark 13:32-37; Luke 17:26-36).

Six working days represents a point in time designated for mankind to repent of their evil ways and turn wholeheartedly unto God. This window of opportunity is six thousand years which is measured on the Jewish calendar of a thirty day lunar month or the average cyclic occurrence between new moon phases. Here we are given a time line or grace period of six thousand years to repent of our rebellion against God. Isaiah 55:6-7 quoting the NASB states: *"Seek the LORD while He may be found; call upon Him while He is near. Let the wicked forsake his way and the unrighteous man his thoughts; and let him return to the LORD and He will have compassion on him, and to our God, for He will abundantly pardon"* (see also Psalm 2:7; 95:7). Six thousand years (6,000) is the allotted time for man to be completed in all aspect of his relationship with his Creator. Notice that six (6), which is the number of man, is followed by three zeros, which is an indication that as the offspring or seed of God, man has finally come to the completion of his rule over the earth and is now ready to be harvested and the wheat will be separated from the tares or weed (Mathew 13:24-40; Revelation 14:1-20).

The LORD said to Ezekiel: *"The gate of the inner court that looketh toward the east shall be shut the six working days."* The inner court represents the soul of man and here is the final clarion call for all mankind to come into the ark of God, His safe haven, which is His Son. As we will look at the number six from its Hebraic origin, we will discover yet another Divine truth that the LORD God is actually giving us insight into the coming of a special day when Yeshua Jesus will re-gather and reestablish Israel. Six is translated **Shishshah** [8337], it is not only identified with the number six, but also points to that which overflows. Looking back we see in Genesis 1:26-27, that man is the overflow or crowning glory of God's creation, as He gave man dominion over the works of His hands. This is a unique overflow as the number six leads us to another important Hebrew word, **Suws** or **Siys** [7797] which speaks of rejoicing. This rejoicing is linked with the celebration of the Sabbath of the Lord called Shavuot also known as the Feast of Weeks or Pentecost. Shavuot will be commemorated as a day of complete rest, liberation and spiritual renewal, when the souls of men will be harvested. At this time there will be the ingathering of the redeemed from the earth as a firstfruits offering of a kingdom of priests and a holy nation unto the LORD (see Exodus 19:6). There is coming to the earth a final outpouring of Holy Spirit, which will be far greater than the Acts 2 upper room experience and it will occurred during a celebration of Shavuot (Feast of Weeks, Pentecost).

Ezekiel 46:1 continues: "... *but* **on** *the Sabbath it shall be opened, and* **in** *the day of the new moon it shall be opened."* Here lies a wealth of information concerning the return of Yeshua Jesus and His reign over the earth. Hidden in these words, the LORD is telling us the exact season when His Son will appear. It must be reinforced that no man knows the day or the hour when Yeshua Messiah will return, but the Father has set forth in His Word the season indicating when this will occur (Acts 1:6-1; Matthew 25:13). "On" the Sabbath indicates the day of Yeshua's return, while "in" the day of the new moon gives us a time line, as well as describing what these coming days will be like. The new moon is also known as Rosh Chodesh or Rosh Hodesh; it can also be interpreted as month, but whether it is the first phase of the moon that appears as a narrow waxing crescent in the night sky or a specified month known only to the Father, it doesn't matter. What matters is our preparedness to endure to the end or succumb to tyranny.

This moon phase is unique as it follows the pathway of the sun. When the new moon is observed from the earth what the natural eyes perceive is total darkness. If one should be in a spacecraft where they could view the moon at a better vantage point they would observe that the backside or un-observable portion, is brilliantly lit. When we see gross darkness covering the earth, those who fear the Lord must not wallow in a feeling of disquiet and despair, because hope and redemption is on the horizon. The prophet Amos spoke of these times by the mouth of the LORD recorded in 5:8-20, which states: "*Seek Him that maketh the* seven stars and Orion, and turneth the shadow of death into the morning, and maketh the day dark with night: that calleth for the waters of the sea, and poureth them out upon the face of the earth: the LORD is His name: that strengtheneth the spoiled against the strong, so that the spoiled shall come against the fortress. They hate him that rebuketh in the gate, and they abhor him that speaketh uprightly. Forasmuch therefore as your treading is upon the poor, and ye take from him burdens of wheat: ye have built houses of hewn stone, but ye shall not dwell in them; ye have planted pleasant vineyards, but ye shall not drink wine of them. For I know your manifold transgressions and your mighty sins: they afflict the just, they take a bribe, and they turn aside the poor in the gate from their right. Therefore the prudent shall keep silence in that time; for it is an evil time. Seek good, and not evil, that ye may live: and so the LORD, the God of hosts, shall be with you, as ye have spoken. Hate the evil, and love the good, and establish judgment in the gate: it may be that the LORD God of hosts will be gracious unto the remnant of Joseph. Therefore the LORD, the God of hosts, the Lord, saith thus; Wailing shall be in all streets; and they shall say in all the highways. Alas! Alas! And they shall call the husbandman to mourning, and such as are skilled of lamentation to wailing. And in all vineyards shall be wailing: for I will pass through thee, saith the LORD. Woe unto you that desire the day of the LORD! To what end is it for you? The day of the LORD is darkness, and not light. As if a man did flee from a lion, and a bear met him; or went into the house, and leaned his hand on the wall, and a serpent bit him. Shall not the day of the LORD be darkness, and not light? Even very dark, and no brightness in it?" This oracle of Amos seals the fate of those who rejected Yeshua and now realize that it is too late to enter into Abba Father's rest as the door of redemption closes, never to be opened again.

A new day is dawning. A new millennium will be established and a new King named Yeshua HaMashiach, whom Gentiles call Jesus, from the tribe of Judah, and a descendant from the seed of David will exercise His Sovereign power on the Sabbath and in the day of the new moon. This Sabbath will be a very special one because it will be the culmination of all Sabbaths. It will be a day of everlasting rest when the darkness that covered the earth for six thousand years is shattered by the glory of God, as Yeshua Jesus is crowned as King over all the earth by Abba Father. This will be a time of eternal rest for the soul. Hebrews

4:1-11 states: "*Therefore, since a promise remains of entering His rest, any of you seem to have come short of it. For indeed a gospel was preached to us as well as to them; but the word which they heard did not profit them, not being mixed with faith in those who heard it. For we who believed do enter that rest, as He has said: "So I swore In My wrath, 'They shall not enter My rest,' "* although the works were finished from the foundation of the world. For He has spoken in a certain place of the seventh day in this way: "And God rested on the seventh day from all His works"; and again in this place: "They shall not enter My rest." Since therefore it remains that some must enter it, and those to whom it was first preached did not enter because of disobedience, again He designates a certain day, saying in David, "Today," after such a long time, as it has been said: "Today, if you will hear His voice, do not harden your hearts." For if Joshua had given them rest, then he would not afterward have spoken of another day. There remains therefore a rest for the people of God. For he who entered His rest has himself also ceased from his works as God did from His. Let us therefore be diligent to enter that rest, lest anyone fall according to the same example of disobedience"* (NKJV, see also Psalm 116:5-7; Jeremiah 6:16; Matthew 11:25-30).

Yeshua Jesus will one day enter by the gate of the Most Holy place towards the east that no one else is authorized to enter. Now is the time for us to come into His rest; now is the window of opportunity open to the entire human race. If you do not know Yeshua Jesus or doubt that He is the Son of GOD, all you have to do is ask Him to prove it. Yeshua has been raised to Supremacy by His Father for our benefit. Romans 14:11-12 states: "*For it is written, As I live, saith the Lord, every knee shall bow, and every tongue shall confess to God. So then every one of us shall give account of himself to God*" (see also Isaiah 45:23). This is the time to prepare for the coming peril that will sweep the entire planet. With this thought in mind let's examine and also ponder a prophetic message that the LORD is giving to us, because He has also revealed two important pieces of information regarding the season prior to Yeshua HaMashiach's return. On the Sabbath and in the day of the new moon Yeshua will return and set up His Sovereign rule. But before His coronation as King many will be martyred for their belief and many will suffer unspeakable oppression, but those who endure to the end will receive the Overcomers crown.

Below is the revelation of the meaning of *on the Sabbath and in the day of the new moon that* will precede the return of Yeshua Jesus.

Taking a look at the emblem of Islam and that of the nation of Turkey one striking feature is observed: they both have a crescent and a star. The crescent and the star here symbolize the leading role of Islam as a religion and Turkey the chief (star) nation that will be highly recognized and acknowledged as its capital. During this period of history the escalation of religious persecution of non-Muslims will be at an all-time high. Jews and Christians especially, will be the target of the greatest forms of torture, but in spite of their sufferings, they will offer sacrifices of praise and thanksgiving unto the LORD and herald Yeshua Jesus as Messiah. Yeshua will then shorten the days, stop the mayhem and send His angels to gather the elect from the earth. Ezekiel 46:1 states: "*Thus saith the Lord GOD; the gate of the inner court that looketh toward the east shall be shut the six working days; but on the Sabbath it shall be opened, and in the day of the new moon it shall be opened.*" On the Sabbath or seventh day and in the new moon the gate of the inner court (entry into the soul) will be accomplished and all Overcomers will enter into the rest of the LORD.

The Hebrew word for new moon is **Chodesh** [2320]; which carries a dual meaning: new moon or month. **Chodesh** is derived from **Chadash** [2318], which means to be made new, rebuild or a time of renewal. In essence the LORD is giving us precise timelines when the Saints of God will be removed from this earth. Following this snatching away Turkey and Islam will rule the earth for a season. This will be a period of great tribulation and Yeshua will break forth triumphantly to restore order. Revelation 21:1-8 states: "*And I John saw the holy city, New Jerusalem, coming down from God out of heaven, prepared as a bride adorned for her husband. And I heard a great voice out of heaven saying,*

Behold, the tabernacle of God is with men, and He will dwell with them, and they shall be His people, and God Himself shall be with them, and be their God. And God shall wipe away all tears from their eyes; and there shall be no more death, neither sorrow, nor crying, neither shall there be any more pain: for the former things are passed away. And He that sat upon the throne said, Behold, I make all things new. And He said unto me, Write: for these words are true and faithful. And He said unto me, It is done. I am Alpha and Omega, the beginning and the end. I will give unto him that is athirst of the fountain of water of life freely. He that overcometh shall inherit all things; and I will be his God and he shall be My son. But the fearful, and unbelieving, and the abominable, and murderers, and whoremongers, and sorcerers, and idolaters, and all liars, shall have their part in the lake which burneth with fire and brimstone: which is the second death." Yeshua will return when Islamic power headquartered in the nation of Turkey dominates the earth.

The emblem of Turkey and that of Islam exhibit similarities to a phase of the moon cycle featured as a narrow crescent which comes after the new moon. The crescent and the star are therefore informing us of the prominent role, location and nature of governmental diplomacy, politics, military and religious dogma that both Turkey and Islam will play in the future. This may seem farfetched, but the Lord GOD has revealed hidden messages regarding the rise of Islam as both a political superpower and religious ideology that will dominate the earth in the future. Here is the Word of God concerning this period of Islamic world domination: *"For nation will rise against nation, and kingdom against kingdom. And there will be famines, pestilences, and earthquakes in various places. All these are the beginning of sorrows. Then they will deliver you up to tribulation and kill you, and you will be hated by all nations for My name's sake. And then many will be offended, will betray one another, and will hate one another. Then many false prophets will rise up and deceive many. And because lawlessness will abound, the love of many will grow cold. But he who endures to the end shall be saved. And this gospel of the kingdom will be preached in all the world as a witness to all the nations, and then the end will come"* (Matthew 24:7-14 NKJV; for further reading see also Matthew 24:15-27; Mark 13:5-27; Luke 21:10-28).

In the book of Genesis the Lord made known that the sun and moon were given to us as an observable calendar; dividing day from night and for signs and seasons, days and years (1:14). The new moon is God's marker in the heavens that measures not only the lunar cycle but also the season when a religious and political ideology rising from Turkey will dominate the earth. The crescent is not only speaking of a moon phase, but also a time on earth when Islam will arise as a political superpower and religious creed. When it seems as if Jews and Gentiles are finally subdued, converted or beheaded; the Prince of Peace who is the root and offspring of David, will return with great power and glory at the rejoicing of the Overcomers.

Yeshua, being a descendant from the tribe of Judah is referred to as Prince just like His brethren. Isaiah 9:6-7 quoting the NKJV states: "*For unto us a Child is born, unto us a Son is given; and the government will be upon His shoulder. And His name will be called Wonderful, Counselor, Mighty God, Everlasting Father, Prince of Peace. Of the increase of His government and peace there will be no end, upon the throne of David and over His kingdom, to order it and establish it with judgment and justice from that time forward, even forever. The zeal of the LORD of hosts will perform this.*" Yeshua is the head of His brethren. He is our reconciler and redeemer and He will enter by the eastern gate in the fulfillment of Bible prophecy.

Ezekiel 46:2 states: "*He shall stand by the post of the gate,*" referring to the fact that it is in Yeshua that all creation is upheld and find grace and forgiveness. He is our Cornerstone and load bearer, our support beam, and our unchanging and immovable post. Colossians 1:15-22 clearly states: "*Christ is the visible image of the invisible God. He existed before anything was created and is supreme over all creation, for through him God created everything in the heavenly realms and on earth. He made the things we can see and the things we can't see such as thrones, kingdoms, rulers, and authorities in the unseen world. Everything was created through him and for him. He existed before anything else, and he holds all creation together. Christ is also the head of the church, which is his body. He is the beginning, supreme over all who rise from the dead. So he is the first in everything. For God in all his fullness was pleased to live in Christ, and through him God reconciled everything to himself. He made peace with everything in heaven and on* earth by means of Christ's blood on the cross. This includes you who were once far away from God. You were his enemies, separated from him by your evil thoughts and actions. Yet now he has reconciled you to himself through the death of Christ in his physical body. As a result, he has brought you into his own presence, and you are holy and blameless as you stand before him without a single fault" (NLT). As sons of the Most High God, we must stay clear of all sin, debauchery and acts of unrighteousness, because the LORD has poured upon us His boundless mercy and grace. A time will come upon the earth when evil leaders and their associates will decide the fate of those who refuse to deny Yeshua Jesus, and like Him, will truly become sheep to the slaughter (Psalm 44:20-22; Romans 8:36; Isaiah 53:7). Will we have the spiritual strength to endure to the end or will we succumb to tyrannical rule?

When all is said and done, the priests will prepare a commemorative burnt offering, which is our voluntary act of fellowship and communion with GOD. Yeshua Jesus became our free will offering so that we in turn, will offer our worship freely back to God. Yeshua will put an end to tyranny, and when these things are fulfilled: the LORD will shut the rescue door of reconciliation just like He did the ark in the days of Noah, because of the overflow of wickedness upon the earth (Genesis 6:5). Simultaneously, the gates to the kingdom of God will also be supernaturally closed forever (Joel 2:1-2; 3:14; Amos 5:18-20). What will it benefit anyone to brush off Yeshua's pleading to enter into His rest? Is the acquiring of worldly possession of more value than the soul?

The LORD now speaks to the prophet concerning the tribe of Judah. In Ezekiel 46:4 the LORD refers to Judah as *"prince,"* the tribe commanded to give their oblation first. Numbers 7:1-12 put forth this understanding quite succinctly: "*And it came to pass on the day that Moses had fully set up the tabernacle, and had anointed it, and sanctified it, and all the instruments thereof, both the altar and all the vessels thereof, and had anointed them, and sanctified them: that the princes of Israel, heads of the house of their fathers, who were the princes of the tribes, and were over them that were numbered, offered: and they brought their offering before the LORD, six covered wagons, and twelve oxen; a wagon for two of the princes, and for each one an ox: and they brought them before the tabernacle. And the LORD spake unto Moses, saying, Take it of them, that they may* be to do the service of the tabernacle of the congregation; and thou shalt give them unto the Levites, to every man according to his service. And Moses took the wagons and the oxen, and gave them unto the Levites. Two wagons and four oxen he gave unto the sons of Gershon, according to their service: and four wagons and eight oxen he gave unto the sons of Merairi, according unto their service, under the hand of Ithamar the son of Aaron the priest. But unto the sons of Kohath he gave none: because the service of the sanctuary belonging unto them was that they should bear upon their shoulders. And the princes offered for dedicating of the altar in the day that it was anointed, even the princes offered their offering before the altar. And the LORD said unto Moses, They shall offer their offering, each prince on his day, for the dedicating of the altar. _And he that offered his offering **the first day** was Nahshon the son of Amminadab, of the tribe of Judah._" Here we see the leaders who are referred to as princes, taking their offerings to the Levites who were set apart as priests unto the LORD in the services of the tabernacle.

The LORD commanded the leaders of Judah to be the first of the twelve tribes in making their offering. Judah is not the first son of Israel, but the LORD requested their offering first because this is the tribe of His promised Redeemer Yeshua Jesus the Messiah, thereby fulfilling Jacob's blessing upon this tribe (Genesis 49:9-12). It is also important to mention two exemplary attributes of Judah's leadership. The first was observed in the way he handled the potentially dangerous situation concerning his younger brother Joseph. Reuben being the eldest son wanted to have no part in the death of Joseph, but instead of protecting his younger sibling by not leaving him with the other siblings who desired to kill him, Reuben left the scene, leaving Joseph behind. This was a very unwise decision on the part of Reuben, which showed a lack of leadership as the eldest. Reuben left the area with the intention of excluding himself from any guilt should his ruthless brothers kill Joseph whom they had thrown into an empty pit at his own advice. Judah on the other hand remained with his brothers, steaming with vehement hatred, and it was at Judah's advice that Joseph's life was spared (Genesis 37:22-36). It was also at Judah's encouraging that Benjamin the youngest brother was carried from Goshen to Egypt, as proof that they were men of integrity and not liars (Genesis 42:33-38; 43:1-9). Judah did not recognize Joseph his own brother who was now the Governor of Egypt neither was he aware that it was only a ploy to gather all the siblings for a surprise family reunion. Once again Judah stood out as a leader; prevailing in honesty and selflessness, and for this he was honored by the LORD. The tribe of Judah was blessed with Yeshua Jesus.

Yeshua became our living sacrifice by laying down His life for the whole human race. These are His words recorded in John 10:11 applying the NASB: *"I am the good shepherd; the good shepherd lays down His life for the sheep."* For those who believe that Yeshua is truly the Son of God and have walked in the path of righteousness; they too, have reciprocated these offerings by their voluntary act of submission, just as He did by giving His life to reconcile us to the Father. The Apostle Paul states in Romans 12:1: *"I beseech you therefore, brethren, by the mercies of God, that you present your bodies a living sacrifice, holy, acceptable to God, which is your reasonable service"* (NKJV).

Ezekiel 46:4 tells us: *"... the burnt offering that the prince shall offer unto the LORD in the Sabbath day shall be six lambs without blemish, and a ram without blemish."* *"Shall offer"* is the Hebrew word **Qarav** [7126], which means to appear before the LORD with an offering as a gift. Here, once more, we see a play on numbers "six lamb" indicate that this offering is given on the behalf of mankind, as six is his assigned number (Genesis 1:26-31). The offering consisting of six lambs memorably and metaphorically is speaking of the offering made for man by the Son of God who is also known as the Lamb that was slain before the foundation of the world (Revelation 13:8; 1 Peter 1:20). The second offering mentioned, is a burnt offering of a single ram, which points to those who have voluntarily surrendered unto the LORD and as an act of worship, have completely devoted their lives to God by keeping the word and testimony of Yeshua Jesus unto the end of their physical life; Leviticus 1:1-17; 6:8-14; 8:18-21; 16:24; 19:22; 28:27 and Genesis 22:13. These will be the offerings made by the Overcomers at the beginning of the seventh millennium when all the enemies of the righteous seed have been crushed by Yeshua.

Verses 9-12

"But when the people of the land shall come before the LORD in the solemn feasts, he that entereth in by the way of the north

gate to worship shall go out by the way of the south gate; and he that entereth by the way of the south gate shall go forth by the way of the north gate: he shall not return by the way of the gate whereby he came in, but shall go forth over against it. And the prince in the midst of them, when they go in, shall go in; and when they go forth, shall go forth. And in the feasts and in the solemnities the meat offering shall be an ephah to a bullock, and an ephah to a ram, and to the lambs as he is able to give, and an hin of oil to an ephah. Now when the prince shall prepare a voluntary burnt offering or peace offerings voluntarily unto the LORD, one shall then open him the gate that looketh toward the east, and he shall prepare his burnt offering, as he did on the Sabbath day: then he shall go forth; and after his going forth one shall shut the gate."

Something very special is mentioned here about the Believer's walk with God which once again, upholds the harmony of His Word. At the appointed time when the people present themselves before the LORD in the solemn feasts, those who entered from the northern gate to assemble for worship could not return that way but instead, were required to exit by the southern gate and likewise those who entered from the southern gate were required to exit from the northern gate. The reason for these instructions lies in the fact that the true Believer is always in a state of advancement; there is no turning back in the kingdom of God. The old man and his un-regenerated soul continue to struggle with the temporary enticements that this world offers. Returning from whence one came symbolically speaks of carnality, missing the mark, being lovers of the world instead of being lovers of God (1 John 2:15-17; James 4:4-10; 2 Timothy 3: 1-9; 4:1-8); As a regenerated being, blood washed and reborn, to turn back to the ways of the world not only shows a lack of faith, but repeatedly crucifies Yeshua who poured out His life giving soul for sinful humanity. Hebrews 10:38-39 states: *"Now the just shall live by faith: but if any man draw back, My soul shall have no pleasure in him. But we are not of them who draw back unto perdition; but of them that believe to the saving of the soul."* Once again the Prince of Israel takes center stage and His name is Yeshua HaMashiach our Righteousness. He will be in the midst of them and they will follow Him wherever He goes. During the assembly of these festive celebrations the required voluntary offerings will be that which one can afford whether rich or poor and this requirement also applied to the seasoning, as oil symbolically represents our voluntary act of worship (Leviticus 2:15-16). The ephah points to the coming perfection of the LORD's Divine Order, not only on earth but also in earth (mankind).

Ezekiel is given instructions once again for the tribal leaders of Israel. When they offer the voluntary burnt and peace offering unto the LORD, the gate located in the east will be left open as these offerings points to Yeshua's own voluntary sacrifice of Himself. At the completion of these oblations, the leaders are required to continue moving forward never looking backwards, as someone else was appointed to close the gate. A final Sabbath of rest will come for the congregation of the LORD. All we are required to do is to be light in this dark world that men may see our good works and glorify God. Our trust and hope is for a wonderful and promising future because we walk by faith and not by sight. The Apostles of old, who walked with Yeshua Jesus, thought they would be eyewitnesses of His second coming, but the season is now ripe for Yeshua's appearing. Whether it is today or that of a thousand years; we must be prepared at all times, as no one knows when Abba Father will send His Son to retrieve His righteous inheritance.

Verses 13-15

"Thou shalt daily prepare a burnt offering unto the LORD of a lamb of the first year without blemish: thou shalt prepare it every morning. And thou shalt prepare a meat offering for it every morning, the sixth part of an ephah, and the third part of a hin of oil, to temper with the fine flour; a meat offering continually by a perpetual ordinance unto the LORD. Thus shall they prepare the lamb, and the meat offering, and the oil, every morning for a continual burnt offering."

A portion of Ezekiel chapter 46 introduces us to the coming reign of the Prince of Judah: Yeshua Messiah. These verses must be viewed as the everlasting memorial of His finished work on the Cross. Yeshua's death, resurrection, and ascension into heaven to be seated at the right hand of the Father is Abba's gift of love to the whole world; He, being the perfect and final sacrifice for all. During His coming reign, all sacrifices will be a memorial of what He had done to reconcile us to the Father. Hebrews 10:1-10 applying the NKJV states: "*For the law, having the shadow of* good things to come, and not the very image of the things, can never with these same sacrifices, which they offer continually year by year, make those who approach perfect. For then would they not have ceased to be offered? For the worshipers, once purified, would have had no more consciousness of sins. But in those sacrifices there is a reminder of sins every year. For it is not possible that the blood of bulls and goats could take away sins. Therefore, when He came into this world, He said: "Sacrifice and offering you did not desire, but a body You have prepared for Me. In burnt offerings and sacrifices for sin You have no pleasure. Then I said, 'Behold, I have come in the volume of the book it is written of Me to do Your will, O God.'" Previously saying, 'Sacrifice and offering, burnt offerings, and offerings for sin You did not desire, nor had pleasure in them (which are according to the law), then He said, "Behold, I have come to do Your will, O God." He takes away the first that He may establish the second. By that will we have been sanctified through the offering of the body of Jesus Christ once for all." The LORD has already given His Son. Therefore these coming sacrifices will be a perpetual memorial of Yeshua's finished work. Therefore, there is no need to recommence animal sacrifices and burnt offering as Yeshua HaMashiach has already established the second and permanent offering unto His Father, by offering His own body voluntarily for the sins of all.

The requirements for the burnt offering in Ezekiel chapter 46 are quite different from the original orders recorded in Leviticus chapters 6 and 7. In Ezekiel 46:13, the burnt offering is prepared every morning as a voluntary or freewill offering of our thanksgiving and worship unto the LORD for His atonement. Yeshua gave up His life as a living sacrifice that we might inherit eternal life, thereby, breaking down the middle wall which separated us from Abba Father. Through Adam all sinned and were found guilty, but Yeshua Jesus became the Way, the Truth and the Life, by taking our sins upon His holy Being thereby restoring and reestablishing our relationship with the Father (see Ephesians 2:1-19). The required measure of the meal offering is a sixth part of an ephah, and one-third of a hin of oil. These are symbolic measures referring to the indwelling of Holy Spirit who commences and will also complete the sanctification process following our salvation.

We are sanctified by position in Abba Father through the atonement of Yeshua Jesus, who gave His Holy Spirit to those who believed in Him, but we also have our part to play. This process is much like the birth of a newborn baby whose food first begins in liquid form; texture is added as the baby matures. If one should remain on a liquid diet their whole life, their growth would be stunted. This same principle applies to the Believer; however, our growth is not based on our age or how long we have been followers of Yeshua Jesus, but by the advanced cleansing and sanctifying power of Holy Spirit within us. As we increasingly yield our bodies (temple) to the Holy Spirit, He transforms us by the renewing of our mind, which is evident by our fruit bearing, thereby advancing the kingdom of God. The sacrifices and offerings now placed on the altar are spiritual, and they are our way of thanking Abba Father for giving Yeshua to us. Hebrews 13:10-15 states: "*We have an altar, whereof they have no right to eat which serve the tabernacle. For the bodies of those beasts, whose blood is brought into the sanctuary by the high priest for sin, are burned without the camp. Wherefore Jesus also, that He might sanctify the people with His own blood, suffered without the gate. Let us go forth therefore unto Him without the camp, bearing His reproach. For here we have no continuing city, but we seek one to come. By Him therefore let us offer the sacrifice of praise to God continually, that is, the fruit of our lips giving thanks to His name.*"

These sacrifices will be a part of our required service, because in the kingdom of God nothing dies and this includes animals. Israel and the body of Yeshua is presently going through the sanctifying process, cleansing us to be presented unto the Father. The "oil," symbolic of Holy Spirit is working the purpose of God in us and also through us, to make us a thoroughly clean dwelling place for their coming reign within us. The Apostle Paul in his letter to the Romans wrote: "*I beseech you therefore, brethren, by the mercies of God, that ye present your bodies a living sacrifice, holy, acceptable unto God, which is your reasonable service. And be not conformed to this world: but be ye transformed by the renewing of your mind, that ye may prove what is that good, and acceptable and perfect, will of God,* 12:1-2. All that Yeshua has done for us will be memorialized in us. Yeshua is a living sacrifice and so will our bodies be presented unto Abba Father. Our sacrifices will be one of praise and our offerings will be one of thanksgiving. This process has already begun by the Holy Spirit to present us unto Yeshua Jesus, who will in turn present us unto His Father, blood bought and purified as the oil of the Lord continues to radiantly burn within us.

Verses 16-18

"Thus saith the Lord GOD; if the prince give a gift unto any of his sons, the inheritance thereof shall be his sons'; it shall be their possession by inheritance. But if he give a gift of his inheritance to one of his servants, then it shall be his to the year of liberty; after it shall return to the prince: but his inheritance shall be his sons' for them. Moreover the prince shall not take of the people's inheritance by possession, to thrust them out of their possession; but he shall give his sons inheritance out of his own possession: that My people be not scattered every man from his possession."

Most of Ezekiel's visions were of a spiritual prophetic nature. In these verses the LORD reverts to giving instructions for the leaders of the twelve tribes regarding the Jubilee and the Day of Atonement of the Lord, Leviticus 25:1-13, 39-43. The LORD reinforced the ground rules regarding observing the Jubilee. Some of Israel's leaders were dishonest and at times oppressed their helpers (see Ezekiel 45:8). This was an admonishing to them to uphold the teachings of the law regarding the year of liberty as it relates to both kindred and bondsmen. That which is given as an inheritance, will remain an inheritance and that which is required by the Mosaic teachings must be upheld without exception.

The year of liberty falls on the holiest day on the Jewish calendar; the Day of Atonement or Yom Kippur. Embedded in this festive celebration is a Messianic prophecy. Yeshua Jesus is in essence, our Jubilee. He came and afforded us rest for the soul and He is honored by the Father as our High Priest after the order of Melchizedek (Hebrews 5:1-10; 6:10-20). He took upon Himself our sins that we might be liberated. Yeshua declared: "*The Spirit of the LORD is upon Me, because He has anointed Me to preach the gospel to the poor; He has sent Me to heal the brokenhearted, to proclaim liberty to the captives and recovery of sight to the blind to set at liberty those who are oppressed; to proclaim the acceptable year of the LORD*"(Luke 4:18 NKJV, see also Isaiah 61:1-3). As sons of God, we too, share in this liberty. The Jubilee is celebrated in the fiftieth year and wrapped in this number is the gift of the multiplied grace of God towards us. Just as we have been forgiven, so we are required to forgive. Ezekiel 46:16-18 are verses that teach us a lesson in honesty, integrity and justice for all.

Verses 19-24

"After he brought me through the entry, which was at the side of the gate, into the holy chambers of the priests, which looked toward the north: and, behold, there was a place on the two sides westward. Then said he unto me, this is the place where the priest shall boil the trespass offering and the sin offering, where they shall bake the meat offering; that they may bear them not out into the utter court, to sanctify the people. Then he brought me forth into the utter court, and caused me to pass by the four corners of the court; and, behold, in every corner of the court there was a court. In the four corners of the court there were courts joined of forty cubits long and thirty broad: these four corners were of one measure. And there was a row of building round about in them, round about them four, and it was made with boiling places under the rows round about. Then said He unto me, These are the places of them that boil, where the ministers of the house shall boil the sacrifice of the people."

There is a common theme in the visions that began in Ezekiel chapter 40. Here, once again, we see the unveiling of a new era for Israel as well as the body of Yeshua Jesus. The LORD continues His discourse with the prophet regarding both the natural and spiritual temple. In the vision of the LORD, the prophet is brought by the Spirit to the entryway facing north which was described as the consecrated chambers of the priests. Because the priests' chambers were facing north; this was a revelation of the new man, finally completely purified and now rightly takes his position of authority as a royal priesthood. The priests will then walk in the perfect holiness of God being fully mature as the Holy Spirit reveals a greater depth of the knowledge of God concerning their purpose during the reign of Yeshua Jesus. During these times, that which is both known and done in part will be fully understood. These visions were also a teaching session for the homesick prophet as they offered him both comfort and hope that one day Israel's glory would not only be restored, but that the twelve tribes would also be completely purified and accepted by God.

Ezekiel was taken through the chambers of the priest and his attention was drawn westward. The west is the designated position of the minister who serves the LORD; therefore, this would be the ideal place for these oblations. After Ezekiel's visit to the altars located in the west, he was next taken to the outer court where he was allowed to pass by the four corners of the court. This was a very important place for the prophet to view, because there he observed something that he had not previously noticed. Located in every corner of the court were secondary courts. The four courts located in the corner of the outer court are symbolic of the completion of God's Divine work in man, while the secondary courts are a picture of His abiding presence and protection.

The outer court relates to the body or the carnal man. This is the area where every war is raged against sin and where the battle is either won or lost. This is the area of our tri-partite being that must first surrender and be presented unto God as a living sacrifice (Romans 12:1). The prophet was amazed to see that within this northern section facing westward, were two sides that were dedicated for the trespass, sin and also the meal offerings. This is the portrayal of the future of man when his cleansing is completed by Holy Spirit. For this reason all four courts are of the same measurement because he is now redeemed, regenerated and made holy and acceptable unto God.

The Lord GOD declared that this area was the holy residence of the priests. Why then were these offerings not made on the brazen altar located inside the courtyard at the gate of the tabernacle? The answer lies in the wonderful fact that these offerings were memorials of the finished work of Yeshua on the Cross! For this reason these offerings were placed as a witness to both Abba Father and man, on the two sides of the residence of the priests towards the west. This was a perpetual memorial of all that Yeshua Jesus had accomplished for the whole world. Mark 14:22-24 states: *"And as they were eating, Jesus took bread, blessed and broke it, and gave it to them and said, "Take, eat, this is My body." Then He took the cup, and when He had given thanks He gave it to them, and they all drank from it. And He said to them, "This is My blood of the new covenant, which* is shed for many" (NKJV). Here we see a picture of the three offerings; the trespass, sin and meal offering being Yeshua's body and blood; broken and poured out for all. Because of this reason, the priests quarters are dedicated as being holy since this is the area where Holy Spirit began His work of preparing us to be both kings and priests (Revelation 1:6; 5:10; 1 Peter 2:9). Within our bodies resides the temple of God bearing the mark of Yeshua our Redeemer and Sanctifier.

The trespass, sin and meal offerings are presented before Abba Father by the priests as an everlasting memorial, displaying Yeshua's stripes and poured out blood for our atonement. 1 Peter 1:15-21 clearly states: "*But as He who called you is holy, you also be holy in all your conduct, because it is written, "Be holy for I am holy." And if you call on the Father who without partiality judges according to each one's work, conduct yourselves throughout the time of your stay here in fear. Knowing that you were not redeemed with corruptible things, like silver and gold, from your aimless conduct received by tradition from your fathers, but with the precious blood of Christ, as of a lamb without blemish and without spot. He indeed was foreordained before the foundation of the world, but was manifest in these last times for you who through Him believe in God, who raised Him from the dead and gave Him glory, so that your faith and hope are in God*" (NKJV). Notice also that the trespass and sin offering was given for sin that was not deliberate, as deliberate sin was a willful act of rebellion. Hebrews 9:11-14 applying the NKJV once more, states: "*But Christ came as High Priest of the good things to come, with the greater and more perfect tabernacle not made with hands, that is, not of this creation. Not with the blood of goats and calves, but with His own blood He entered the most holy place once for all, having obtained eternal redemption. For if the blood of bulls and goats and the ashes of a heifer, sprinkling the unclean, sanctifies for the purifying of the flesh, how much more shall the blood of Christ, who through the eternal Spirit offered Himself without spot to God, cleanse your conscience from dead works to serve the living God?*" It will be required by the LORD that a memorial be made of these offerings because Yeshua Jesus our High Priest made us to be righteous; reconciling us to Abba Father, therefore we are viewed as His priests (see also 2 Corinthians 5:17-21).

186

This was not a natural temple being viewed, neither was it one to be built in the near future, instead, it was a representation of the grace of God upholding and strengthening man, His fourth and final dwelling place. For this reason all four inner supportive courts were of the exact measurement: forty cubits long and thirty cubits wide, indicating that they were rectangular structures with an area of 1200 square cubits. This is a symbolic number signifying unity, witness and the completion of the government of the LORD, as He installs His own new leaders from the twelve tribes of Israel. This number points to their future perfection before Abba Father.

The number forty speak of many things; Israel's chastisement for unbelief as seen in their forty years of wandering in the wilderness; a new beginning and era of grace and the completion of Abba Father's Divine order. On the other hand, thirty is symbolic of how wide the multiplied grace of God is given to His people, bringing them back to His Divine order. A square consists of four equal sides, which points to the perfect cohesive nature and unity of the Godhead. Because of this reason the measurements within the court were rectangular since man's unbelief was measured by God's grace. These measurements are telling us a story that although we have sinned and missed the mark, the LORD God has forgiven us because of His grace.

Surrounding these four courts are also rows of buildings for offerings made by boiling. To understand what this all means, let's look at the LORD'S instructions given to Moses for Aaron and his sons who were commissioned for priestly duties: "*And Moses said to Aaron and his sons, boil the flesh at the door of the tabernacle of the congregation: and there eat it with bread that is in the basket of consecrations, as I commanded, saying Aaron and his sons shall eat it. And that which remaineth of the flesh and of the bread shall ye burn with fire. And ye shall not go out of the door of the tabernacle of the congregation in seven days of your consecration be at an end: for seven days shall he consecrate you. As he hath done this day, so the LORD hath commanded to do, to make an atonement for you*" (Leviticus 8:32-34). The priests are separated by way of consecration and atonement. These too are symbolic in nature and also points to Yeshua's finished work on the Cross. He became our offering unto the Father, so that the new man in Him will bear the mark and reflection of all that it took for our redemption.

Notice the priests were called ministers and a minister has the pure heart of a bondservant and not that of a slave. That which he does is motivated by his free will of thanksgiving and pure love for the Father to whom he belongs. There is nothing more that man can offer, than that which has already been offered in his behalf. So with great appreciation, he bears in his body the suffering of Yeshua and carry his own cross as His disciple, which is his act of thankfulness, honor and love For his Savior and Lord (Matthew 16:24-26; Luke 9:23-25). We bear in our body's the dying of our Lord knowing that the time is close at hand when we will be raised up with Him (2 Corinthians 4:7-14). To reject this precious offering that Abba Father extends to us, is a rejection of Yeshua's blood sacrifice and those who do so will be eternally separated from the Father of life and light, to accept eternal darkness, damnation and anguish.

Chapter 47

Verses 1-12

"Afterward He brought me again unto the door of the house; and, behold, waters issued out from under the threshold of the house eastward: for the forefront of the house stood toward the east, and the waters came down from under from the right side of the house, at the south side of the altar. Then brought He me out of the way of the gate northward, and led me about the way without unto the utter gate by the way that looketh eastward; and behold, there ran out waters on the right side. And when the man that had the line in his hand went forth eastward, he measured a thousand cubits, and he brought me through the waters; the waters were to the ankles. Again he measured a thousand, and brought me through the waters; the waters were to the knees. Again he measured a thousand, and brought me through; the waters were to the loins. Afterward he measured a thousand; and it was a river that I could not pass over: for the waters were risen, waters to swim in, a river that could not be passed over. And he said unto me, Son of man, hast thou seen this? Then he brought me, and caused me to return to the brink of the river. Now when I had returned, behold, at the bank of the river were very many trees on the one side and on the other. Then said he unto me, These waters issue out toward the east country, and go down into the desert, and go into the sea: which being brought forth into the sea, the waters shall be healed. And it shall come to pass, that every thing that liveth, which moveth, withersoever the rivers shall come, shall live: and there shall be a great multitude of fish, because these waters shall come thither: for they shall be healed; and every thing shall live whither the river cometh. And it shall come to pass, that the fishers shall stand upon it from Engedi even unto Eneglaim; they shall be a place to spread forth nets; their fish shall be according to their kinds, as the fish of the great sea, exceeding many. But the miry places thereof and the marishes thereof shall not be healed; they shall be given to salt. And by the river upon the bank thereof, on this side and on that side, shall grow all trees for meat, whose leaf shall not fade, neither shall the fruit thereof be consumed: it shall bring forth new fruit according to his months, because their waters they issued out of the sanctuary: and the fruit thereof shall be for meat, and the leaf thereof for medicine."

As we approach the end of the book of Ezekiel, we will embark on more information that will prove to us that this book is indeed writings of Yeshua's love, justice and redemption; not only for His beloved Israel, but for all those who worship the God of Abraham, Isaac and Jacob, who are redeemed from the corruption of this world. There will be an outpouring of Holy Spirit in the last days when evil has thoroughly saturated the whole earth. At this point in human's history, many will turn to the LORD, while those who continue to reject Him will be left without Him forever. Romans 8:11 states: "But if the Spirit of Him who raised Jesus from the dead dwells in you, He who raised Christ Jesus from the dead will also give life to your mortal bodies through His Spirit who dwells in you" (NASB).

Great distress will be the order of the day before the second return of Yeshua Jesus. Weeping will be echoed before the throne of GOD, but the Holy Spirit's final mark of adoption and son-ship would have already been made and the door of salvation left opened for six thousand years finally closed forever by the LORD God. The Holy Spirit continues to work through imperfect people whom He empowers and transforms to do great exploits for the glory of Abba Father. He will get His point across to those who are searching for truth for at the end of the day we will only find truth and everlasting peace in God. These writings were not embarked upon to present mankind with another book to read or to bring honor and recognition to the scribe who was commissioned for this tremendous task. Be it known that the Holy Spirit had a tough time getting His child to commence this project. But one morning He spoke sternly: "You are stubborn!" As His voice echoed with these three words, His scribe tearfully repented and the rest is history.

The book of Ezekiel can be compared to the sand dunes in a desert, where precious archeological artifacts have laid hidden for thousands of years only to be discovered after years of relentless and meticulous excavation. These closing chapters of Ezekiel's writings will reveal a message that has been sealed since mankind graced this planet as a final act of a loving, compassionate, and ever gracious Father, beckoning His wondering children to return to the safe haven of home. Time is about over, it is already midnight on the calendar of the LORD!

The bride and body of Yeshua are in their final stages of purification. Ezekiel's vision is approaching its end and the Spirit of the LORD God takes the prophet to the entrance of the temple once again. Ezekiel had been there before, but with this final trip he expressed unrestrained joy because of the changes that had taken place in this reconstructed temple not built by human hands. Ezekiel now gazes at the regenerative work of the Holy Spirit in man, graciously adorned as the bride of Yeshua Jesus and waiting to be presented to Abba Father. The Apostle states in Ephesians 4:1-6: *"I therefore, the prisoner of the Lord, beseech you that you walk worthy of the vocation wherewith ye are called, with all lowliness and meekness, with longsuffering, forbearing one another in love; endeavoring to keep the unity of the Spirit in the bond of peace. There is one body, and one Spirit, even as ye are called in one hope of your calling; One Lord, one faith, one baptism, One God and Father of all, who is above all, and through all, and in you all."* Here the Apostle Paul unveils a picture of the coronation of both Jews and Gentiles, joined forever as ONE NEW MAN and Ezekiel the prophet of the Lord was granted this unique opportunity to see his unveiling. Man, the crowning glory of the Lord's creation, reconstructed and recreated with a renewed mind; holy, pure, righteous and redeemed from the curse of the law. Galatians 3: 26-29: clearly states: *"For ye are all the children of God by faith in Christ Jesus. For as many of you as have been baptized into Christ have put on Christ. There is neither Jew nor Greek, there is neither bond nor free, there is neither male nor female: for ye are all one in Christ Jesus. And if ye be Christ's, then ye are Abraham's seed, and heirs according to the promise."*

On Ezekiel's return trip to the entrance of the temple, he observed waters coming from an easterly direction flowing from under the threshold of the temple. "Waters," used here in its plural form, indicates that it had only one source but many tributaries, symbolizing the coming outpouring of Holy Spirit upon every nation, tribe and tongue. Joel 3:17-18 states: *"You will be convinced that I the LORD am your God dwelling on Zion, my holy mountain. Jerusalem will be holy conquering armies will no longer pass through it. On that day the mountains will drip with sweet wine, and the hills will flow with milk. All the dry stream beds of Judah will flow with water. A spring will flow out from the temple of the LORD, watering the Valley of Acacia Trees"* (NET). Keeping in mind the spiritual prophetic nature of portions of these visions, Joel's oracle is referring to this coming move of God, and the time of its fulfillment is at hand. Located near the Dead Sea is the Valley of Shittim or Acacia Trees and looking beyond this natural valley, the LORD was about to reveal a much greater truth.

A valley is found between highlands, which forms a natural conduit for life sustaining water. Allegorically speaking, it is a representation of the life giving flow of Holy Spirit. The Shittim or Acacia tree grows and survives under very harsh conditions. Not only are these trees resistant to decay, they flourish under the most adverse circumstances; much like the palm trees which points to the life and existence of the Believer in Yeshua. From the beginning of the Believer's confession and profession of Yeshua as his Savior, the devil begins a lifelong battle to steal, kill and destroy his soul in Sheol. These are the words of Paul which reminds us to hold fast to the end: *"Who shall separate us from the love of Christ? Shall tribulation, or distress, or persecution, or famine, or nakedness, or peril, or sword. As it is written, For thy sake we are killed all the day long; we are accounted as sheep for the slaughter. Nay, in all these things we are more than conquerors through Him that loved us"* (Romans 8:35-37). No matter what occurs, when it appears as though everything around us is likened to the "Dead Sea," there will be a fountain that flows from the throne of GOD that will sustain us. The valley mentioned in the book of Joel was barren, but nearby was water, however this was not potable or life sustaining as the name of this body of water was the Dead Sea. The outpouring of waters in this valley from the heavens would therefore be necessary to both give and sustain life.

The source from which the water flowed in Ezekiel chapter 47 gives us another revelation. A threshold is described as the support for an entryway that is under a doorsill; without this support the entryway would be unsafe. Yeshua describes Himself as being the door; He is also the threshold, way or doorway to the Father (John 10:9; 14:6). Yeshua said: *"He that believeth on Me, as the Scripture hath said, out of his belly shall flow rivers of living water, (But this spake He of the Spirit, which they that believe on Him should receive: for the Holy Spirit was not yet given; because that Jesus was not yet glorified)"* (John 7:38-39). The flowing waters from beneath the threshold are symbolic of the Holy Spirit who will be poured out immeasurably in the final hours upon the Believers in Yeshua. Revelation 22:17 is our hope and comfort: *"And the Spirit and the bride say, "Come!" And let him who hears say, "Come!" And let him who thirsts come. Whosoever desires, let him take the water of life freely"* (NKJV).

The waters cascading from the right side of the house is symbolic of a place of power and authority. It flowed towards the south side of the altar; the place of the watchman or prophet, who now bears the mantle of a priest, making intercession for a mighty move of the outpouring of Holy Spirit in us. Ezekiel is then taken towards the northern gate where man's authority is now erected, approved and sustained by the LORD. Ezekiel was escorted to the outer gate on the east side of the temple and was overwhelmed with joy and gladness because of what he had seen. Now the prophet clearly understood the working of the Holy Spirit within man, and he saw the days ahead when God's Spirit would not only rest upon His people but reside within them. Ezekiel now gazes with expectancy, as he observed the waters that he first saw flowing from beneath the threshold, now pouring from the right side also. Yeshua walks ahead of Ezekiel and measures a thousand cubits before accompanying the prophet through ankle deep waters. Now let's examine the spiritual prophetic interpretation of these verses that will stir our souls to pursue holiness.

One thousand contains four numbers; 1-0-0-0. One is the mark of unity; zero is the reproducing seed and four is the number that completes all that God has made universally. Hidden within this thought is the fact that the Genesis account extends to another dimension. Not only did God create and completed everything necessary for this inhabited heaven and earth, He also created a parallel universe much the same as earth which He calls the new heaven and earth. John who was a close disciple and friend of Yeshua Jesus wrote: *"And I saw a new heaven and a new earth: for the first heaven and the first earth were passed away; and there was no more sea"* (Revelation 21:1, see also Isaiah 65:17-20; 66:22-23; 2 Peter 3:13-14). *"Sea"* is however not referring to a body of water as the angel explained to John: ... *"The waters, which you saw, where the harlot sits, are peoples, multitudes, nations, and tongues"* (Revelation 17:15).

The number one (1) speaks of the Divine unity of the Godhead; while the three zeros (0-0-0) tells the story of the ever reproducing seed. Zero or its Hebrew equivalent zera reveals that everything was created by the Lord God and the entire human race is their offspring, having gained a favorable inheritance in Yeshua Jesus. Colossians 2:6-10 applying the NET states: *"Therefore, just as you received Christ Jesus as Lord, continue to live your lives in him, rooted and built up in him and firm in your faith just as you were taught, and overflowing with thankfulness. Be careful not to allow anyone to captivate you through an empty, deceitful philosophy that is according to human traditions and the elemental spirit of the world, and not according to Christ. For in him all the fullness of deity lives in bodily form, and you have been filled in him, who is the head over every ruler and authority."* We have a solid foundation on which we are built upon, in the person of none other than Yeshua Jesus. 2 Corinthians 5:21 states: *"For He made Him who knew no sin to be sin for us, that we might become the righteousness of God in Him"* (NKJV). At this point we will examine the revelation of the four unique features of 1,000 cubits.

Fist 1000 cubits – *The waters were ankle deep*

The "man," as Ezekiel describes Yeshua, had a line in His hand. The very first and most important point to get from the onset is the fact that the line is a form of measurement which connects end to end. The line also speaks of dimensions as well as comparing standards of one thing against another. This is not man judging man, but Yeshua's dealings with us. Ephesians 4:11-16 states: *"And He Himself gave some to be apostles, some prophets, some evangelists, and some pastors and teachers, for the equipping of the saints for the work of ministry, for the edifying of the body of Christ, till we all come to the unity of the faith and the knowledge of the Son of God, to a perfect man, to the measure of the stature of the fullness of Christ; that we should no longer* be children, tossed to and fro and carried about with every wind of doctrine, by the trickery of men, in the cunning craftiness of deceitful plotting, but, speaking the truth in love, may grow up in all things into Him who is head Christ from whom the whole body joined and knit together by what every joint supplies, according to the effective working by which every part does its share, causes growth of the body for the edifying of itself in love" (NKJV). It is only by Yeshua's standards that we will one day be judged, because all our spiritual measurements are found in Him, and the first place He starts to measure man is at the ankles where we cross over from death into everlasting life.

The ankle is made up of seven bones which connect the foot to the leg; it is a symbol of strength, stability, our point of balance and mobility. Interestingly, there are seven bones in our ankle, which points to the process of spiritual perfection beginning with our walk with God. The Hebrew word for ankle is **Ephec** [657], it means cause to cease or come to an end. It is linked to **Aphec** [656], which means to bring to an end or cease to be; which is also linked to **Ephec Dammiym** [658], which gives the boundary of drops of blood. Also associated with the ankle is yet another Hebrew word **Dam** [1818], which means the shedding of the blood of the innocent. The Hebrew transliteration for "ankle," reveals the shedding of the blood of the innocent, which could only be that of the Son of God whose innocent blood was poured out to take away the sins of the world and offer the redeemed eternal life for being partakers in His death and resurrection. It was therefore the pre-incarnate Son of the Living God, who stepped into the water first as He led Ezekiel through this spiritual prophetic vision. 1 John 1:7 states: "*But if we walk in the light, as He is in the light, we have fellowship one with another, and the blood of Jesus Christ His Son cleanseth us from all sin.*" Again Romans 6:3-11 applying the NLT reminds us: "*... Have you forgotten that when we were joined with Christ Jesus in baptism, we joined him in his death? For we died and were buried with Christ by baptism. And just as Christ was raised from the dead by the glorious power of the Father, now we also may live new lives. Since we have been united with him in his death, we will also be raised to life as he was. We know that our old sinful selves were crucified with Christ so that sin might lose its power in our lives. We are no longer slaves to sin. For when we died with Christ we were set free from the power of sin. And since we died with Christ, we know we will also live with him. We are* *sure of this because Christ was raised from the dead, and he will never die again. Death no longer has any power over him. When he died, he died once to break the power of sin. But now that he lives, he lives for the glory of God. So you also should consider yourselves to be dead from the power of sin and live to God through Christ Jesus."*

The beginning of this journey reveals the undeniable truth pertaining to the shedding of Yeshua Jesus' innocent blood: the price paid for our redemption, and for this reason, the first 1,000 cubit commences with the waters at the ankles; a symbol of the starting point of man's walk with God. The shedding of Yeshua's innocent blood was therefore the necessary pre-requisite for the endowment of Holy Spirit. Yeshua Jesus sates in John 16:13: *"Howbeit when He, the Spirit of truth, is come, He will guide you into all truth: for He shall not speak of Himself; but whatsoever He shall hear, that shall He speak: and He will show you things to come."* It was also noted that "ankle" is mentioned only twice in Scripture; first in Ezekiel 47:3 and next in Acts 3:7. In Ezekiel 47:3, it is Yeshua both measuring and taking man through the waters indicating that He is acquainted with us in every area of our lives. When the waters of difficulties overwhelm us, it is the waters or presence of Holy Spirit that sustains us. Yeshua is the living water and the Holy Spirit whom Yeshua left with us is also described as waters because He is able to empower and satisfy every weak, parched and dying area of our soul by flushing out all impurities. In essence the Holy Spirit is Living water, much like Yeshua Jesus, because both are a part of the Godhead. The first 1,000 cubits symbolizes Yeshua's sacrifice for sin. Those who call upon His name must now take up their cross and follow Him all the way with the Divine Helper, which is Holy Spirit, the earnest of our inheritance. Yeshua's innocent blood was our down payment therefore He takes the first step into the waters to guide our footsteps because He is pure light. Jesus said: *"... I am the light of the world. The one who follows me will never walk in darkness, but will have the light of life"* (John 8:12 NET). The ankle points to the Pesach or Passover, as we take our very first step from bondage and death to eternal life in Yeshua Jesus.

At the second 1,000 cubits mark – *The waters were knee deep*

Once again Yeshua measures the waters before taking Ezekiel to the next level of purification. Purification comes with pain and each level is a reflection of our walk with God. First of which is our ability to walk and next is our ability to both walk and run. Hebrews 12:1 states: "*Therefore we also, since we are surrounded by so great a cloud of witnesses, let us lay aside every weight, and the sin which so easily ensnares us, and let us run with endurance the race that is set before us, looking unto Jesus, the author and finisher of our faith, who for the joy that was set before Him endured the cross, despising the shame, and has sat down at the right hand of the throne of God*" (NKJV). Our first move in the right direction begins with a single step. We must first begin with baby steps and by the time this process is mastered, we move on to running, which incorporates both the use of our feet and knees to make long strides. Should the ankle sustain injury, our journey becomes hampered and painful. The comfort we have as we move forward, lies in knowing that Yeshua Jesus is always there with us, because He is acquainted with our weaknesses. This is our hope and assurance that even when we walk through the valley of the shadow of death we should not fear because the Lord is always present with us (Psalm 23).

Ezekiel documented that the second set of measurements were doubled as the waters had risen another 1,000 cubits. The second level points to the decision we have to make to pursue holiness and win others for Yeshua no matter what the price; therefore, the waters were described as being at the knees. The Apostle Paul best describes the life of a Believer as he serves the Lord: "*And when they had come to him, he said to them: "You know, from the first day that I came to Asia, in what manner I always lived among you, serving the Lord with all humility, with many tears and trials which happened to me by the plotting of the Jews; how I kept back nothing that was helpful, but proclaimed it to you, and taught you publicly and from house to house, testifying to Jews, and also Greeks, repentance toward God and faith toward our Lord Jesus Christ. And see, now I go bound in the spirit to Jerusalem, not knowing the things that will happen to me there, except that the Holy Spirit testifies in every city, saying that chains and tribulations awaits me. But none of these things move me; nor do I count my life dear to myself, so that I may finish my race with joy, and the ministry which I received from the Lord Jesus, to testify to the gospel of the grace of God"*, (Acts 20:18-24 NKJV).

If we get ahead of Yeshua we make a mess of everything because we lose both sight as well as focus of Him. Note carefully that the verse did not say He measured and the waters had risen two thousand cubits; instead, when Yeshua measured a second time, the waters had risen another thousand cubits. This is a very important observation, because all measurements are intimately connected with the Godhead, therefore, the understanding and interpretation of the second measurement of one thousand cubits remains indicative that the presence of Father, Son and Holy Spirit accompanies us on this sanctifying journey.

The knees were identified as the location of the body where the second 1,000 cubits was measured. In human anatomy the knee is made up of three joints, and is described as being the largest and most complex. The knee aids ambulation and joins the thigh to the leg. When we walk or run, the knees flex and extend with a very slight rotation. Being the largest and most intricate of all joints, the knee is by far the most likely to be injured, so we must pay very close attention to it. We are most vulnerable at the knee level in our walk with God. It is at this level that the devil unleashes darts and demons to stop us, knowing that we will snatch millions from the jaws of Sheol. The Lord did not make any mistake when He designed the human body: as the ankle is made up of seven bones, indicating the process of spiritual perfection; the knee consists of three joints which points symbolically to our determined and unshakable stance as His witness in this earth as we grow spiritually. Without the knees, one would be disabled in warfare and therefore succumb to the fiery darts of the enemy. The knees are therefore important in our warfare as they are to our worship.

The Hebrew word for knee is **Berek** [1290], it is a part of the word **Barak** [1288], which conveys the idea that one falls to the knees in worship. It points to Shavuot or Pentecost and speak of our total devotion, adoration, and love. Most important of all, the knees are associated with the complete surrender of your will to the Holy One who is greater than us. Unless the knee sustains injury it is usually taken for granted. If the knee is injured, not only will it affect our ability to walk, but it will also displace pressure on the ankle to carry the weight of our body.

Figuratively speaking, the knee level anointing or flow of Holy Spirit is the most vulnerable time in our walk with the Lord. The Believer must be very careful at the knee level anointing, as pride can creep in and instead of leading others to worship God, we might find ourselves in the precarious position of robbing the Lord of the glory that is due to Him. For this reason Yeshua Jesus is always ahead of the Saint as our example to follow, and if we keep our eyes on Him, we will be victorious over every diabolical scheme placed in our path from the host of hell. If we are not careful we will fall into the pit of pride at the knee level anointing and by the time we become aware of our state; the mantle we once wore has become polluted, as the presence and imparted power and anointing of the Holy Spirit departs.

The inner man is strengthened when our ankles and knees are rooted and grounded in love. Ephesians 3:14-19 states: *"For this cause I bow my knees unto the Father of our Lord Jesus Christ, of whom the whole family in heaven and earth is named, that He would grant you, according to the riches of His glory, to be strengthened with might by His Spirit in the inner man; that Christ may dwell in your hearts by faith; that ye, being rooted and grounded in love, may be able to comprehend with all saints what is the breadth, and length, and depth, and height; and to know the love of Christ, which passeth knowledge, that ye might be filled with all the fullness of God."* Blessed are those who put their trust in God; we must yield completely to Holy Spirit as His rivers of living water will only flow from a clean vessels. The choice is ours as freewill agents because our measurements are founded either in Yeshua or anti-Christ.

Two levels measuring 1,000 cubits have already been attained; the decision is up to us to remain permanently at either level or go on to deeper and greater things in God. The ankle anointing is good, the knee anointing is better, but now we must embark on the anointing that has reached the loins, which is best and has the greatest potential. For those who make it to this level, there is a bonus prize which is the crowning glory of the Father. Only a few Saints will attain to this greater level of sanctification in this life, because they pursued the passion of the Lord fervently. They have broken free from the trappings of this world and view their time on earth as that of a pilgrim who presses even farther and deeper to a higher calling. Philippians 3:8-16 NLT states: *"Yes, everything else is worthless when compared with the infinite value of knowing Christ Jesus my Lord. For his sake I have discarded everything else, counting it all as garbage, so that I could gain Christ and become one with him. I no longer count my own righteousness through obeying the law; rather, I become righteous through faith in Christ. For God's way of making us right with himself depends on faith. I want to know Christ and experience the mighty power that raised him from the dead. I want to suffer with him, sharing in his death, so that one way or another I will experience the resurrection from the dead! I don't mean to say that I have achieved these things or that I have already reached perfection. But I press on to possess that perfection for which Christ Jesus first possessed me. No, dear brothers and sisters, I have not achieved it, but I focus on this one thing: Forgetting the past and looking forward to what lies ahead, I press on to reach the end of the race and receive the heavenly prize for which God, through Christ Jesus, is calling us. Let all who are spiritually mature agree on these things. If you disagree on some point, I believe God will make it plain to you. But we must hold on to the progress we have already made."* At the ankle, knee, and loin level in the process of our walk with God, we can still turn back and walk away. Those who pursue the Lord with passion are those who are willing to go the extra mile, forsaking all. Here, at this point, the Spirit of the Living God fully takes over and the child of God now finds him or herself being taken without resistance, effortlessly where the Spirit wills. Be it known that He will only take us if we want to go, because the choice to press on or turn back is always up to us.

At the third 1,000 cubits mark – *The waters were to the loins*

At the first 1,000 mark we are welcomed into the family of God through the sacrificial blood of the Innocent One: The second 1,000 mark is our decision to continue on this life changing journey, while the third makes that choice clear. Throughout this process it has been Yeshua who goes forth and measures the waters, then takes Ezekiel through. Isaiah the prophet spoke these words: *"And I will bring the blind by a way that they knew not; I will lead them in paths that they have not known: I will make darkness light before them, and crooked things straight. These things will I do unto them, and not forsake them"* (42:16). As we walk with the Lord, we will not faint and as we continue to run after Him we will not grow tired or weary. Now we must take a stand for Him and this will require the mustering of all the strength that we possess.

The loin is the anatomical region of the body where the hips, lower abdomen and reproductive organs are located. It is our point of balance and strength, truth and endurance, stability and productivity. It is stated in 1 Peter 1:13-21: "*Therefore gird up the loins of your mind, be sober, and rest your hope fully upon the grace that is to be brought to you at the revelation of Jesus Christ; as obedient children, not conforming yourselves to the former lusts, as in your ignorance; but as He who called you is holy, you also be holy in all your conduct, because it is written, "Be holy for I am holy." And if you call on the Father, who without partiality judges according to each one's work, conduct yourselves throughout the time of your stay here in fear; knowing that you were not redeemed with corruptible things, like silver and gold, from your aimless conduct received by tradition from your fathers, but with the precious blood of Christ, as of a lamb without blemish and without spot. He indeed was foreordained before the foundation of the world, but was manifest in these last times for you who through Him believe in God, who raised Him from the dead and gave Him glory, so that your faith and hope are in God*" (NKJV).

At this third 1,000 cubits level located at the loins, it will take all boldness and spiritual initiative in our pursuit of holiness. The water to our loins is indicative of our complete abandonment and trust in the Lord. We are now at a point of spiritual maturity where no room is left vacant for carnality or the exposure of our weaknesses, because the things of the flesh are now finally subdued. We will leave the bondages of spiritual Egypt with God before us and His mighty hosts behind us. Girding the loins points to our freedom in Yeshua Jesus so that we may partake in the Passover (see Exodus 12:5-14). Another vital aspect of the loin entails our warfare (Ephesians 6:14) and our effectiveness in preaching the gospel. With this confidence and assurance, many will enter into the kingdom of God and also be used as proselytes, which is the revolutionary mark of our productivity. John 7:37-39 states: "*In the last day, that great day of the feast, Jesus stood and cried, saying, If any man thirst, let him come unto Me, and drink. He that believeth on Me, as the Scripture hath said, out of his belly shall flow rivers of living water. But this spake He of the Spirit, which they that believe on Him should receive: for* the Holy Spirit was not yet given; because that Jesus was not yet glorified." At the loin level one's mind is firmly made up, the standard has been acquiesced, to do all that can be done for the advancement of the kingdom of God in the earth from the life giving river that flows from within.

At the fourth 1,000 cubits mark – *It was an impassable river*

The fourth measurement of 1,000 cubits came with a distinct change. All along as Yeshua measures the water, He then proceeds to take the prophet through, but in this final measurement, He cautioned Ezekiel to observe all that had taken place so far. Ezekiel who represents the children of God, could by unwavering faith decide to continue on the journey with Yeshua, remain at this point at the river, or choose to turn back because of fear. At this level his final decision to go all the way with His Lord came at a self-sacrificing price: forsaking all, to be identified with his crucified Lord! The Apostle Paul knew what it meant to be crucified with Yeshua Messiah, he states in one of his several letters to fellow Believers: "*I am crucified with Christ: nevertheless I live; yet not I, but Christ liveth in me: and the life which I now live in the flesh I live by the faith of the Son of God, who loved me, and gave himself for me*" (Galatians 2:20).

For the Overcomer this pilgrimage is over, as he finishes the race and is rewarded by Abba Father as His new creation. Man no longer considers his life as his own and with great excitement and jubilation, prepares himself to receive his inheritance. We read in Ephesians 1:9-14: "*Having made know unto us the mystery of His will, according to His good pleasure which He hath purposed in Himself: That in the dispensation of the fullness of times He might gather together in one all things in Christ, both which are in heaven, and which are on earth; even in Him: In whom also we have obtained an inheritance being predestinated according to the purpose of Him who worketh all things after the counsel of His own will: that we should be to the praise of His glory, who first trusted in Christ. In whom ye also trusted, after that ye heard the word of truth, the gospel of your salvation: in whom also after that ye believed, ye were sealed with that Holy Spirit of promise, which is the earnest of our inheritance until the redemption of the purchased possession, unto the praise of His glory.*"

At this fourth measurement we now become a new creation in God, old things have passed away and all things are made new. We are taken from levels of water where we are most vulnerable and comfortable, to a level in God where His cleansing power now completely purifies and perfects us, not through the keeping of the law, but by the all-inclusive saving grace of Abba Father. The Apostle Paul's conviction recorded in Galatians 2:21 is now the anthem of the Overcomers: "*I do not set aside God's grace, because if righteousness could come through the law, then Christ died for nothing*" (NET).

Before concluding this section, the understanding of the Hebrew words for *brink, bank* and *river* will be explained. It is noted that the words "brink" and "bank," mentioned in Ezekiel 47:6-7 is derived from the same Hebrew word **Saphah** or **Sepheth** [8193]; it is transliterated "mouth," which is our organ of speech. This Hebrew word conveys the idea of rejoicing and exaltation in every language and dialect. Embedded in this word is the understanding that there will be an exuberant outburst of praise, echoed by those who have been cleansed by this end time move of Holy Spirit's purifying process.

Next is the Hebrew word **Nashal** [5158]; which is transliterated "river," it originates from **Nachal** [5157] which indicates that one has received his or her inheritance. When **Nachal** is linked with **Saphah** or **Sepheth**; we can clearly understand the reason for such a celebration: the Overcomers have finally received their inheritance. Revelation 21:5 -7 states: "*And He that sat upon the throne said, Behold, I make all things new. And He said unto me, Write: for these words are true and faithful. And He said unto me, It is done. I am Alpha and Omega, the beginning and the end. I will give unto him that is athirst of the fountain of the water of life freely. He that overcometh shall inherit all things; and I will be his God, and he shall be My son.*" The fourth measurement of 1,000 cubits is the inheritance of the Overcomers. "*And the Spirit and the bride say, Come. And let him that heareth say, Come. And let him that is athirst come. And whosoever will, let him take the water of life freely*" (Revelation 22:17). Let's recapitulate:

- The first 1,000 cubits – this measurement is the poured out blood of Yeshua Jesus for all, the innocent dying for the guilty so that we, too, may be partakers in the kingdom of God, however this is a personal choice that comes with a price as man takes the first step to walk with God. In essence, every step he takes he bears his cross as he follows Yeshua. At this point man passes over from death to everlasting life.

- The second 1,000 cubits – This measurement is the decision we make as free will agents to accept or reject God's reconciliatory offering of salvation. Man's growth becomes evident yet he will stumble many times. With determination, his knees becomes his warfare as well as his worship, where he prays for strength for the journey and rejoice in the Lord and the power of His might. It is also at this level that he is most likely to give up and run away from the presence of God. This journey began at Shavuot (Pentecost) over two thousand years ago.

- The third 1,000 cubits – This measurement indicates that the decision has been made and the standard is now set in motion to be holy as our Redeemer is holy. Man presses through, and heaven rejoices because he overcame by the blood of the Lamb and by the word of his testimony. His flesh is now crucified with Yeshua and ready for the fourth and final mark of God in his life.

- The fourth 1,000 cubits – This is man's final level of purification where he partakes of the Pesach or Passover. He spiritually passes over from the bondage of sin to the liberty of salvation and from death to life. He overcame all adversities and now receives his inheritance as a joint heir with Yeshua.

The spiritual prophetic interpretation of the measurements marked off in 1,000 cubits, expresses the unity of the Godhead (Elohim) to recreate man, and therefore rebuild his temple as a holy habitation through four unique levels of measurement in Yeshua Adonai.

As we approach these days of the greatest peril that man will ever face on earth, remember these words of the LORD spoken by Isaiah and recorded in 43:1-19: applying the NET: "*Now, this is what the LORD says, the one who created you, O Jacob, and* formed you, O Israel: "Don't be afraid, for I will protect you. I call you by name, you are mine. When you pass through the waters, I am with you; when you pass through the streams, they will not overwhelm you. When you walk through the fire, you will not be burned; the flames will not harm you. For I am the LORD your God, the Holy One of Israel, your deliverer. I have handed over Egypt as a ransom price, Ethiopia and Seba in place of you. Since you are precious and special in my sight, and I love you, I will hand over people in place of you, nations in place of your life. Don't be afraid, for I am with you. From the east I will bring your descendants; from the west I will gather you. I will say to the north, 'Hand them over!" And to the south, 'Don't hold any back!' Bring my sons from distant lands, and my daughters from the remote regions of the earth, everyone who belongs to me, whom I create for my glory, whom I formed yes, whom I made! Bring out the people who are blind, even though they have eyes, those who are deaf, even though they have ears! All nations gather together the peoples assemble. Who among them announced this? Who predicted earlier events for us? Let them produce their witnesses to testify they were right; let them listen and affirm, 'It is true,' you are my witnesses, "says the LORD, "my servant whom I have chosen, so that you may consider and believe in me, and understand that I am he. No god was formed before me, and none will outlive me. I, I am the LORD, and there is no deliverer besides me. I decreed and delivered and proclaimed, and there was no other god among you. You are my witnesses," says the LORD," that I am God. From this day forward I am he; no one can deliver from my power; I will act, and who can prevent it?" This is what the LORD says, your protector, the Holy One of Israel: "For your sake I send to Babylon and make them all fugitives, turning the Babylonians' joyful shouts into mourning songs. I am the LORD, your Holy One, the one who created Israel your king." This is what the LORD says, the one who made a road through the sea, a pathway through the surging waters, the one who led chariots and horses to destruction, together with a mighty army. They fell down, never to rise again; they were extinguished, put out like a burning wick: "Don't remember these earlier events; don't recall these former events. "Look. I am about to do something new. Now it begins to happen! Do you no recognize it? Yes, I will make a road in the desert and paths in the wilderness."

After Ezekiel was shown the coming of the regenerated man in Yeshua, he was escorted to the bank of the river and to his astonishment, observed many trees on both sides of the river which he never noticed before. Trees here symbolize the life giving power of God that will sustain those who have been justified by faith. The coming healing of the waters that flows from the LORD, will bring peace to the nations of the world as there will be a magnanimous outpouring of Holy Spirit in the last days as a final act of Abba Father's grace. Many will be reborn into the kingdom of God during this time; being swept in His presence by tribulations and a realization that the God of the Hebrews is the only true God. The fishers are disciples and proselytes who will proclaim the word of God to both Jews and Gentiles in these final hours. Yeshua while walking by the Sea of Galilee called unto two brothers and said unto them, *"Follow Me, and I will make you fishers of men"* (Matthew 4:19, see also Mark 1:17). Those who reject this final call will be memorialized as salt just like Lot's wife who looked back because she loved the world more than she loved God (Genesis 19:16-26; Luke 17:31-32).

Ezekiel 47:12 introduces us to the joy that awaits the family of God and this promise is vividly expressed in Revelation 22:1-4: *"And he showed me a pure river of water of life, clear as crystal, proceeding from the throne of God and of the Lamb. In the middle of its street, and on either side of the river, was the tree of life, which bore twelve fruits, each tree yielding its fruit every month. The leaves of the tree were for the healing of the nations. And there shall be no more curse, but the throne of God and of the Lamb shall be in it, and His servants shall serve Him. They shall see His face, and His name shall be on their foreheads"* (NKJV). We will offer wave offerings of praise and thanksgiving to the Father being forever grateful for all that He has done to redeem us from our sinful nature through the unblemished sacrifice of the second Adam, the Son of God, who redeemed us from the curse of the law. The prophet Ezekiel, whom Yeshua showed these things, represents the Jewish nation of Israel, but non-Jews should also rejoice because Abba Father did not forget them. Yeshua said: *"I am the good shepherd; and I know My sheep, and am known by My own. As the Father knows Me, even so I know the Father; and I lay down My life for the sheep. And other sheep I have which are not of this fold, them also I must bring, and they will hear My voice, and there will be one flock and one shepherd"* (John 10:14-16 NKJV).

As we come to the end of these great teachings that the LORD gave unto Ezekiel the prophet more than twenty-five hundred years ago, we must realize that if He so chooses to reveal the mysteries of this prophetic Book, it is a sign that He is about to do something in the earth. The following verses will prove that the land of Israel will increase its borders during the last of the last days, as Abba Father aids Israel once again to a miraculous victory over their enemies. The world will then be dumbfounded and declare "The God of Israel is the One and only true God!"

Verses 13-23

"Thus saith the Lord GOD; This shall be the border, whereby ye shall inherit the land according to the twelve tribes of Israel: Joseph shall have two portions. And ye shall inherit it, one as well as another: concerning that which I lifted up Mine hand to give it unto your fathers: and this land shall fall unto you for inheritance. And this shall be the border of the land toward the north side, from the Great Sea, the way of Hethlon, as men go to Zedad; Hamath, Berothah, Sibraim, which is between the border of Damascus and the border of Hamath; Hazarhatticon, which is by the coast of Hauran. And the border from the sea shall be Hazar-enon, the border of Damascus, and the north northward, and the border of Hamath. And this is the north side. And the east side ye shall measure from Hauran, and from Damascus, and from Gilead, and from the land of Israel by Jordan, from the border unto the east sea. And this is the east side. And the south side southward, from Tamar even to the waters of strife in Kadesh, the river of the Great Sea. And this is the south side southward. The west side also shall be the Great Sea from the border, till a man come over against Hamath. This is the west side. So shall ye divide this land unto you according to the tribes of Israel. And it shall come to pass, that ye shall divide it by lot for an inheritance unto you, and lo the strangers that sojourn among you, which shall beget children among you: and they shall be unto you as born in the country among the children of Israel; they shall have inheritance with you among the tribes of Israel. And it shall come to pass that in what tribe the stranger sojourneth, there shall ye give him his inheritance, saith the Lord GOD."

These verses makes it quite clear that the earth belongs to the Lord GOD (Psalm 24) who has the legal right to divide it to whomever He will. Genesis 15:18-21 states: *"In the same day the LORD made a covenant with Abram, saying, Unto thy seed have I given this land, from the river of Egypt unto the great river, the river Euphrates: the Kenites, and the Kenizzites, and the Kadmonites, and the Hittites, and the Perizzites, and the Rephaims, and the Amorites, and the Canaanites, and the Girgashites, and the Jebusites"* (see also 12:5-7). The Land of Israel along with its borders was given to the Hebrew descendants of Abraham, Isaac the son of Sarah his wife, and Jacob. Esau was the legal heir of this covenant birthright, but he dishonored God, by dishonoring His gift to him, and so Jacob became the recipient of its blessing. In this final distribution of land, the LORD included all foreigners and their offspring who joined themselves to Israel, which meant that the engrafted Gentile's will be beneficiaries like Yeshua's brethren in Israel's inheritance, as the kingdom of Israel and its original borders are reestablished.

Chapter 48

Verses 1-8

"Now these are the names of the tribes. From the north end of the coast of the way of Hethlon, as one goeth to Hamath, Hazarenan, the border of Damascus northward, to the coast of Hamath; for these are his sides east and west; a portion for Dan. And by the border of Dan, from the east side unto the west side, a portion for Asher. And by the border of Asher, from the east side even unto the west side, a portion for Naphtali. And by the border of Naphtali, from the east side unto the west side a portion for Manasseh. And by the border of Manasseh, from the east side unto the west side, a portion for Ephraim. And by the border of Ephraim, from the east side even unto the west side, a portion for Reuben. And by the border of Reuben, from the east side unto the west side, a portion for Judah. And by the border of Judah, from the east side unto the west side, shall be the offering which ye shall offer of five and twenty thousand reeds in breadth, and in length as one of the other parts, from the east side unto the west side: and the sanctuary shall be in the midst of it."

Here we will see the unveiling of a divine message from Abba Father. Seven tribes were mentioned in these verses with a double portion going to Joseph through his sons Manasseh and Ephraim. The number seven indicates that the LORD is perfecting the tribes that will be saved and unite all twelve, but before doing so He named seven first. When these tribes are placed in the order in which they were given in these verses, this is what the Holy Spirit unveiled through the meaning of their names:

Dan – I will serve judgment and vindicate

Asher – and bring prosperity and happiness

Naphtali – for your wrestling and struggles

Manasseh – I have caused to be forgotten

Ephraim – to make you fruitful

Reuben – for I have seen and known

Judah – your praise.

Israel as a people sinned and rebelled against God, but the statement above carries a dual interpretation that we will understand even better when it is completed. Not only will we see the LORD judging and vindicating the house of Israel, we will also understand Yeshua's finished work on the Cross for our redemption. 2 Peter 1:2-4 states: "*Grace and peace be multiplied to you in the knowledge of God and of Jesus our Lord, as His divine power has given to us all things that pertain to life and godliness, through the knowledge of Him who called us by glory and virtue by which have been given to us exceedingly great and precious promises, that through these you may be partakers of the divine nature, having escaped the corruption that is in the world through lust*" (NKJV).

Verses 9-22

"*The oblation that ye shall offer unto the LORD shall be of five and twenty thousand in length, and of ten thousand in breadth. And for them, even for the priest, shall be this holy oblation; toward the north five and twenty thousand in length, and toward the west ten thousand in breadth, and toward the east ten thousand in breadth, and toward the south five and twenty thousand in length: and the sanctuary of the LORD shall be in the midst thereof. It shall be for the priests that are sanctified of the sons of Zadok; which have kept My charge, which went not astray when the children of Israel went astray, as the Levites went astray. And this oblation of the land that is offered shall be unto them a thing most holy by the border of the Levites. And over against the border of the priests the Levites shall have five and twenty thousand in length, and ten thousand in breadth: all the length shall be five and twenty thousand, and the breadth ten thousand. And they shall not sell of it, neither exchange, nor alienate the firstfruits of the land: for it is holy unto the LORD. And the five thousand, that are left in the breadth over against the five and twenty thousand, shall be a profane place for the city, for dwelling, and for suburbs: and the city shall be in the midst thereof. And these shall be the measures thereof; the north side four thousand and five hundred, and the south side four thousand and five hundred and on the east side four thousand and five hundred, and the west side four thousand and five hundred. And the suburbs of the city shall be toward the north two hundred and fifty, and toward the south two hundred and fifty, and toward the east two hundred and fifty, and toward the west two hundred and fifty. And the residue in length over against the oblation of the holy portion shall be ten thousand eastward, and ten thousand westward: and it shall be over against the oblation of the holy portion; and the increase thereof shall be for food unto them that serve the city. And they that serve the city shall serve it out of all the tribes of Israel. And the oblation shall be five and twenty thousand by five and twenty thousand: ye shall offer the holy oblation foursquare, with the possession of the city. And the residue shall be for the prince, on the one side and on the other of the holy oblation, and of the possession of the city, over against the five and twenty thousand of the oblation toward the east border, and westward over against the five and twenty thousand toward the west border, over against the portion for the prince: and it shall be the holy oblation; and the sanctuary of the house shall be in the midst thereof. Moreover from the possession of the Levites, and from the possession of the city, being in the midst of that which is the prince's, between the border of Judah and the border of Benjamin, shall be for the prince."*

All tribes will receive the same allotment of land with the exception of the tribe of Levi because their inheritance is in the LORD (Numbers 18:20-21; Deuteronomy 10:8-9; 18:1-2; Joshua 13:14, 33). Once again the LORD has kept His people Israel without discrimination, because of His intense love towards them. These final measurements reinforce the manifold compassion, mercy and grace of Abba Father. The LORD refers once again to His devoted priest Zadok, whose descendants were approved to minister in His presence. That which was given to the children of Israel could not be revoked, sold or exchanged; neither could they keep the firstfruits of the land for themselves. The firstfruits belonged to the LORD and were set aside as a gift or wave offering, indicating their voluntary act of worship. The firstfruits however, were much more than our act of worship, because it spoke of three persons: Yeshua, the Holy Spirit and indeed the redeemed Saint of God (1 Corinthians 15:23; Romans 8:23 and Revelation 14:4). We have addressed the meaning of these measurements as revealing a picture of the unfathomable grace of Abba Father towards mankind. The introduction of the measurement four thousand five hundred (4,500), points to the closing of time as we know it and therefore its implication and understanding will be explained at the end of this chapter.

The allotted land dedicated to the city of God was in the shape of a square, which is symbolic of equality and unity of the Godhead. There was neither strife nor exertion for preeminence or recognition in the Godhead; they work as a Divine team and the death and resurrection and glorification of Yeshua Jesus now draws mankind also into this same relationship. All things will be made new as the allotment of land will be the same, however, the size of our mansions will be as a direct result of our fervent walk with God upon this earth. We must therefore be very careful and make sure that our foundation is built upon Yeshua Jesus. The Apostle Paul wrote in his first letter to the Corinthians: "*The one who plants and the one who waters work as one, but each will receive his reward according to his work. We are coworkers belonging to God. You are God's field, God's building. According to the grace of God given to me, like a skilled master-builder I laid a foundation, but someone else built on it. And each one must be careful how he builds. For no one can lay any foundation other than what is being laid, which is Jesus Christ. If anyone builds on the foundation with gold, silver, precious stones, wood, hay, or straw, each builder's work will be plainly seen, for the Day will make it clear, because it will be revealed by fire. And the fire will test what kind of work each has done. If what someone has built survives, he will receive a reward. If someone's work is burned up, he will suffer loss. He himself will be saved, but only as through fire. Do you not know that you are God's temple and that God's Spirit lives in you? If anyone destroys God's temple, God will destroy him. For God's temple is holy, which is what you are*" (3:8-17 NET). In essence we decide what our mansion will be like, therefore we must be very careful to live a life that is holy, acceptable and pleasing unto the Lord.

As Ezekiel's vision reverts to the natural once again, he is given instructions for his brethren concerning the future division of the land of Israel. In Ezekiel 48:9-13 we observe that the land by its measurements is actually rectangular in shape. However, the measurement of the land given in Ezekiel 48:8 to be set apart as holy, has in its center the sanctuary that measures 25,000 cubits long and 25,000 cubits wide, which is a square. The outer rectangle consisting of four right angles outlines the first tabernacle in the wilderness which symbolically represents mankind's body (outer court), soul (inner court), and spirit (Most Holy Place); having fallen short of the glory of GOD, which is represented by its two equal short sides and two equal long sides. Ephesians 2:8-10 states: *"For by grace you have been saved through faith, and that not of yourselves: it is the gift of God, not of works, lest anyone should boast. For we are His workmanship, created in Christ Jesus for good works, which God prepared beforehand that we should walk in them"* (NKJV). The sanctuary which is centrally located bears similarities to the outer rectangle, by also possessing four right angles, however this is in the shape of a square, which is a picture of the all-encompassing true sanctuary and presence of God the Father, the Son and, Holy Spirit living within us as a Divine Unity. It is important to note that these measurements are devisable by five, which is a picture of Abba Father's endless grace. The Levites as well as the eleven other tribes of Israel repeatedly disappointed the LORD, yet He proved His faithfulness to them over and over again. As for the Levites, the LORD chose the sons of Zadok as ministers (Ezekiel 48:11-12). A free will offering of cities and suburbs will be given by each tribe from their portion of land to the priests and Levites because their inheritance is in the LORD (Numbers 35:1-8).

Ezekiel 48:10 states: *"And the sanctuary of the LORD will be in the midst thereof."* This information is repeated in Ezekiel 48:21-22 as belonging to the Prince. The Prince spoken of here is none other than Yeshua the Prince of Peace (reference to the center portion of land set apart for Him connects also with Ezekiel 48:8). Hebrews 8:1-2 states: *"Now of the things which we have spoken this is the sum: We have such a High Priest, who is set on the right hand of the throne of the Majesty in the heavens; a Minister of the sanctuary, and of the true tabernacle, which the Lord pitched, and not man.* This allotted land is described as being a holy sanctuary because the throne of GOD will be in its center as His tangible presence among His people. Revelation 21:3 states: *"And I heard a great voice out of heaven saying, Behold, the tabernacle of God is with men, and He will dwell with them, and they shall be His people, and God Himself shall be with them, and be their God."* We must make sure that the Lord is central is our lives for what will it profit a man to gain the world at the expense of losing his soul? What can we offer for its redemption?

The squared middle sanctuary has four corners made up of ninety degree angles and the sum of these internal angels is 360 degrees. This measurement gives a panoramic view of the revolving wheel of the Word of God, transforming our lives thereby making it a holy abode for the presence of God. The liquidity of the Word of God takes a circuit of 360 degrees changing everything that it touches. Isaiah 55:10-11 applying the NASB states: *"For as the rain and the snow come down from heaven, and do not return there without watering the earth and making it bear and sprout, and furnishing seed to the sower and bread to the eater; so will My Word be which goes forth from My mouth; it will not return to Me empty, without accomplishing what I desire, and without succeeding in the matter for which I sent it."* The Word is embodied in a person, it is documented in the New Covenant: *"In the beginning was the Word, and the Word was with God, and the Word was God. He was in the beginning with God. All things came into being through Him, and apart from Him nothing came into being that has come into being. . . . What was from the beginning, what we have heard, what we have seen with our eyes, what we have looked at and touched with our hands, concerning the Word of life and the life was manifested, and we have seen and testify and proclaim to you the eternal life, which was with the Father and was manifested to us"* (John 1:1-3; 1 John 1:1-2 NASB).

It is the Word, who is known as Yeshua our Prince of Peace who will reign among His people and the consolation of the Gentiles is they too, are partakers in this glorious benefit. Romans 8:16-17 and Ephesians 2:4-16 states: *"The Spirit Himself bears witness with our spirit that we are children of God, and if children then heirs – heirs of God and joint heirs with Christ. If indeed we suffer with Him, that we may also be glorified together. . . . But God, who is rich in mercy, because of His great love with which He loved us, even when we were dead in trespasses, made us alive together with Christ (by grace you have been saved), and raised us up together, and made us sit together in the heavenly places in Christ Jesus, that in the ages to come He might show the exceeding riches of His grace in His kindness toward us in Christ Jesus. For by grace you have been saved through faith, and that not of yourself; it is the gift of God not by works, lest anyone should boast. For we are His workmanship, created in Christ Jesus for good works, which God prepared beforehand that we should walk in them. Therefore remember that you, once Gentiles in the flesh – who are called Uncircumcision by what is called the Circumcision made in the flesh by hands that at that time you were without Christ, being aliens from the commonwealth of Israel and strangers from the covenants of promise, having no hope and without God in the world. But now in Christ Jesus you who once were far off have been brought near by the blood of Christ. For He Himself is our peace, who has made both one, and has broken down the middle wall of separation, having abolished in His flesh the enmity, that is, the law of commandments contained in ordinances, so as to create in Himself one new man from the two, thus making peace, and that He might reconcile them both to God in one body through the cross, thereby putting to death the enmity"* (NKJV). In that day when Yeshua reigns as Prince we will not be separated or segregated as Jews and Gentiles, but will be known as One New Man; His residue, His remnant and His chosen people.

Verses 23-29

"As for the rest of the tribes, from the east side unto the west side, Benjamin shall have a portion. And by the border of Benjamin, from the east side unto the west side, Simeon shall have a portion. And by the border of Simeon, from the east side unto the west side Issachar a portion. And by the border of Issachar, from the east side unto the west side, Zebulun a portion. And by the border of Zebulun, from the east side unto the west side, Gad a portion. And by the border of Gad, at the south side southward, the border shall be even from Tamar unto the waters of strife in Kadesh, and to the river toward the Great Sea. This is the land which ye shall divide by lot unto the tribes of Israel for inheritance, and these are their portions, saith the Lord GOD."

The tribe of Judah and Benjamin formed an alliance that was called the southern kingdom, while the remaining ten tribes made up the northern kingdom (1 Kings 12:21-24). As Ezekiel's final vision draws to a close the LORD concludes His prophetic message which He started in the opening verses of this chapter. The first seven tribes of Israel commenced with Dan which was a part of the northern kingdom and ended with Judah from the southern kingdom, to demonstrate His reconciliatory work among these brethren. This He continued in Ezekiel 48:23-29, by completing the coded message; beginning with the tribe of Benjamin and adding four other tribes from the northern kingdom. Scholarly thinkers of the past, who bore a mighty prophetic mantle, did not miss these revelations by intellectual or spiritual oversight, but it was by providence that the Almighty GOD chooses to reveal them in these last days.

First of all Judah is the son of Leah, Jacob's first wife. By ending the first list with Leah's son Judah (Ezekiel 48:8) and commencing the second with Benjamin, Rachel's son (Ezekiel 48:23) we see the LORD reuniting the twelve sons or tribes thereby tearing down the wall that separated them. This is a picture of Israel as one, because in the reign of Yeshua Jesus, there will not be a northern and southern kingdom; only the kingdom of God. Also take into consideration that the sons of Jacob (Israel) were not mentioned in the chronological order of their birth which completes the message of Abba Father began at the beginning of chapter 48.

> **Benjamin** – You are the son of my right hand
>
> **Simeon** – I have heard you
>
> **Issachar** – and will reward
>
> **Zebulun** – the honored dwellers
>
> **Gad** – who I will call my troop and distribute my fortune.

Here we see Abba Father not only talking about Israel, but also all that He had to put His only begotten Son Yeshua Jesus through to redeem us. This is the full message which the LORD began in Ezekiel 48:1-8.

"I will serve judgment and vindicate and bring prosperity and happiness for your wrestling and struggles, which I have caused to be forgotten to make you fruitful. I have seen and known your praise; you are the son of My right hand, and I have heard you and will reward the honored dwellers whom I will call My troop and distribute My fortune."

Ezekiel 48:28 is also mentioned in 47:19 which will be explained here. Gad borders Tamar on the south unto the waters of strife in Kadesh that is towards the Dead Sea. The Dead Sea is in close proximity to another great body of water known as the Mediterranean. Embedded in this statement are great truths. The verse states: *"And by the border of Gad, at the south side southward, the border shall be even from Tamar unto the waters of strife in Kadesh, and to the river toward the great sea."* For now, our focus will be on the name "Tamar." Other references to Tamar in Scripture includes: Judah's daughter-in-law who subsequently bore him twins after the death of her husband, which was his son, Genesis 28:12-30; King David's daughter, 2 Samuels 13:1; David's grand-daughter who was the daughter of Absalom, 2 Samuels 14:27; the name of a place located in the wilderness, 1 Kings 9:18, and lastly the name of the town mentioned in Ezekiel 47:18 and 48:28. The focus however, is not the fact that the name "Tamar" referred to in Ezekiel is a town, but rather what the name essentially implies, because in all its usage, the meaning remains the same, and that is: "palm tree." What about the palm tree that is so significant that the LORD repeatedly refers to it in the book of Ezekiel? Is He trying to reveal something to us that we have not yet grasped?

The palm tree grows and flourishes under very adverse conditions yet every part of it is useful. Psalm 92:12-15 states: *"The righteous shall flourish like the palm tree: he shall grow like a cedar of Lebanon. Those that be planted in the house of the LORD shall flourish in the courts of our God. They shall still bring forth fruit in old age; they shall be fat and flourishing; to show that the LORD is upright He is my rock, and there is no unrighteousness in Him."* The palm tree is also a symbol of the righteous ones who are now called Overcomers. They pursued the passion of their Lord and Savior by leading others to the path of righteousness even as grave danger loomed over their shoulders. Being vigilant, they resisted and overcame the darts of wicked opposition and declared the good news of the Gospel.

These are they that are likened unto palm trees. Tying in with the nature and profitability of the palm tree (Tamar) is the understanding of what the name "Gad" means, which is, "*Who I will call my troop and distribute my fortune.*"

The LORD is informing us that the Overcomers are the righteous ones that will be rewarded, because they kept the faith through many adversities. The very nature of the palm tree as being useful, also describes the nature of Abba Father as a provider. The name Tamar has so much to say about GOD's dealings with us. We see also in the book of Ezekiel, living palm trees and also carvings of its leaves on the doors of the temple. The palm tree points to our usefulness to the Father in every area of our lives. As the palm tree flourishes in very hostile climatic conditions yet remain comprehensively productive, so it is intended for the Believer, because our spiritual worth comes into view when we are most vulnerable. The palm tree is also associated with the feast of tabernacles (Leviticus 23:39-41); Yeshua's entry into Jerusalem on the colt of a donkey (John 12:13) and the sealing of the twelve tribes of Israel in the book of Revelation (Revelation 7:3-10); yet the embodiment and main characteristic of the name "Tamar," is righteousness. Next we will discuss the second half of Ezekiel 48:28 which ties in with 47:18.

The water of strife also known as Meribah, means provocation. This body of water located in Kadesh is said to be towards the river of the Great Sea. Kadesh is known by many names: Qadesh-Barnea; Kadesh-Barnea; or the Fountain of Judgment. After being eye witnesses of the awesome power of GOD on their behalf against the Egyptians, and knowing that the battle is the Lord's; instead of conquering the land and its inhabitants that was promised to their forefathers by the LORD GOD, they feared the giants living there (Deuteronomy 9:23-29; Numbers chapter 13; 14:1-24). Ezekiel 48:23-29, unveils the story of how the children of Israel, are again taken to the same location where they were first given their portion of real estate and forfeited it.

Coming full circle once again, the children of Israel are given a second chance to reclaim their inheritance at the fountain of God's judgment against them in Kadesh-Barnea, and by the waters of strife: Meribah; where they provoked the LORD which resulted in their judgment. Kadesh was a symbol of their lack of trust and faith in Abba Father. Now the children of Israel will remember their past misfortunes and not make the same mistake again, because this was their final chance to enter the land of Canaan and be blessed.

Kadesh will be memorialized as what could have been, if only they had not doubted the integrity of the LORD. Forty wasted years of their history was the end result of their fear and unbelief. Psalm 95:8-11 states: "*Harden not your heart, as in the provocation, and as in the day of temptation in the wilderness: when your fathers tempted Me, proved Me, and saw My work. Forty years long was I grieved with this generation, and said, It is a people that do err in the heart, and they have not known My ways: unto whom I swore in My wrath that they should not enter into My rest.*" The water of strife also called Meribah, was Israel's provocation of the LORD, while Kadesh-Barnea was His declared judgment against them. It is recorded in Psalm 106:32-35: "*They angered Him also at the waters of strife, so that it went ill for Moses for their sakes because they provoked his spirit, so that he spake unadvisedly with his lips. They did not destroy the nations, concerning whom the LORD commanded them but were mingled among the heathen, and learned their works.*" The children of Israel left excited to possess the land of Canaan, but the truth of the matter was, they were seeking an opportunity to rationalize their way out of combat to possess their inheritance. Because of their unbelief and hardness of heart they suffered greatly (see Numbers chapter 13; 14:1-24).

The Dead Sea is a river towards the Mediterranean Sea. Salt is good but the high salinity of the Dead Sea can be destructive. Symbolically the Dead Sea speaks of the hardness of the heart of men towards God. Unbelief and rebellion against Abba Father hardens the soul and the unbelieving are unable to recognize His vision for their future. God has a plan for this unproductive body of water as well as the unproductive man. Zachariah 14:8-9 quoting the NIV states: "*On that day living waters will flow out of Jerusalem, half of it east to the Dead Sea and half of it west to the Mediterranean Sea, in summer and in winter. The LORD will be king over the whole earth. On that day there will be one LORD, and his name the only name.*" The allotment of inheritance began with Dan whose name means "I will serve judgment and vindicate," and ends with Gad whose name implies, "who I will call my troop and distribute my fortune." Typically we see throughout the Word of God, he whom the Lord vindicates, He also endows with good fortune.

Verses 30-35

"And these are the goings out of the city on the north side, four thousand and five hundred measures. And the gates of the city shall be after the names of the tribes of Israel: three gates northward; one gate of Reuben, one gate of Judah, one gate of Levi. And at the east side four thousand and five hundred: and three gates; and one gate of Joseph, one gate of Benjamin, one gate of Dan. And at the south side four thousand and five hundred measures: and three gates; one gate for Simeon, one gate for Issachar, one gate for Zebulun. At the west side four thousand and five hundred, with their three gates; one gate of Gad, one gate of Asher, one gate of Naphtali. It was round about eighteen thousand measures: and the name of the city from that day shall be, The LORD is there."

The LORD still has much more to share with us. First of all 4-5-00 refers to the final act of His grace. The number 4 is a symbol of all that Elohim has created and therefore nothing can be added or subtracted. Next is the number 5 which is the stamp of His grace that He freely bestows upon mankind. It is next followed by two zeros (00) which implies that there is about to be a change in the family of GOD; not for evil but for good as we will see in these last verses. For within 00 is the story of life; the seed that is the regenerated, the recreated house of Israel and body of Yeshua Jesus, which is the church. We must endeavor to conquer sin in our lives and be liberated by the grace of God.

The Apostle Paul clearly states: *"What shall we say then? Are we to continue in sin so that grace may increase? May it never be! How shall we who die to sin live in it? Or do you not know that all of us who have been baptized into Christ Jesus have been baptized into His death? … Even so consider yourselves to be dead to sin, but alive to God in Christ Jesus. Therefore do not let sin reign in your mortal body so that you obey its lusts, and do not go on presenting the members of your body to sin as instruments of unrighteousness; but present yourselves to God as those alive from the dead, and your members as instruments of righteousness to God. For sin shall not be master over you, for you are not under law but under grace"*(Romans 6:1-3; 11-

220

14 NASB). This new temple, this splendiferous structure, has a foundation and a building permeated by the grace of God, and this temple is man, made up of both Jews and Gentiles! The book of Ezekiel is all about Yeshua Jesus, and it is the prayer of this scribe that many will wail at the wall in repentance. In these closing verses a second message is given. Here we see the sons of Israel been named, but in this list, unlike the first, not only was Levi and Joseph added, but the order of their names were rearranged. With this in mind let's see the revealed message imbedded in the meaning of their names and Holy Spirit's second message to the world:

Reuben – I have seen and known

Judah – your praise

Levi – you are joined to me

Joseph – and I have added

Benjamin – you are the son of my right hand

Dan – I will serve judgment and vindicate

Simeon – I have heard you

Issachar – and will reward

Zebulun – the honored dwellers

Gad – whom I will call my troop and distribute my fortune

Asher – and bring prosperity and happiness

Naphtali – for your wrestling and struggles.

Once more the LORD makes it quite clear that Yeshua and His brethren, and all Believers in the GOD of Abraham, Isaac and Jacob will be rewarded for their endurance.

The gates of the city are now assigned names after Israel's twelve sons beginning from the north, then east, south and west. This order is different from the Revelation 21:13 account of east, north, south and west; with south and west retaining their position. This is not a mystery, because the temple being constructed in Ezekiel is not the New Jerusalem descending from heaven (Revelation 21:10). The temple of Ezekiel's visions is much smaller and there is a reason for this. In Ezekiel chapter 40 we see both a natural and spiritual component to it. The spiritual prophetic component was greatly emphasized as the message pertained to the recreated and regenerated NEW MAN in Yeshua Jesus comprised of both Jews and Gentiles. It speaks of a coming temple made spotless for the habitation of the Divine Godhead. The new temple of the recreated man must first be built to live in the New Jerusalem of GOD. 1 Corinthians 3:16-17 reminds us: *"Do you not know that you are the temple of God and that the Spirit of God dwells in you? If anyone defiles the temple of God, God will destroy him. For the temple of God is holy, which temple you are"* (NKJV, for further readings see also 1 Corinthians 6:15-20; 2 Corinthians 6:16-18). We are the temple of God and the temple under construction in Ezekiel is that of man. The Holy Spirit is reconstructing man from the outer court (his body), the inner court (his soul), to the Most Holy Place (his spirit); preparing us for the coming consummation of Israel and the body of Yeshua Jesus.

In the regeneration and reconstruction of man as a home for the Godhead, the north is first mentioned; this is man ruling as priest and king, it is his position of authority as a new creation. Next is the east; the place of the lion, which is man in Yeshua. This is next followed by the south; the watchman or prophet and last the west a picture of the willing minister or bondservant. This is not all as we will see in the list of names when the message is broken down to address the nature of man in Yeshua Jesus. All positions will tie in with the position of the faces of the living creatures at the beginning of the book of Ezekiel. Let's place the messages beside each position and the assigned sons of Israel and see what is been said about man in Yeshua, his authority, his servitude, and also his prophetic mantle.

North gate – Reuben, Judah and Levi
I have seen and known your praise, you are joined to me.

East gate – Joseph, Benjamin and Dan
I have added, you are the son of my right hand and I will serve judgment and vindicate.

222

South gate – Simeon, Issachar and Zebulun
I have heard you and rewarded the honored dwellers

West gate – Gad, Asher and Naphtali
Who I will call my troop and distribute my fortune and bring prosperity for your wrestling and struggles.

There is however more to the message as two more facts will be highlighted here. First of all, the LORD repeats Himself a third time with the hope that all Israel will finally understand the depth of His passion, which reinforces His immutability to give them what rightfully belongs to them, not by their own merit, but through His never ending covenant of love, mercy and grace. Highlighted by the first named son of Israel for each position, Abba Father now speaks of the new man in Yeshua Jesus, who is neither Jew nor Gentile but the manifested sons of God:

North Side – Reuben

East Side – Joseph

South Side – Simeon

West Side – Gad

The LORD begins with Reuben, the first son of Jacob by his first wife Leah. The next son mentioned was Joseph, who was also the first son of Israel's by his second wife and the love of his life, Rachel. The third son mentioned was Simeon the second child of Leah. Lastly was Gad, the seventh son of Israel and firstborn of Zilpah, Leah's handmaiden who was not legally married to Israel (Genesis 29:31-35; 30:1-24). The name Zilpah means sprinkling or dropping, which alludes to a small quantity or amount being dispersed. The LORD was very specific in His choosing of these sons of Israel. Notice He did not select any sons born to Rachel's handmaid Bilhah, because her name means simple or foolish; otherwise, one lacking in wisdom and judgment. Ruben being the first son of Israel was so assigned because the number one declares unity. Next mentioned was Joseph, Israel's eleventh son and this number points to that which has fallen short of two important offices: first is ten; GOD'S Divine Order and next is the number twelve; His governmental control. The third mentioned was Simeon who was Israel's second son and the number two speaks of the choice we must make. Last of all is Gad, who is the seventh son of Israel, whose mother was Zilpah. Because Zilpah was not legally married to Israel, she represents in a typological setting the engrafted Gentile family. The number seven now completes God's spiritual perfection. These four sons of Israel were chosen based on their birth order and not by their character to portray a divine truth. As we examine the numerical birth order of these sons of Israel: Reuben, Joseph, Simeon, and Gad to head each gate, we see God's promise to both Jews and Gentiles unfolding. Abba Father has bestowed upon us His grace when we are united and even when we miss the mark, or make bad choices and fall from His grace.

Abba Father has the power to reclaim and perfect us whether we are Jews or Gentiles. Deuteronomy 28:8-10 states: "*The LORD shall command the blessing upon thee in thy storehouses, and in all that thou settest thine hand unto; and He shall bless thee in the land which the LORD thy God giveth thee. The LORD shall establish thee a holy people unto Himself, as He hath sworn unto thee, if thou shalt keep the commandments of the LORD thy God, and walk in His ways. And all people of the earth shall see that thou art called by the name of the LORD; and they shall be afraid of thee.*" True and everlasting prosperity comes from the LORD, which He gives to those who live by His teachings. Yeshua inherited all things from the Father and so will the house of Israel along with the engrafted Gentiles. The Apostle Paul in his second letter to the Corinthians implores all Believers to be reconciled unto God (5:14-21).

To be reconciled unto God means we are His new creation, His new dwelling place residing in the Holy city: the New Jerusalem prepared for the elect and this beautiful city, will usher in His everlasting reign. The perimeter given for the city was 18,000 measures, but it is not known whether this was its height or width, therefore, the LORD is revealing something about His Divine grace as it covers the temple of man. If we look at 18,000 as 1-8-000 we are better able to understand the spiritual prophetic interpretation of the numbers.

1 – Restoration of unity, by the abolishment of division
8 – The Lord completes with the number 7 and the addition of 1 more is a new beginning, which is the eighth.

000 – A mark that the seed has been given a new life, a new lineage, and a new legacy.

This is a picture of the new man, he has been restored and given a fresh start, his old life is now dead and he is welcomed back into the family of God. That which was lost by the first Adam, is regained by the second: Yeshua Jesus. The Apostle Paul wrote in 1 Corinthians 15:22, 45: "*For as in Adam all die, even so in Christ shall all be made alive. . . . And so it is written, the first man Adam was made a living soul; the last Adam was made a quickening Spirit*" (see also Romans 5:14). As the visions of Ezekiel the prophet comes to an end, and the final measurements of man are made; his glorious temple looked more like a city, as man is regenerated and reconstructed from the outer court (his body), to the inner court (his soul) and lastly the Most Holy Place (his spirit). All walls of separation have been demolished and finally man gains the approval of being called the temple of God. From that day on, man will be the abode of the ever present Jehovah Shammah: the LORD living in us!

This has been an awesome journey through the book of Ezekiel. We see the grace of God reflected in His love for both Jews and Gentiles. The LORD God sent His Son Yeshua, our Redeemer who took Ezekiel on these tours of Israel's past, present and glorious future. Their disobedience as well as that of the Gentiles who lived among them had dire consequences. The LORD however had a plan, to reconstruct man once again in a final attempt to reconcile us unto Himself. For this task Yeshua HaMashiach who is called by the Gentiles, Jesus the Christ was sent as a final sacrifice and a freewill offering, to purchase our redemption. To the Jews He is Yeshua or Yehoshua, but to the Gentiles, He is Jesus the selfsame One who died for all.

The axe is now laid at the root of the tree. The Lord will redeem only those whose heart have been circumcised and are walking in the newness of life. Yeshua Jesus said to the Pharisees a strict sectarian group of teachers: "*I know that you are Abraham's descendants, but you seek to kill Me, because My word has no place in you. I speak what I have seen with My Father, and you do what you have seen with your father.*" *They answered and said to Him, Abraham is our father.*" *Jesus said to them, If you were Abraham's children, you would do the works of Abraham. But you seek to kill Me, a Man who has told you the truth which*

I heard from God. Abraham did not do this. You do the deeds of your father." Then they said to Him, "We were not born of fornication; we have one Father God." Jesus said to them, "If God were your Father, you would love Me, for I proceeded forth and came from God; nor have I come of Myself, but He sent Me. Why do you not understand My speech? Because you are not able to listen to My word. You are of your father the devil, and the desires of your father you want to do. He was a murderer from the beginning, and does not stand in the truth, because there is no truth in him. When he speaks a lie, he speaks from his own resources, for he is a liar and the father of it. But because I tell the truth, you do not believe Me. Which of you convicts Me of sin? And if I tell the truth, why do you not believe Me? He who is of God hears God's words; therefore you do not hear because you are not of God" (John 8:38-47, NKJV; see also Mathew 3:7-11).

We must be ever watchful. Those who love their life in this world will lose it and those who lose their life in this world for Yeshua Jesus will find it (Mathew 10:39; 16:25; Luke 17:33; Mark 8:35). The question remains; are we ready and willing to take up our cross and follow Him? Will we denounce the Bread of Life from heaven for a morsel of bread on this earth, or will we boldly declare the Lordship of Yeshua Jesus and at the end of our physical life drop to our knees and triumphantly shout to the heavens, "I have fought a good fight, I have finished my course, I have kept the faith: O LORD my God and everlasting Redeemer, COME!"

www.ingramcontent.com/pod-product-compliance
Lightning Source LLC
Chambersburg PA
CBHW070348090426
42733CB00009B/1327